D0442613

THE
DIGITAL
ENTERPRISE

THE MOVES AND MOTIVES OF THE DIGITAL LEADERS

Karl-Heinz Streibich

ISBN 978-0-9897564-0-2

Editing by Dr. Robert J. Weiss, 507 Mize Court, Uniondale, NY, U.S.A.
Cover design by Software AG
Interior layout/typesetting by 1106 Design, LLC, 610 E. Bell Rd, Suite 2-139,
Phoenix, AZ 85022, U.S.A.
Printed by Bang Printing, 3323 Oak St, Brainerd, MN 56401, U.S.A.

First Printing, 2013

The earnings of this book will be donated to the social foundation Software AG — Stiftung, Am Eichwäldchen 6, 64297 Darmstadt, Germany.

Contents

PART III

Foreword

By Marc Benioff

Every decade, we witness a major shift in technology. Today, we are in the midst of an incredible revolution where the world is being reshaped by the convergence of mobile and social cloud computing, along with the ability of brands to develop one-to-one, personalized relationships with customers. The combination of these technologies enables us to connect everything together in a new way, and it is dramatically transforming the way we live and work. It's a phenomenal time.

I started salesforce.com in 1999 inspired by the rapid evolution of the of the consumer web. We stood on the shoulders of consumer companies like Amazon, eBay, and Yahoo!, and we leveraged their innovations to develop a better way to serve enterprise customers. Soon, the adoption of the cloud computing model changed everything, introducing a new business and technology model for enterprise software. And, ultimately, the Industrial Internet spawned an incredible wave of innovation over the past decade.

Today, everything is changing again. The devices, the networks, and even the computers we use to connect are all new. Exciting new mobile and social cloud apps are delivered via powerful LTE wireless networks to literally billions of connected computers. And, these connected computers are not just the mobile phones in our pockets. Rather, they are different kinds of connected computers — our watches, our cameras, our cars, our refrigerators, even our toothbrushes. In this new world, everything is connected on the network, as well as in the cloud. This is the third wave of computing, which will unleash a new wave of innovation that will transform business.

There are more than 4.5 billion people connected on social networks. Going further, research firm IDC reports that there will be 3.5 billion networked products by 2015. Compare that to 1.7 billion networked PCs, and it's clear that the "Internet of Things" has arrived. With more people, products, and apps connected to the network than ever before, we are entering an amazing new world of possibilities.[1]

In this connected world, customers are no longer anonymous. They are known. They are not just a number or an account; rather, they are unique human beings with a distinct set of needs. They want a two-way relationship where they are at the center of your world. They expect brands to deliver consistent, personalized experiences across every channel.

Companies must transform themselves to meet the rising expectations of modern customers. Innovative companies are connecting customers, partners, employees, and even products in new ways. I call them "customer companies." Becoming a customer company is not an option; it is mandatory for any business looking to grow in the coming years.

We tend to focus on the consumer internet companies as the leaders in technology innovation. The fact is, however, that today many companies across many different industries are embracing new technologies and are rapidly innovating. These companies are building connected products that can communicate status updates, reports, and other information in real time. And they are creating very sophisticated yet very easy-to-use mobile apps to connect with their customers, wherever they are. These companies are getting closer to customers and are redesigning the future of business.

I'm inspired by what I see our customers doing, just as I was energized by the examples in these pages. This book is filled with stories of global companies tapping mobile, social, and cloud technologies and using

Big Data to manage their supply chains, create new products, and better connect with customers via personalized experiences.

I was pleased to see GE, one of our customers, profiled here. It's amazing how GE Aviation is building closer connections to its customers — and making its products more socially connected. The new GEnx jet engine — currently flying on Boeing's new 787 Dreamliner — is a connected product that provides real-time data about engine performance from both GE and the airline customers to communities of service technicians. Service teams on the ground can access the data while the plane is mid-flight, providing an entirely new model of customer service for GE to offer its customers.

In another example, Toyota is connecting its cars to the network. It is using salesforce.com to integrate customers, dealers, and cars into a community. Toyota's cars now have the capability to send tweet-like status updates to their drivers to alert them of low tire pressure or to offer them a coupon for their next check-up. This new model of proactive customer service helps Toyota get closer to its customers to build brand loyalty and drive future sales opportunities. Shigeki Tomoyama, managing officer at Toyota, calls it "a new kind of car, almost like an iPhone on wheels."

Philips, a visionary consumer-centric company, is using technology to deliver innovations that matter to its customers. It is connecting millions of products — from toothbrushes and coffeemakers to new LED lighting products — into a single customer network. (I'm looking forward to the connected next-generation toothbrush that will send a report to my dentist.)

As any of the leaders of these companies will tell you, becoming a digital company, a connected company, a customer company, is a journey.

You need to start as early as possible, and there is no finish line. After all, when it comes to technology, the only constant is change.

However, this revolution is nothing to fear. Just the opposite, it is something to foster. This is a magical time. The future is limited only by our imagination about what's possible. Turn the page if you want to see what we have to look forward to.

Preface

When Software AG initially approached me to work with Karl-Heinz Streibich's book project team, I was a bit puzzled. Software AG has long been known for products like Adabas, Natural, webMethods, and ARIS. In my mind, the company was more into IT plumbing than digital innovation. I was wrong.

My first step was to research Software AG's recent acquisitions including Terracotta, LongJump, and Apama. With in-memory, platform-as-a-service (PaaS), and complex event-processing capabilities, Software AG is well positioned to help its customers exploit advanced analytics, cloud computing, and other technology-enabled innovations.

Besides, IT is entering a new phase, as Karl-Heinz shared with me in an early conversation. He had just viewed Dr. Thomas Enders, CEO of EADS, the manufacturer of Airbus planes and other aviation and defense products, deliver the keynote address at the March 2013 CeBIT event in Hanover, Germany. As described in Chapter 1, Dr. Enders's presentation highlighted the heightened expectations that every industry has concerning IT. That is the new IT, Karl-Heinz observed. It is focused much more on the front office than on the back office and infrastructure.

As I interviewed Software AG executives — Dr. Wolfram Jost, Ivo Totev, Dr. John Bates, Bjoern Brauel and others — I got a fascinating view of customers' innovations from their locations in Germany, Hong Kong, The Netherlands, California, and elsewhere.

Karl-Heinz then informed me that one of his favorite business books is *In Search of Excellence,* the bestseller by Tom Peters. One reason he found the book so valuable is "because it was full of use cases. The technology world similarly has plenty of innovation stories." Karl-Heinz then opened up his contact list and provided me with an amazing list of C-level executives in a variety of industries and countries.

This book reflects Karl-Heinz's optimism about the industry and the richness of his contacts. Throughout the book you will encounter the vision of "Industrie 4.0" that is driving innovation across a wide spectrum of industries around the globe. You will read about GE's vision of the Industrial Internet and how it will bring massive efficiencies to aviation, utilities, and many other industries. You will discover how banks and insurance companies and oil companies and museums and casinos are innovating using a wide range of other technologies.

In a book I published in 2012 titled *The New Technology Elite,* I described the "enterprising of consumer tech" — Apple's industry-leading retail metrics, Google's hyper-efficient data centers, Amazon's stunning logistics, and other innovations that mask their complex operations to make consumer technology seem simple and easy to use. This book focuses more on enterprise class innovation. It is about technology executives who talk technical jargon like "M2M" and "CEP" but actually are relentlessly focused on business results. Their business philosophy is product-centric and customer-centric. Even where these executives are back-office focused, they deliver massive efficiencies and speed. They have no need to talk ROI — the payback of their efforts is exponentially greater than what IT has delivered for decades.

You will also read about innovation in places you may not expect. Take railroads, for example. In several chapters you will read about trackside sensors that support predictive maintenance for high-speed, high-risk networks. There are mobile ticketing innovations in an industry that offers countless fare combinations. There's China's high-speed rail network. The "old" industry is being revitalized in hundreds of ways.

Or, consider Singapore. The island nation manages to evolve its workforce every few years to stay abreast of technology-enabled opportunities. It also boasts a highly evolved system of mobile-enabled taxis.

Your definition of innovation might not classify railroads or Singapore as "mainstream." In that case, we provide you with plenty of other choices. The book includes 22 guest executive perspectives and more than 300 innovation cameos representing more than 20 industries in more than 25 countries. In terms of technologies, the Gartner "nexus of forces"[2] — the convergence and mutual reinforcement of social, mobility, cloud, and information patterns that drive new business scenarios — is discussed in many sections of the book. In addition, advanced cybersecurity, robotics, wearable computing, various green technologies, and many other promising technologies are also presented.

We have organized the book into three parts. Part I, which consists of Chapters 1–2, conveys Karl-Heinz's passion about why every enterprise, irrespective of the industry or the geography in which it operates, needs to become a Digital Enterprise.

Part II, which comprises Chapters 3–17, explores the many opportunities available to the Digital Enterprise. Each chapter focuses on a specific opportunity. All of these chapters are comprised of three segments:

- Commentary from Karl-Heinz on the Digital Enterprise

- Roughly 10–20 cameos of innovations in that opportunity

- Interviews with 1–3 executives and thought leaders that describe their digital journeys in their unique industries and geographies

Digital Journeys

Finally, Part III, Evolving the Digital Enterprise, Chapters 18–19, concludes the book by envisioning what's next for Digital Enterprises — emerging technologies and approaches.

This is a really exciting time for most technology executives. For too long IT has been an expensive and low-payback back-office investment focused on "systems of record." Today, however, by embedding IT into their products and front-office projects, technology is becoming fun — and profitable. The enterprises profiled in this book illustrate how today's organizations are building systems that help them to differentiate themselves from their competition.

This book project has itself been a "Digital Enterprise." When Tom Peters wrote his classic in the early 1980s that inspired Karl-Heinz and countless other executives, he traveled extensively around the world to interview the subjects of the use cases he profiled. In contrast, the Software AG team of editors, graphic designers, project managers, and translators who worked on this book leveraged a variety of widely available collaboration infrastructure. The interviews that appear in the book reflect hours of cross-border VoIP calls, and they were captured on a Zoom digital recorder and backed up in the Google Cloud. The graphics leveraged the Adobe Creative Suite. The book, then, is the product of plenty of digital creativity and collaboration.

Over the past decade, we have witnessed a glorious stream of consumer technology innovations. Get ready for an even greater wave of industrial innovation. Welcome to the Digital Enterprise!

Vinnie Mirchandani

PART I

EVERY ENTERPRISE NEEDS TO BECOME A DIGITAL ENTERPRISE

1

Introducing the Digital Enterprise

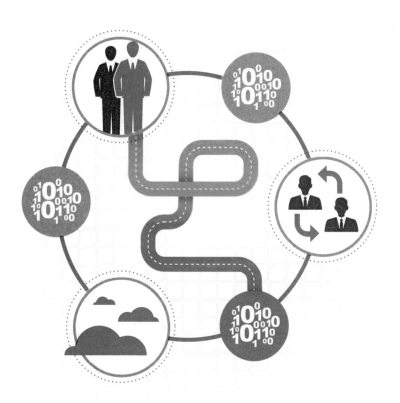

CeBIT, held each year in Hanover, Germany, is the world's largest event for digital IT and telecommunications solutions. In 2013 some 285,000 visitors from 120 countries attended the meeting.[3]

During the opening ceremony, Dr. Thomas Enders, CEO of EADS, the manufacturer of Airbus planes and other aviation and defense products, delivered his keynote speech.[4] Dr. Enders walked through a mock-up of Martian rocks and introduced the next-generation (next-gen) Mars Rover, called Bridget, that EADS is building in collaboration with the European Space Agency. "But I need to bring you back to reality," Enders informed the largely IT audience. "The Rover is incredible, but it uses computing concepts from the 1990s when the IT industry is today talking about spray-on Wi-Fi and DNA-based storage."[5]

Enders then laid out his vision of how IT could help to innovate the aerospace and defense industries.

- Make planes lighter. Perhaps use optical wireless to reduce the more-than 300 miles of wires contained in an Airbus A380?

- Reduce the current two-year lag between plane design cycles and certification.

- Assist with the development of Flightpath 2050, the "European Aviation Vision." Essentially, Flightpath 2050 envisions an air transport system that will integrate all of Europe. Among its goals is door-to-door service anywhere on the continent in 4 hours.[6]

Then, without needing to emphasize the point too strongly given his industry's safety requirements, he added: "Without compromising security."

Dr. Enders's speech was a watershed event. This was the first time a non-IT executive had keynoted a CeBIT event. His vision exemplified the heightened expectations that IT is creating in every executive.

"Your (IT) industry is increasingly relevant for us" was the core message throughout his talk.

In this chapter we consider some additional examples of the higher expectations generated by IT developments. In Part II we drill down into 15 opportunity areas for the Digital Enterprise.

From Standard Mass Production to Mass Customization

It all began with Tin Lizzie — the Model T. Henry Ford's slogan was "you can have any color so long as it is black."[7] For decades the mass production of the same product was the basis of economic growth and prosperity in manufacturing-based societies. However, during these years companies invested a great deal of effort and intelligence in two systems: (1) just-in-time production, intended to reduce capital spending; and (2) build-to-order to better align products with customer needs. Put simply, companies strove to make products that reflected and appealed to customers' individuality.

Despite these investments, however, the gap remained: Customers were demanding individualized products in sectors where the most cost-efficient mode of manufacturing was to mass-produce relatively uniform goods. One well-known example comes from Asia, where for many years tailors have been able to produce a tailored suit within three hours. These clothes, however, were made by hand with cheap labor, rather than mass-produced in highly efficient manufacturing environments. Consequently, closing the gap between the century-old, Frederick Taylor-influenced mass production and the large-scale manufacture of customized products was and is the famous classroom puzzle of "squaring the circle."

The advent of the consumer web using Facebook, Twitter, and similar applications and, today, the Internet of Things, marked the initial stages in the creation of the technological framework to close the gap between production efficiency and product individualization. However, implementing these technologies requires production sites to adopt a new paradigm. The traditional approach was to introduce increased intelligence into the production machineries and tools; however, the product itself remained passive. In contrast, the Internet of Things technologies bring each product to life, meaning the product acquires the intelligence to instruct the machine as to how it should look. At this point the mass production of individualized products was born. All of this activity is facilitated by other technological breakthroughs — for example, a drastic reduction in the cost of memory. This development was critical because the Internet of Things creates previously unimaginable volumes of data. During the last 50 years the cost of memory has declined by a factor of 500 million.[8] As a result, we now have software technology that can measure, analyze, and respond to on-the-move mass data streams.

In Chapter 3, Rob James describes how Echo Entertainment's VIP customers, who constitute only 0.1% of total visitors, nevertheless generate more than 30% of revenues. He further explains why technologies to personalize services to these customers are so important. In Chapter 9, Prof. Dr. Wolfgang Wahlster discusses how semantic memories promise to revolutionize mass customization and reshape the manufacturing and logistics of many products.

From Repairing to Preparing
Former Corning President Bill Decker supposedly told his R&D group, "Glass breaks ... why don't you fix that?" That simple challenge led Corning to produce many versions of damage-resistant glass, including the Gorilla Glass that now protects millions of consumer electronics devices including portable computer screens and mobile phones.[9]

Breakage has long been a concern with technological products. Historically to break and then be repaired was the destiny of technological devices, products, and systems of any size. There was no proactive element in this methodology, only a reactive one. Meanwhile, forward-looking technicians have pondered for years about how to reduce the time required to repair technology products. Some of the key strategies they proposed were improvements in quality, regular proactive maintenance, and enhanced ease of use (many product failures are due to improper usage).

Driven by both safety and economic concerns, experts developed the practice of proactive maintenance with the goal of predictive maintenance; that is, to anticipate a potential failure of a device, product, or complex system well before it actually malfunctioned. By performing proactive maintenance both producers and consumers could ensure that the product would remain functional more-or-less forever.

Significantly, experts had developed very intelligent solutions to realize this goal a decade or two ago. However, implementing these solutions required technologies that could analyze the vast amounts of real-time data that were produced by any component within a larger system efficiently, ideally in real time. Until fairly recently these technologies simply didn't exist.

This situation changed with the advent of the Internet of Things, combined with Big Data real-time analytics. It is now possible to measure the behavior of any system component with hundreds of millions of sensors and then analyze the data in real time to respond proactively before a device fails.

Thus, a dream came true. After several decades the technology finally emerged that could transform the concept of predictive maintenance into reality. What a breakthrough in the efficiency of production systems, in the safety of life-critical systems, and in the availability of any convenience system!

In Chapter 4, José Manuel Inchausti Pérez describes how the auto insurance industry in general and MAPFRE in particular is using driver analytics to better predict risks in their business. Auto repair is a significant expense for that industry. In Chapter 10, William Ruh describes how aircraft engines, wind turbines, MRI scanners, and other GE products are "communicating" their state of health to allow for more proactive monitoring.

From IT Products to Digital Projects

During the past five decades, IT has undergone several waves of innovation. This process began with deciding which mainframe to buy and then progressed to which server to choose, which application to develop, and which standard software package to use. Massive IT projects sometimes lasted for more than five years. Many of these projects failed because the customers' wish lists evolved during this extended period of development. Consequently, the applications or products had become obsolete by the time their creation projects were finalized.

It became increasingly obvious that the business side did not understand product-related IT strategies and concepts. In this context IT was too cryptic for business; it couldn't be understood by non-IT professionals. As a result, businesspeople treated IT as an infrastructure cost center rather than as an innovation center for the enterprise. What a waste of resources and opportunities, for decades.

For the past few decades, IT has focused primarily on *systems of record*. These are ERP-type systems that businesses utilize to manage their operations — our financials, HR, etc. They are focused on controls and numbers.

Today, many enterprises are entering an exciting new phase: information systems for competitive advantage. The companies that contributed cases to this book are embedding technology in their products and services, moving to technology-enabled business models, and utilizing technology to redefine their distribution channels. They are implementing digital technologies in both product-facing and customer-facing areas. This is IT that helps generate revenue. And it is happening in every industry.

In Chapter 3, Celso Guiotoko describes the sophistication of auto industry product evolution at Nissan Motor Company. At the other extreme, Max Hollein describes in Chapter 4 how even industries from which we do not expect digital leadership are reinventing themselves with technology — for example, Städel, a leading European museum located in Frankfurt am Main, Germany.

For decades, IT shops had been called "data centers." However, they have evolved from hardware operation centers to application development/implementation and operation centers. Data were stored in mechanically accessible hard discs — the slowest existing devices in the data centers — and were accessed through a database using data-retrieval techniques that were suboptimal even for structured data. With the emergence of the Internet with its almost unlimited capacity for text, pictures, and videos, the volume of available data increased exponentially, along with the desire to utilize and analyze this new data format. These developments spurred the innovation of software that could utilize the increasingly inexpensive chip-based memory as a real-time storage device for large data volumes, called Big Data. The result was in-memory computing, which made data visible and transparent in real time. The emergence of in-memory computing coincided with innovations like cloud computing, social collaboration platforms such as Facebook in the consumer area, mobile devices, and business process management (BPM).

Thus, for the first time companies acquired the capability to entirely digitize their data generation, data analysis, and data-based decision making. Machine-to-machine collaboration, as well as human collaboration, enables enterprises to execute business processes with unprecedented speed and insight, in real time. Going further, cloud-based applications, because they are relatively easy to use, enable businesses to add value by implementing digital projects even if these businesses don't possess a particular expertise in IT. In such cases the business can outsource the planning, building, and operation of their digital projects to partners who offer digital tools directly to business users. The final result of IT projects is driven through the proliferation of digital solutions for the business.

From Mobile Phones to Smart Mobile Data Processing Devices, the Smartphones

When we hear the term "digital societies" we generally envision technologically advanced regions such as North America, Europe, and East Asia — but not necessarily or historically Africa. Major waves of innovation such as mainframe computers and PCs didn't make nearly the kinds of inroads in that continent that they did elsewhere, with some exceptions, most noticeably South African companies. Perhaps surprisingly, then, today Africa is spearheading the use of mobile smart devices. In this process it is leapfrogging several technological evolution steps, thereby also promoting the democratization of information in the digital society. A prominent example is M-Pesa, a money transfer and micro-financing service that customers access via mobile phones. M-Pesa is already flourishing in emerging economies like Kenya and Tanzania. In Chapter 5, Jan Verplancke of Standard Chartered PLC describes the Breeze mobile banking rollout. In contrast, in more developed Western economies, mobile payments are still an immature technology and are not widely used.

The global success of smartphones required a distinctive breakthrough IT innovation:

1. Massive processing power on a low-energy-consumption chip, such as the chip innovated by ADR, a UK-based chip design company and a global leader in its field

2. Broadband network investments, enabled through a massive cash flow generated by national telecom companies, global mobile providers, and landline cable providers

3. User interfaces for non-IT people; for example, the gesture-driven touch screens developed by Apple

4. The invention of mobile apps formats, as innovated by Apple, Google, and other companies

5. Big Data analysis tools to manage the exponentially growing volumes of data contained in social networks, in in-memory systems such as Apache Hadoop and BigMemory from Terracotta, and in other technologies.

The combination of all these new technologies combined with up-to-date collaboration tools empowered people to interact at unprecedented levels. Overall, then, the emerging nexus of smart mobile devices, digital collaboration platforms, Big Data transparency, and cloud applications promises to transform the ways people throughout the world live and work. In Chapter 6, Esat Sezer of Coca-Cola Enterprises describes how mobile apps are revolutionizing the merchandising process in the bottling industry. Heinz Kreuzer of TUI Infotec then follows with a perspective on how the travel industry is experiencing a wave of innovation driven by mobile computing.

Digital Citizens Demand Digital Government Services
To appreciate the transformative impact of the digital revolution in the governmental sphere, consider the stunning success of Estonia. After suffering through decades of stagnation, Estonia has evolved into one of the most "networked" countries in the world. Its "Tiigrihüppe" ("tiger leap") initiative provides its population with a highly digitized lifestyle that can serve as a role model for other nations. Banking, elections, parliamentary proceedings, healthcare, and education are all highly digitized and are widely accepted and trusted by its citizens.[10] In

Chapter 17, Prof. Dr. Henning Kagermann explains how acatech — the National Academy of Science and Engineering — is acting as "glue" to facilitate innovative collaboration between the German government, businesses, and academia.

Digital citizens demand digital government services. Citizens who are digital natives don't accept outdated government bureaucracies in which people wait in long lines and then ask for services from public institutions. In addition, governments are creating more regulations that businesses must comply with, without automating their systems to expedite the compliance processes. The result is higher costs for businesses, adding to bureaucracy costs. The obvious solution to this problem is to provide all citizen- and business-oriented government services online, based on secure and trusted data and document exchanges. This type of innovation will help countries remain competitive while simultaneously reducing the size and improving the efficiency of government bureaucracies.

The adoption of digital platforms by government agencies is the foundation for creating digital processes based on digital content provided through open government or open data. Significantly, the technologies needed to achieve this goal already exist. What is needed is the political will to establish a trusted digital relationship with their citizens, as Estonia did, and then implement the digital solutions. The budgetary squeezes and the multiple levels of bureaucracy that characterize most Western countries should be a sufficient incentive for nations to follow the route of digital government services for their digital citizens. If the disparity between the expectations of digital citizens concerning government services and the services governments actually provide becomes too great — and it is already sizeable — the result will be an ever-increasing gap between governments and their citizens. Conversely, those nations that adopt digital government services in an efficient, trusted, and prudent way will have significant competitive advantages compared to their analog counterparts in which citizens queue to request a form sheet or a signature.

Protect the Franchise

Everyone knows that when you work in a store you lock the door after you close up. You also lock your cash register when you leave the cashier station. You similarly lock up your warehouse, your home, and your valuables. These types of security concerns apply to the digital world as well.

Closely related to security is privacy. The word "privacy" has both a factual and an emotional meaning to people throughout the world. Essentially, although most people value both privacy and security, expanding one often involves limiting the other. In addition, across countries and cultures people hold different views regarding the "trade-off" between privacy and security, as evidenced by the recent controversies regarding privacy issues involving government agencies in the United States and the UK.

Security and privacy needs exist in the digital world to the same extent they do in the physical world. In the digital public world you are sharing common platforms with other digital users. You don't have a physically separate area as you do in the real world. In the digital world we are *all* virtually in the same room.

Given this reality, why are so many consumers in digital environments still so relaxed regarding security? One possible reason is that the digital crossroads, platforms, and meeting places are invisible and are located remotely from the users, thereby creating a false sense of security based on physical distance and lack of visibility.

Unfortunately, criminal misuse of digital content is steadily increasing. In fact, the growing number of digital criminal acts is potentially the greatest obstacle impeding the proliferation and acceptance of the digital world. For the digital revolution to become universally embraced, governments and private enterprises need to develop security and privacy regulations and applications that mirror those that exist in the physical world. Without these protections, the digital world could become just a pilot program that failed. Fortunately, throughout history humans have exhibited a tremendous capacity for solving problems and meeting challenges. Digital technologies offer tremendous potential for human societies; moreover, the trend toward digitization is probably irreversible. Therefore, preparing for its stable development is in the interest of all of us. Hopefully, as more people come to accept this reality, we will apply our collective energies and intelligence to enhancing digital security and privacy.

In Chapter 15, Prof. Dieter Kempf explains how his company, DATEV, brings to thousands of small- and mid-sized businesses the convenience and security that dedicated IT staff provide in much larger companies

Machine-to-Machine (M2M) Is the Next Big Thing

Keyboard-based human interaction is where it all started. Machine-to-machine (M2M) interaction is the next big thing. M2M is a cross-disciplinary phenomenon that extends into all areas of life, including the Internet of Things. The Internet of Things is the basis of "Industrie 4.0," which is also called the Fourth Industrial Revolution.

M2M touches on and has the potential to revolutionize almost all areas of life. In this section we consider just a few of the myriad possibilities arising out of M2M technological advancements. In many of these cases M2M will bring about actual technological breakthroughs. M2M can make driving safer, homes more secure, health support instantly available, logistic processes more predictable and transparent, new energy grids possible, government agencies and enterprises easier to navigate, retailers more efficient, and consumer goods more intelligent. In sum, M2M automates anything, anywhere, at any time. It also creates new business opportunities both for provider industries such as telcos, software companies, and network equipment providers and for user industries that utilize these technologies. The following examples only scratch the surface, but they illustrate the potential of M2M technologies.

1. M2M in Energy Grids

Germany's decision to abandon nuclear power could serve as the catalyst for a huge technological leap forward. To stabilize energy supplies, the nation will need to develop massive amounts of renewable energy sources. It will also need to optimize its use of these energy supplies. As one example, households will be equipped with smart meters that can help to optimize energy consumption by adjusting usage to fluctuations in energy costs. Smart homes will communicate via control centers, which give commands to devices based on such factors as personal usage patterns, outside temperatures, security input, and other active feedback mechanisms.

In sum, M2M-managed production, supply, and consumption of energy will be the cornerstones for a successful transformation to alternative energy sources in the post-nuclear energy era. In Chapter 13, Dr. Michael Gorriz and Dr. Kai Holzweißig of Daimler discuss the promise of "Linked Data" as the language that connects a growing number of M2M networks.

2. M2M in Supply Chains, Transport, and Logistics

Logistics services are in many ways commoditized services. Competitive differentiations for logistics providers are based on a series of factors:

- Cost advantages generated by the efficient use of the business infrastructure

- Predictability of shipments to and services for customers

- Real-time tracking of goods wherever they are

- Routing optimization

- Data logging of environmental conditions for sensitive goods; for example, temperature monitoring of healthcare shipments

Enhanced customer satisfaction, more competitive pricing, more efficient resource usage, and environmental benefits are just some of the breakthrough benefits of fully digitized, M2M-based logistics and supply chains.

3. M2M in Commerce

M2M can benefit retailers and consumers by helping them optimize demand and supply. Retailers can reduce their capital spending on goods on the shelf or in the warehouse by monitoring demand and supply in real time. In addition, they can increase the availability of their self-service sales mechanisms such as vending machines by utilizing online predictive maintenance concepts. For their part, consumers can enjoy flexible payment systems that eliminate the need for cash and enable customers to purchase goods in a more cost-efficient and thus less-expensive way. For example, mobile advertisements inform selected consumers of special offers and the availability of desired goods, in real time. Ultimately, M2M will create a win-win situation that will be the primary driver behind the digitization of the consumer goods provision system that includes shops, vending machines, and other outlets.

4. M2M in Home Security

The benefits generated by fraud reductions will significantly boost the proliferation of surveillance for both private households and businesses. In turn, this development will result in fewer damages and losses, lower insurance premiums, and reduced resource consumption resulting from fewer security interventions. Furthermore, it will significantly increase the perceived as well as the actual quality of life for homeowners and apartment dwellers.

Another benefit of M2M is that property owners, fire and police departments, and other concerned parties can be alerted remotely, in real time, in cases of fire, burglary, water damage, and problems resulting from wind and severe weather. Going further, M2M technologies can detect the exact spot where the damage or impact occurred. This information is invaluable for first responders and repair specialists.

5. M2M in Remote Healthcare

Technologies that enable the surveillance of remote infrastructures are also the basis for remote healthcare. Indeed, the spectrum of possibilities ranges from prevention and fitness information, to medical assistance in cases of health difficulties, to assisted living for elderly people. The benefits include the following:

- Management of preventive healthcare behaviors

- Reductions in healthcare costs despite increased usage of the healthcare system by an aging society

- Management of preventive healthcare and assisted living for elderly people and persons with disabilities.

Digitizing the entire healthcare system, including measuring vital bodily functions in cases of weakness or illness, can dramatically increase the provision of healthcare in modern societies.

6. M2M in Public Sector Infrastructure Services

Public sector infrastructure services are burdened by budget reductions in federal, state, and local governments. Providing quality services under these challenging conditions requires greater efficiencies such as the following:

- More efficient use of resources

- Proactive infrastructure support and maintenance through monitoring of remote places

- Bureaucracy reduction through automated information exchange among citizens, businesses, and agencies

- Process automation

- Data integration and consolidation

Moreover, all of these changes must occur within a remote and holistic process of infrastructure management.

7. M2M in Traffic Management Systems

The key beneficiaries of M2M-based traffic management systems are infrastructure providers, drivers, auto manufacturers, and fleet managers. The primary objective of traffic management is to alleviate traffic congestion, particularly in densely populated cities. Achieving this objective will generate multiple benefits:

- Less smog and pollution in general

- An enhanced quality of life for people who live in, work in, or visit the city

- More predictable logistics

- Reduced fuel consumption

- Cost reductions for fleet management

Reduced traffic congestion will also benefit auto manufacturers because their products will contribute to CO_2 reductions and minimize the time drivers are trapped in frustrating circumstances. For motorists, digitized vehicle services can increase traveling comfort, optimize the routing of cars through congested areas, help prevent accidents by identifying potential accident sites, and inform service stations in the event of a vehicle breakdown. Fleet managers can optimize the utilization of their cars through informed routing decisions, enhanced vehicle tracking, fewer accidents as a result of higher safety standards, and the detection of unusual driving behaviors. Finally, connected cars can provide vital traffic information to other cars as well as to traffic-management agencies, radio stations, and other traffic-related institutions.

M2M provides instant information and intervention possibilities, without depending on human activities. Not only can M2M detect a defect in real time, but in many cases it can contain the problem and initiate instant remedial actions. A new world of new business opportunities is arising out of the digital M2M connectivities.

2

The Digital Journey

Digital is synonymous with new and exciting. Consumers line up for hours outside Apple stores and then emerge from the store happy and thrilled with their new iPhone or iPad. Ask most children what they want for the holidays, and more likely than not they will ask for something digital.

In the previous chapter we discussed Dr. Thomas Enders's expectations for digital innovation. In many ways, however, digital products that replace complicated analog devices are even more difficult to create. Breaking down information into bits and bytes is one thing, but improving the analog experience involves a great deal more effort. Among other things this process requires speed, ultimately speed in real time, because the day-to-day human experience unfolds in real time.

More specifically, processing information in real time requires exceptionally fast processors. For the past 30 years, processing capacity has followed Moore's Law, which predicted that the number of transistors contained on a microchip would double every 18 months.[11] As chip complexity and capacity have steadily increased, processing speeds have increased in tandem. Real-time reaction makes it possible to store and to process ever larger amounts of data. The price curve, coupled with the increased capacity of disk storage, has improved the economics of digital innovation. Finally, advances in telecommunications and memory have made the physical distance between the data and the processor less of an issue.

As a result, digital data can be processed and manipulated wherever they reside (in the cloud or on the premises), by consumers wherever they are located (mobile users), both on their own and connected to any interested parties (collaboration), regardless of the volume of data (Big Data). This development transcends simply reproducing what was possible in the analog world. Rather, it dramatically extends the range of our human senses, making us virtually omnipresent anytime, with anyone.

What does all of this mean? Essentially, we live in a digital world where digital users demand digital infrastructures at home, in the company they work for, and, last but not least, from the administrations they deal with. The digital user, the digital consumer, demands a digital way of living. The analog alternative is no longer an option. Analog behavior means waiting when you go to a public agency; it means being an uninformed consumer; it means being unconnected; and it means spending much more money for a slow way of getting something that frequently is not exactly what you want.

Technology is clearly the enabler for the digital revolution. The driver to use technology, however, is the consumer, the private consumer — you and me and everyone else. This reality creates pressure for anyone in any institution, public or private, whom the private person, the normal citizen, deals with. The digitally savvy consumer doesn't accept analog behavior. Rather, he or she dismisses it as inefficient and antiquated.

For perhaps the first time in modern history, consumers are driving the technological advancements of both private enterprises and public institutions. Today, the recent college graduate who goes to work for a company frequently has a more sophisticated IT setting at home than does a classical workplace: digital gaming, graphical user interfaces (GUIs), collaboration networks such as Facebook, mobile connections to anyone at any time through smartphones, and countless other technologies.

The industry refers to this trend as the "consumerization of IT." This and other digital trends put pressure on the IT departments of all types of enterprises to upgrade, to modernize, and to implement what Gartner calls the nexus of forces: the convergence and mutual reinforcement of social, mobility, cloud, and information patterns that drive new business scenarios.[12]

In addition to private businesses, public institutions and other nonprofits also need to become digital as quickly as possible. The digital citizen does not appreciate having to stand in line for a title or a license, to appear in person to provide a signature, or to wait for weeks for a document to arrive in the mail. Going further, the adoption of digital technologies by governments provides competitive advantages for their economies by making the processes that public administrators utilize more efficient. For example, digital advancements are significantly reducing the costs of bureaucracy for both citizens and businesses. In Germany bureaucracy costs are as high as € 30 billion per year.[13] Significantly, digital advancements in government agencies often have to be enabled through legislation.

So, how does the enterprise or government transform itself into the Digital Enterprise and the digital government? The purpose of this book is to show the direction that enterprises and public institutions have taken and the specific strategies they have adopted to achieve this objective.

As private enterprises and public institutions embark on their inevitable digital journey, they need to focus on certain basic requirements:

- Digitize the relevant content as well as all of the affected contracts and relevant information

- Digitize and integrate all processes that cross departments and enterprises

- Provide security and governance for the management and utilization of digital content

- Provide insight and visualization as needed in a real-time enabled world

Within this process, "mobile" is the buzzword. Mobile is the major disrupter for any industry that is seeking to expand its digital capabilities. Essentially, mobility enables the "anywhere, anytime, with anyone" aspects of the digital society.

The question remains, Why is the pressure for companies and institutions to become digital so intense? There have been so many hypecycles in the IT industry in the recent past that the natural tendency is to respond "so what" or "let's wait and see." The key difference between these "false alarms" and the digital revolution is that today the payback is tangible. Digital solutions provide countless benefits for consumers as well as for enterprises and government institutions.

Let's focus on consumers first. The key benefits for consumers are:

1. A 24 hours/7 days relationship with anyone, with real-time interaction. "Anyone" encompasses not only suppliers of goods and services but also friends, family members, emergency facilities, medical providers, public agencies, and almost any other individuals or institutions you can think of.

2. Full transparency of supply and demand. The digital revolution has created the opportunity for today's consumers to be better informed than any previous generation. Customers are increasingly empowered to demand the best buy and best fit, including the best price. Consequently, companies need to implement new strategies or face serious economic consequences. From the perspective of the business, this new model offers benefits as well as challenges. Specifically, it will reduce the rate of returns of purchased goods, thereby lowering logistics costs and improving competitive advantage.

3. Crowd opinions help to make purchasing decisions. Ratings for "likes" or "dislikes" can either foster or destroy a product's market potential. Businesses can utilize these data as real-time ratings for their products and services as well as for the entire customer experience with their products and services. Public institutions can use them to measure citizen satisfaction, which exerts a major influence on election results in democratic nations.

The benefits to public institutions and enterprises include the following:

1. Unlimited customer- and citizen-reach, anytime, anywhere, for the company or the institution's products and services and, more importantly, for the proactive adjustment of demand and supply. The continuous link to customers and potential customers enables companies to modify their products and services, their logistics, and even their overall strategy more quickly and effectively than was conceivable in the traditional analog business.

2. Unlimited business scalability. The greatest challenge to growth in virtually any business is not market demand itself. Rather, it is the business's capability to scale its organization. Traditionally, businesses executed their functions in departmental silos rather than in workflows oriented toward the customer value-creation chains. Consequently, companies configured their IT to support departments, not workflows. IT thus created walls between departments due to the incompatibility of data formats and a general lack of cross-departmental integration. Processes frequently were neither documented nor automated. The consequence of this disjointed system was limited growth. In contrast, Digital Enterprises possess the capability to scale as demand requires.

3. Digital Enterprises have total business performance transparency for their managerial and operational excellence, as well as for all required government regulations. The resulting benchmarking

benefit provides digital companies and digital institutions with the capabilities for continuous improvements, wherever and whenever they are required. As the proverb goes, you can manage only what you can measure.

4. Real-time support of management decisions. A business's ability to adjust to changing circumstances as expeditiously as possible is a critical success factor. The Digital Enterprise has the capability to learn on the go and to decide on the go, because it has real-time access to all of the information it needs. Contrast this model with the analog world of uninformed, unconnected, nontransparent businesses. Can you imagine the competitive advantage for digital companies whose management is up to speed on all relevant business aspects, anytime, anywhere?

5. Real-time support for any worker, at any level. This benefit creates unprecedented opportunities. Companies can now make decisions at the point of operations anywhere in the company — decisions that help to optimize whatever function the worker is responsible for. For example, a shop clerk obtains the information about a customer at the time he or she enters the shop, through recognition systems that identify the person, through social media like Facebook that record his or her preferences, and from LinkedIn, which conveys information about his or her career status and plans. The key here is mass customization. The information is there. The task to be mastered is to utilize it to the maximum benefit of both the company and the customer.

In sum, every business must become a digital business, regardless which industry it operates in. The critical questions include how to create a strategy to convert this objective into a reality, how to implement this strategy, what is the succession of actions, and so on. To answer these questions, businesses should adopt the following implementation pattern:

1. Define your enterprise digital platforms, which are built on top of your existing IT application environment. Implement a digital layer so you can begin the digitization process as quickly as possible. The digital layer consists of the following capabilities: integration bus as a backbone, business process management (BPM) platform visualization/analytics, and the Big Data management layer.

2. Define the personal digital enablement tools and systems that are at your employees' disposal. These resources are personal enablers and personal productivity tools.

3. Define the functional digital enablement; that is, the digital systems for specific departments such as salesforce.com for sales and marketing, SAP SuccessFactors for HR, and so on. These systems of records optimize the resource pools in the various departmental functions.

4. Finally, create a roadmap for transforming your organization into a Digital Enterprise or a digital public agency. If you have not already begun this transition, then start now. Time is your biggest enemy!

In Part II, we outline 15 digital opportunity areas. For each area we provide real-life examples of how business enterprises and government agencies have improved their customer-facing, manufacturing, logistics, information security, governance, and other operational areas.

PART II

OPPORTUNITIES AVAILABLE TO THE DIGITAL ENTERPRISE

3

Create Smarter Products

We hear a lot of references today to smart products. What exactly *are* smart products?

Smart products are digitally enabled products that are often equipped with sensors to measure, transmitters to communicate, and energy-efficient usage patterns. Smart products are embedded in an infrastructure that makes the products smart. The mass of the products' intelligence typically lies in central cloud-based systems that process the data delivered by millions of smart products or sensors.

These observations hold true whether we are referring to smart cloth for sports uniforms, to medically supportive smart products for people who are ill or who have disabilities, to industrial systems like proactive maintenance for jet engines, or to entire systems in industrial plants that identify maintenance requirements before the systems fail. Smart predictions of consumption patterns are a great source of revenue generation for vending machine content providers such as Coca-Cola.

Smart products help you plan your day easily, they help you maintain the security of your home, and they help you know where your kids are. What's more, they provide this information whenever you want it.

So, to make products smart is not an "if or if not" issue. Rather, it is a basic development to simplify life by making systems more efficient, secure, reliable, and simply smarter.

In recent years, most enterprises have had to come to grips with a trend called "consumerization of IT," as employees clamor to use their favorite mobile device, social networks, or personal email accounts at work. Consequently, enhancing the security and supporting the diversity of Android, iOS, and other devices and consumer-centric apps has become a major IT focus.

At the same time, a number of companies have exploited the major opportunities offered by "Consumerization" with a capital C. They are asking the question: "If people increasingly live in the world of PlayStations and iPhones, can we rethink our products to make them more appealing to today's tech-savvy customers?"

Prompted by this question, industry after industry is looking to make its products "smarter" by utilizing technologies such as software, sensors, and satellite support. In some cases this process is as basic as enhancing a product with LEDs or Bluetooth connectivity or creating YouTube how-to manuals. In other cases it is far more sophisticated. In this chapter we examine technological innovations that are occurring within a number of industries. We begin with a very popular product — cars.

The Much Smarter Car

The automobile industry is experiencing a digital revolution sparked by innovative technologies for electric batteries, "infotainment," mobile apps, and safety applications. Indeed, even an "outsider" to that industry — Google — has excited the world with its autonomous (self-driving) concept car. The car drives at the speed limit it has stored on its maps, it uses its sensors to maintain a safe distance from other vehicles, and its cameras read and interpret traffic lights and other signs. Going further, in tests the car has demonstrated the ability to handle complex turns and heavy traffic.[14] In fact, the results have been so impressive that they have generated policy debates on how traffic signals and speeding fines will have to evolve as more cars become driverless.

Although the driverless car may be the car of the future, elements of this functionality have been available for some time from automakers like Mercedes. For example, the Mercedes adaptive cruise control, which uses its Distronic radar to maintain a safe distance from other cars, has been available since the late 1990s. More recently, Mercedes has offered attention-assist functionality to intervene if the driver is drowsy. Blind-spot assist detects cars beside you, and it prevents you from merging into their lane. Lane-keeping assist alerts you when you're drifting out of your lane. Finally, the Mercedes Parktronic guidance system helps you parallel-park.[15]

Mercedes' competitor, BMW, has been innovating with its connectivity, navigation, entertainment, and other technology-enabled features. BMW's Connected Drive suite of technology enables real-time traffic information, and it enhances the vehicle's navigation functionality with smarter routing and detour suggestions. This technology suite also supports BMW's Heads-Up Display and safer nighttime vision by employing infrared sensors. In addition, the technology interacts with a wide variety of mobile apps. For example, drivers can be integrated via voice commands with email, Google Search, Facebook, and other applications.[16] This connectivity enables the car to function as a wireless hotspot for the car's occupants. In many ways, the car has evolved from a vehicle to much more of a companion in daily life.

Tesla, the U.S. electric car, offers mobile apps that allow owners to interact with their Model S to monitor their car's electric charge and to precondition their car on very hot or cold days.[17]

In a practitioner guest column that appears later in this chapter, Celso Guiotoko, CIO of Global IS at Nissan Motor Co., Ltd., discusses other auto innovations such as "steering-by-wire," which the aviation industry pioneered.

While Mercedes, BMW, and Tesla focus on premium cars, automakers in all price categories are bringing technology-driven innovations to mass markets. For example, Hyundai, the Korean automaker, has been experimenting with interfaces based on driver eye tracking and gestures.[18] Škoda, the Czech automaker, has been offering its Adaptive Frontlight System (AFS) to improve visibility since 2008.[19] Even the ultra-cheap Tata Nano in India — priced at under €2,000 — came equipped with a radio system that supported MP3, USB, and Aux-in functionality.[20]

The Smarter Shower
You could argue that the auto industry has always been technically savvy and they are just raising the technology bar in their products. But, how do we explain the technology innovations in our showers?

Consider, for example, the Gerloff Magic Shower. This system includes electronic controls for adjusting the water temperature and switching between rainshower and hand-held showerhead flows. Going further, the system also controls music playback and mood lighting to enhance the shower experience.[21]

Gerloff's competitor, Moen, offers a "vertical spa" that comes complete with a number of body sprays, showerheads, and hand showers. Its ioDigital control device allows users to customize temperature and water delivery options. It also remembers those options, so different family members can personalize their settings.[22]

Smarter Toys
A widely watched YouTube video shows a baby who tries to use gestural controls on a printed magazine. The video is titled "An iPad which does not work."[23] There is no question the younger generation of consumers is more comfortable with technology, and they expect almost everything they purchase or use to be high-tech. It's no wonder, then, that toys and games have to become more digital.

As an example, Mattel's Mindflex Duel game uses a brain machine inter-face developed by NeuroSky. Players move a ball through an obstacle course, using only the power of their minds.[24] Lego, the famous Danish maker of plastic toy bricks, has introduced an augmented reality app that allows users to view a digital, 3D image of what they are assem-bling.[25] The English toymaker MakieLab enables its young customers to create "Makie dolls" using an iPad app to customize eye and skin color, hairstyles, and clothing choices. It then uses 3D printers to cre-ate the dolls, and it ships them to the customers.[26]

Technology for the Older Demographic

Creating technology-enabled products for youthful customers seems rather obvious. However, a very different demographic is increasingly adopting digital products: elderly people. On many flights you see older travelers reading eBooks on their Kindles. Does this surprise you? If so, then think about it for a minute. Carrying an e-reader is much less cumbersome than lugging hardback books. In addition, eBook users can easily increase the font size. And, if they are tired, the machine can read aloud to them.

In Japan, service robots are increasingly being used for elderly care. These are not the bulky robots employed in yesterday's plants. These machines are so fine-tuned they can spray water and shampoo people's hair and then massage the scalp with their mechanical fingers.

From electric scooters to assistive technology for individuals who are hearing and visually impaired, modern companies are developing a growing number of technologies for a demographic that in many cases never owned a PC. For example, Intel and other firms are focusing on a novel approach to patient care called "ageing in place." They include "beds that can monitor patients' vital signs as they sleep, stoves that can turn themselves off when their owners forget, and video games that can detect early signs of dementia."[27] These services rely on newly created monitoring technologies that may eventually replace retirement homes and assisted living centers.

Whereas most of the products we have just discussed are aimed at ever-more-savvy tech customers, even more elaborate products are evolving for professionals across various fields. The remainder of this chapter focuses on three areas: hospitals, farms, and casinos.

The Smarter Hospital

Contemporary healthcare embraces the concept of the "five rights": the right patient receiving the right dose of the right medication at the right time via the right delivery method. The U.S. medical company Hospira has been developing infusion systems to help practitioners achieve that goal. These systems support bidirectional wireless data communication that matches patient, authorized caregiver, order, and pump data by scanning bar codes and ID badges. If all of this information is correct, then the system checks the order against the drug library and the dosing guidelines. After everything has been verified, the system can automatically program the pump, and the infusion can begin. Going further, the software- and sensor-enabled checks and balances free up the nursing staff to tend to other duties. They can also alert nurses that their attention is needed using various visual and audio signals.[28]

The Smarter Farm

An even more elaborate set of technologies has been designed by John Deere for its farming community. Deere's FarmSight connects farming equipment, owners, operators, and dealers.[29]

FarmSight assists in three areas:

- Machine Optimization — using precision technology for higher levels of productivity and increased uptime

- Logistics Optimization — using technology to develop fleet management solutions and to improve machine-to-machine (M2M) communication

- Agriculture Decision Support — obtaining machinery and agronomic data essential to making proactive management decisions

The Smarter Casino

In a guest column later in this chapter, Rob James, former Chief Technology Officer at Echo Entertainment, describes how casinos are utilizing digital technologies like RFID and facial recognition to provide better customer service.

Summary

Embedding digital technology in products presents a major opportunity for Digital Enterprises in every industry. You need only look at companies like Daimler, founded in 1890, and Moen, founded in 1937, which are delivering smarter products. These companies are not startups, by a long shot. Of course there is also a fear factor: If our customers don't view our products as smart, then will they increasingly view them as dumb? And, if they do, will they desert us for our competitors? Now that we've examined the process of making products smarter, we conclude the chapter with two practitioner perspectives — Nissan Motor Co., Ltd., and Echo Entertainment.

Nissan's Digital Journey

Celso Guiotoko, Corporate Vice President and CIO, Global IS Division, Nissan Motor Co., Ltd.

Nissan Motor Co., Ltd., headquartered in Yokohama, Japan, is part of the Renault-Nissan Alliance. We sold nearly 5 million vehicles in 2012, and we are renowned for our exciting and innovative products. We are considered a leader in zero-emission mobility with products like the Nissan LEAF, an affordable, pure-electric vehicle; our pre-announced, ultra-compact two-seater electric vehicle; the e-NV200, an electric compact van; and e-Atlas, an electrically powered truck.

Within the Nissan culture, product innovation receives the greatest emphasis in our technology-investment strategy. "Innovation" refers both to technology to make our *products* smarter and to technology to make the *processes* of manufacturing and supporting our products smarter.

An example of making our product smarter is the "steering-by-wire" technology that is being introduced in the Infiniti Q50. A conventional steering system directs tire movements by transmitting steering inputs to the tires via a mechanical link. In contrast, in steering-by-wire, the messages are electronic. Basically, the steering wheel "talks" to a computer, and the computer "talks" to the wheels. Even on a road surface with minor ridges or furrows, the driver no longer has to grip the steering wheel tightly and make detailed adjustments. This improvement makes traveling on the intended path more comfortable. We expect Q50 drivers to enjoy benefits similar to those delivered by "fly-by-wire" in the aviation industry over the last couple of decades — reduced weight, lower maintenance costs, and enhanced steering precision.

To augment the "steering by wire," we have developed a "straight-line stability system." Using a camera mounted above the vehicle's rearview mirror, the system analyzes the road ahead, recognizes the lane direction, detects changes in the vehicle's direction, and transmits this information as signals to multiple electronic control units.

Another exciting innovation is our Electric Vehicle Telematics Program, which enables Nissan LEAF owners to remotely monitor and control selected vehicle functions utilizing either their smartphone or a secure website. Owners can monitor the state of their vehicle's charge, control door locks, and turn the air conditioning on or off. In addition to these benefits for car owners, the program also allows Nissan to monitor battery-related issues and perform predictive failure analysis for customers' cars. Nissan can use this information to proactively alert LEAF owners of potential problems.

Our electric vehicle differentiation is also on display with our EV Power Station. This system uses the high-capacity lithium-ion batteries used in the Nissan LEAF to store and supply electricity. LEAF owners can use the station to store electricity during the night when the demand is low (and rates are likely lower) and then supply it to their home during daytime when the demand is high.

Yet another example of Nissan's drive toward innovative technology is our Connected Service Platform. Starting in 2015, Nissan will offer our customers enhanced safety and a wide variety of new conveniences like accident-avoiding driving intervention technologies, electric vehicle charging reservations, and a music player that adapts to the listener's moods. All of these features will be enabled by wireless and cloud-based technologies. Shorter term, the Connected Car is generating plenty of "Big Data," which allow us to monitor quality issues, analyze charging performance, and evaluate various other metrics across the customer community.

In addition to all of these innovations, Nissan has moved into digital mockups. The digital design process allows us to present 3D data early in the design cycle, realize the image with a reduced workforce downstream, and facilitate early collaboration with other departments in areas such as package planning and aerodynamics. In effect, we can perform more concurrent versus sequential engineering, thereby reducing our product development lifecycles by half.

To assist us in our efforts to manufacture the most up-to-date and driver-friendly vehicles, we have adopted a policy of monitoring social networks for new product feature ideas; for feedback concerning our competitors' features, sales, and service; and for other valuable information. Given the long lead time in auto product lifecycles compared to those for consumer products, the feedback from early pilots is extremely helpful.

Clearly, then, Nissan's digital journey has accelerated, especially when you measure it in terms of our product features and development life-cycle. The auto industry is going through an extremely innovative time when it comes to fuel efficiency, connectivity, and safety, and Nissan is well positioned to lead the market.

Celso Guiotoko is Corporate Vice President and CIO, Global IS Division of Nissan Motor Co., Ltd.

Echo Entertainment

Rob James, former Chief Technology Officer, Echo Entertainment Group Ltd.

Echo Entertainment Group is one of Australia's largest publicly listed companies. We are active in four vibrant business areas — hospitality, dining, nightlife, and gaming. We also operate four casinos: The Star in Sydney, Jupiters on the Gold Coast, Treasury in Brisbane, and Jupiters in Townsville.

The lifeblood of our business is the VIP customer, also called the "whale" or "high roller" in the industry vernacular. These individuals represent only 0.1% of the customers who visit our casinos (we don't support online gambling). Nevertheless, they generate more than 30% of our revenues. Not surprisingly, then, much of our innovation is driven by a desire to service VIP customers as effectively as we can.

Although gaming appears to be highly automated with the slot machines and the dazzle in our nightlife, many of the industry processes are still largely manual and regulated. Consequently, in any given year we evaluate several innovation projects. In this column I describe six projects we have either implemented or piloted.

One strategy we employ to prioritize our innovation projects is to assign them scores based on the following criteria (1 being the lowest and 5 the highest):

- Complexity to test the idea (5 being easy, 1 being difficult)

- Complexity to scale the idea into production (5 being easy, 1 being difficult)

- Value of the return on success (using multiples of costs to execute is simplest; i.e., 1 for hard to break-even, 2 for profits in the 2x return on investment, 3 for 3x up to 5 for 5x or more in return on investment)

- Size of market opportunity (1 for we don't have this market, we'll need to get it, through 5 for we have this market and understand it well)

- Our experience (1 for we've never done anything like this before, through 5 for we possess a great set of skills and expertise to execute the idea)

Now that I've explained Echo's philosophy and methodologies, let's review some of our recent innovation projects and pilots.

Electronic Chip Purchase Voucher (eCPV)

One recent innovation we have implemented is the eCPV. A CPV (chip purchase voucher) is a funds-release function designed expressly for VIP players. Much like a withdrawal at a bank, we have created a process to ensure these players have sufficient funds with the casino, have validated their ID, and can withdraw the amount in the form of chips all at the same time without disrupting the game.

Traditionally, this function has been executed through a paper-based process that takes 20 minutes to complete. This process involves printing a CPV contract form that is then signed by the player, the dealer, and the pit manager before any chips can be released. This process can be very time consuming, particularly when all parties are not immediately available. In contrast, the digital eCPV process uses iPads. Rather than creating paper contracts, we provide VIP players with a PIN at the start of the process when they deposit their funds. Later, when they require funds at their table, they simply enter the desired amount along with their PIN. The pit manager then enters his sign-in PIN, and the chips are released. In contrast to the old paper-based system, the eCVP process takes less than 2 minutes.

Mobility

Mobile devices and mobility are critical to our casino organization, where fewer than 9% of the staff is sitting behind a dedicated desk. Echo is working on multiple innovations in this space. For example, we have developed a slot-tracking system for mobile devices that surveys current activity to find large bets on slot machines. Slot hosts can utilize this information to locate high-value players who are not currently participating in our loyalty program and approach them to sign up.

We have also implemented hotel mobile check-ins for our staff that allow them to get out from behind the check-in desk and greet guests. Two other major innovations are (1) mobile business intelligence-management panels on mobile devices that enable slot technicians to manage slot machines and (2) customer dashboards that allow casino hosts to easily access players' profiles and service them accordingly.

Video Analytics

One of the essential operational functions of a casino is managing the yield on its tables. In a casino with hundreds of tables, managing the number of open tables, the games played on those tables, the denomination of the casino chips, and the number of guests in the casino represents a formidable challenge. Traditionally, casinos have performed these functions through historical analysis. By taking into account previous days in the last week, month, and year, we try to manage a "spread" (table roster) for the next four weeks. The operational staff such as the casino manager then makes decisions on the day based on observations and, most likely, on "gut feel!"

The fundamental shortcoming of this approach is that these data are generally tracked manually and typically quite inaccurately. Tracking players at a table involves a manual process of keying in an estimate by the dealer. Additionally, decisions about how fast a game should be dealt or how many bets are being placed are made without accurate data.

By leveraging our investment in video technology, Echo has implemented video machine learning analytics to track this information more accurately. We have cameras pointed at every table in case disputes with players arise. We can use the same video stream to analyze the data in real time to more accurately determine both the number of bets being played at a table per hand and where the bets are being placed (in the case of Baccarat player, banker, or tie bets). (The number of bets is much more important information than the number of players at a table because many people either don't play every hand or are simply spectators.) This system also enables us to estimate the value of the bets by analyzing the size of the pile along with the colors to determine the denomination.

This tool is incredibly powerful because, by estimating the number of bets, along with their value and frequency, we are able to calculate table yield live. By performing these calculations on a casino-wide scale, we can start to run analytics to determine whether we should be opening tables, closing tables, changing the game being played, or changing the minimum bets allowed on the tables.

Ultimately, Echo plans to deliver dashboards to the dealers so that KPIs can be driven to them. For example, based on the game and the number of bets being played, are the cards being dealt too quickly or too slowly?

Facial Recognition

Facial recognition is becoming increasingly accurate. In a casino environment where hundreds, if not thousands of cameras have been installed, this technology can provide substantial benefits. From a security and compliance perspective, we can utilize it to keep out excluded patrons, or the "bad guys." More generally, we can use it to provide a more enjoyable customer experience.

As an example, cameras located in the hotel lobby could focus on customers who are waiting to check in. The front desk host could utilize the facial recognition technology to identify the VIPs, automatically check them in, and cut a key for them. He or she could then personally walk up to these individuals, hand them their keys, and direct them to their room. From the patrons' perspective, it's just a nice touch that the hotel operator either remembered them or was told who they are. The reality, however, is that there is a lot of technology driving this special treatment.

Of course, the "creep" factor needs to be considered here. Customers don't want to be greeted everywhere they go by staff who seem to know them! Therefore, this service needs to be sufficiently subtle to balance guests' appreciation of the personal attention they receive with their desire for privacy.

Event-Based Notifications

The casino car park provides a reserved level for VIP patrons. VIPs can access this special benefit by swiping their loyalty card. The event of swiping a card can be captured, and a casino host can be notified when a VIP has arrived. This capability can be extended to provide additional benefits, such as understanding guests' relationships with other patrons. For example, a husband and wife may have a hotel reservation under the wife's name while the loyalty membership is under the husband's name. By being aware of this association, the hotel could pre-check the couple in when the husband swipes into the car park.

Another focus of technology innovation is event systems that are processed by complex event processing (CEP) engines. An example use case is to track a combination of spend on the bar and gaming play, along with historical and location information, to make very targeted and specific offers. For example, after several hours of playing games and running up a bar tab, if the patron is walking through the property and we sense that he or she has passed a restaurant, we could SMS a special offer.

RFID Chips

One innovation we have considered but not invested in is RFID chips. The initial business driver for RFID chips was security. If someone were to steal RFID chips — as happened in 2010 when US$1.5 million of chips were stolen from the Bellagio in Vegas — the chips can be immediately rendered worthless by deactivating the RFID tags.

RFID chips are considerably more expensive to stock than traditional ceramic or clay chips. This expense, however, also represents an investment to protect the casino from those rare occurrences when chips are actually stolen. We have also considered other drivers for RFID chips; for example, optimizing cage processes, automating tray counts at tables, automating the value of bets on a table, and automating bet tracking in VIP salons.

Once again, many of these innovations required additional technology investments. Although the costs associated with RFID have come down, making the business case easier to drive, it's interesting to find other technologies also accelerating around RFID costs to provide even more options like the video analytics described above.

Gaming has always been an exciting industry. We are constantly using technology-enabled innovation to make it even more so.

Rob James is former Chief Technology Officer at Echo Entertainment Group Ltd.

4

Make Your Services Agile

Smart products and their sensors are providing the primary input for smarter services. Smarter services are based on the aggregation, combination, and analysis of data generated by a single, hundreds, thousands, or even millions of sensors located within a targeted serviceable environment.

Proactive behavior is one element that was understood and targeted, from an intellectual point of view, years ago. Large industrial systems, large medical systems, and even the health status of an individual could be monitored to determine the required actions to keep the systems or the person's health stable.

The intellectual comprehension of proactive behavior was one thing. Putting it into action, however, requires today's highly advanced technology, smart mobile usage, smart products, collaboration platforms, cloud operations, and the ability to analyze these massive amounts of data in real time.

Modern technologies enable services to do just that. The results are stunning. Consider the following developments:

- Jet engines deliver terabytes of data that enable pilots and crews to avoid serious mishaps by responding quickly to potentially hazardous situations.

- Large industrial systems increase their availability to unprecedented levels, in some cases achieving 100% availability.

- Medical systems proactively monitor people's health, enabling professionals to intervene before people suffer severe health damage.

- Collaborative medical systems can provide data for millions of patients, where professionals can analyze patterns and detect diseases earlier.

- Logistics systems perform at optimal levels, reduce fuel consumption, decrease the number of accidents, and detect erratic or dangerous driving behavior.

Compare the composition of the annual *Fortune 500* list of companies for the last decade to that from 30 or 60 years ago. The number of service companies — banking, insurance, and so on — has grown considerably. Moreover, even in product industries, the revenue mix has been trending towards more of a product/services hybrid — plus installation, delivery, repair, and warranty services including unprecedented availability warranties.

As service industries have assumed a larger role within modern economies, technology has become an increasingly vital element within these industries. Most banks began to offer ATMs in the 1970s; service call centers became common in the 1980s; and frequently asked questions (FAQs) have been a fixture on websites since the 1990s. Today, a new generation of smart services that leverage telematics, predictive analytics, and social networks is reshaping every industry. Let's look at a few examples.

Banking

CaixaBank in Spain is reporting that its mobile transactions have almost totally supplanted its ATM transactions. Transactions through its physical branches now represent less than 10% of overall business, compared to more than 30% just a decade ago. Almost 3 million customers use more than 60 applications in the bank's CaixaMóvil App Store. Some of these apps allow customers to execute routine transactions like paying bills and transferring funds. However, the bank also offers highly creative features. For example, one app varies the volume of your music to reflect how the stock markets are performing.[30]

In the United States, Chase is pursuing a mixed mobile and branch strategy. Because paper checks are still a major form of payment, Chase supports mobile deposits where customers can take photos of the front and back of their checks with their smartphones. In general, the bank's branches are increasingly defined by technology. For example, in addition to all the typical ATM functions, the branches now offer next-gen kiosks that cash checks and dispense cash in multiple denominations. Going further, by introducing machines that can create debit cards on the spot, Chase can empower customers to make card purchases as soon as they leave the branch. Finally, the branches offer videoconferencing with off-site bank specialists who can sell various products and services and serve customers who speak other languages.[31]

Insurance

Another service that is becoming increasingly technology driven is the insurance industry. For example, as José Manuel Inchausti Pérez, Managing Director of Technology and Process at MAPFRE, the leading Spanish insurer, describes in his executive guest column later in this chapter, his company offers a telematics-enabled concept for younger drivers in its YCAR program. MAPFRE also provides mobile apps to this younger customer base that enable them to locate their cars, calculate fuel costs, share travel journals on social networks, and estimate future insurance premiums.

Debeka, a German insurer that sells travel insurance, has a mobile app that provides vaccination information by country, tips for first aid, and GPS coordinate transmission by email in case of emergencies.[32]

Finally, Nationwide Insurance's iPhone application allows customers to collect and exchange accident information, take pictures of the accident scene, initiate a claim, display their insurance card and other account information, and locate nearby tow trucks and authorized repair shops.[33]

Government Services

Estonia, barely two decades removed for a long period of Soviet domination and economic stagnation, now provides its citizens with one of the world's richest set of digital services. Included here are free universal Wi-Fi, an ID card with certificates to authenticate identity and enable digital signatures, a highly efficient tax-filing process, online balloting, electronic medical and real estate records, parking payments via mobile phone, and an e-School administration that allows parents to monitor their children's activities from home.[34]

Governments are also utilizing innovative technologies to alleviate transportation headaches. In particular, heavy and oversize-load transports represent a very serious challenge for people, materials, and logistics. Not all routes are suitable for this type of transport, so special arrangements such as roadblocks and police escorts are frequently required to guide special transports safely to their destination. The x-trans.eu website plays a central role as a facilitator in this process, gathering information for a transport permit only once and then communicating it in an appropriate manner to the authorities in the individual European countries. A pilot project is being tested between the states of Bavaria in Germany and Upper Austria in Austria. The broader goal of this project is to streamline an array of government processes that require approvals across multiple jurisdictions and agencies.[35]

Another critical area of government activity is surveillance. Today most government agencies have access to massive amounts of surveillance video. Their challenge is to process those data quickly and efficiently. An impressive use case comes from the Law Enforcement and Emergency Services Video Association (LEVA) Forensic Video Analysis Response Team. LEVA is a nonprofit corporation dedicated to training law enforcement and emergency services in the most up-to-date video technologies. In one of its most impressive efforts, the company processed more than 5,000 hours of video evidence related to the June 15, 2011, Stanley Cup Riot in Vancouver, Canada.[36] Within a two-week period it had reviewed and tagged the video and documented 15,000 criminal acts committed by 300 rioters.[37]

Museums, a vital part of the local communities in all major cities, are already using digital technology to better showcase their artifacts and to enhance the experience for people visiting the museum in person and experiencing it over the web. This technology is already more-or-less state of the art. However, the museum world is about to experience another seismic disruption brought on by digitization.

To secure their long-term survival and to become even more relevant, museums need to secure donors. Unfortunately, local donors are a rare and precious resource. Consequently, there is intense competition among museums to attract remote donors who are frequently located in other museum vicinities. Because museums can offer a digital virtual presence of the entire museum experience in unprecedented ways, the competition for donations will enter into a new stage. Specifically, it will leave its local barriers of the analog world. In other words, it will globalize.

How will this development transform the museum world? Essentially, any museum that fails to exploit the opportunity to internationalize its reach by establishing a digital virtual presence will experience new remote competition for its donors at its doorsteps from other museums that maintain such a presence. The solution is not a classic home page, but, instead, innovative strategies to present artwork to their new and remote target audience.

In his guest column, Max Hollein, Director of the Städel Museum in Frankfurt, Germany, describes his museum's digital journey.

Mobile and social technologies are also exerting a major impact on the travel industry. For example, the MGM Mirage in Las Vegas has launched a virtual reality app that provides a multidimensional experience of the city's hotels, restaurants, and attractions.[38] Hotels have historically trained their staff to be very observant of their guests' unique needs. Social media is allowing them to "listen" even more. The St. Regis Bora Bora Resort, for example, conducts Google searches on guest names prior to their arrival. It then shares guest profiles from that intelligence with their department heads to help them provide more personalized service.[39]

Technology is also reshaping the guest room. Hotels like The Plaza in New York are making devices like the iPad the centerpiece of the guest experience. The tablet in each room allows guests to order a meal via room service, make restaurant reservations, book wake-up calls, print out boarding passes, control the room's lighting and air conditioning, and process many other guest requests.[40] The Radisson chain has Sleep Number beds in its rooms. These beds allow guests to adjust the firmness of the mattress with a control device. Because many guests have these types of beds at home, they can adjust the hotel bed to their specific comfort scale number so it feels like their own bed.[41]

Hong Kong launched the Octopus stored-value smart card in 1997 to collect fares for its mass transit system. Today customers can use the smart card for stores, restaurants, parking meters, vending machines, and other venues. A testament to Hong Kong's importance as a global hub is the fact more than 20 million cards are in circulation, which is 3 times Hong Kong's population.[42]

In Singapore, the taxi service ComfortDelGro runs a fleet of more than 16,000 cars and books more than 30 million rides annually. In 2010 the company launched a location-aware app that enables mobile users to book taxis. This system wirelessly connects taxis using in-vehicle mobile data terminals (MDTs). This massive amount of booking and GPS data has led to a story that has been making the rounds of Big Data conferences. A project to triangulate weather satellite data with hundreds of millions of GPS records revealed an interesting pattern: Many taxis did not appear to be moving during rainstorms. Further analysis discovered that the root cause was a company policy that stated that cab drivers involved in accidents would have their pay docked while the accident was being investigated. The policy was leading taxi drivers to pull over during rain showers. The drivers had decided that the fares were not worth the risk.[43]

Auto Service

Two fundamental changes in the auto services business relate to where and how these services are delivered. Services like Safelite, which fixes shattered car glass, now go to the customer rather than expect the customer to bring the car into a repair shop. After the company has confirmed a mobile repair appointment, it sends the customer an email containing the name, picture, and background information of the technician they are sending to work on the vehicle.[44]

Another example of innovation in auto services is Mercedes-Benz, which equips its cars with its mbrace2 telematics system. This system "includes features such as Facebook, Google, open browsing, stocks, Yelp!, and news headlines" in addition to "new remote access capabilities [that] include Travel Zones/geo-fences, remote vehicle health diagnostics, Curfew Minder, Driving Journal, Speed Alerts, Valet Protect, and Remote Horns & Lights."[45] Owners can automatically update mbrace2 via over-the-air (OTA) technologies. This cloud offering reduces trips to the dealer for new software updates. Once you go to the dealer, you can see from the error codes on the onboard diagnostics how much the modern auto technician has to know about sensors, software, satellite signals, and other technologies.[46]

Summary

As products become smarter and are embedded with increasing amounts of technology services to install, maintain, and repair, by definition become more technologically sophisticated. Traditional services industries are also making their services smarter using mobile, social, and other technologies.

Now let's look at three practitioner perspectives — first from MAPFRE and then from DB Systel GmbH and, finally, the Städel Museum.

MAPFRE — How Satellites Are Transforming Auto Insurance

José Manuel Inchausti Pérez, Managing Director of Technology and Process, MAPFRE S.A.

Some of you may associate MAPFRE with our sponsorship of the tennis star Rafael Nadal. Others may be aware that we offer health coverage for athletes. We do that and much more. MAPFRE is a €25-billion insurance company — the insurance market leader in Spain and the largest provider of insurance other than life insurance in Latin America.

In addition to health and life insurance, MAPFRE is a major player in the auto insurance industry. In this column I discuss how our products are being transformed by technology, particularly by satellites and digital maps. Three of our leading satellite-enabled innovations are YCAR, Futura, and MAIassist.

YCAR

YCAR is an offering aimed at "Generation Y" consumers. We connect a telematics device to the insured car's on-board diagnostics outlet without obstructing the driver's line of sight. The satellite tracking provides us with information concerning driving patterns — miles driven each day, nighttime driving, how often the driver makes hard stops, and so on. We then analyze this information to offer discounts to safe drivers.

YCAR began in 2007 when MAPFRE launched a pilot that was limited to 10,000 drivers between the ages of 18 and 27. (We had 65,000 customers by June 2013.) The pilot data revealed interesting trends, such as the days and hours when young drivers use their cars. One key finding is that road safety correlates more closely to the length of the drive than to the age of the driver.

MAPFRE learned from that experience, and we have since been adding services to the YCAR platform. One example is pay-per-use insurance. In addition, we send emergency services to an accident site, and we offer tracking in the event of theft. Significantly, our auto theft costs have gone down dramatically thanks to the tracking capabilities. We also provide our customers with a tele-diagnosis service. Consumers appreciate these services even more than the discounts. Figure 4-1 illustrates other value-added services we are considering adding to YCAR.

YCAR Value-Added Services

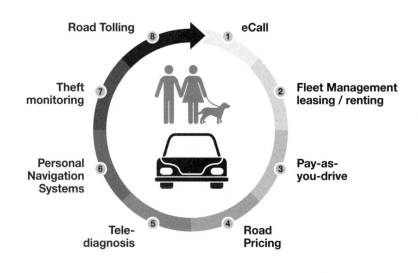

Figure 4-1: YCAR Value-Added Services

Significantly, YCAR uses GPS data for only some of the emergency services due to concerns with that system's privacy protection. MAPFRE utilizes what we call the privacy firewall that AENOR (the Spanish Standards body) certifies. One reason we implemented this policy was to avoid some of the privacy issues that Progressive experienced with their GPS pilot in Texas in the late 1990s.

Futura

Futura is a system we developed to automate the roadside assistance process. When we (or a client who uses our software) receive a call from an insured driver, our system determines the best service provider. It then automatically generates a service request to the provider's mobile device that includes location information and other important details.

Futura integrates satellite positioning technology (GPS), mobile networks, and state-of-the-art digital cartography applications to provide optimal service. In addition, Futura makes the entire process transparent to the insured parties, to the provider, and to MAPFRE. Our clients report quicker service, providers report greater utilization of their vehicles, and our staff report that administration processes such as managing invoices have become less complicated.

MAlassist

MAlassist is a mobile technology that extends the Futura concept. With MAlassist, customers can select from their mobile device the type of assistance they need: accident, theft, or breakdown. The MAPFRE assistance systems then detect the client's exact location via GPS, and they automatically initiate the assistance-management process. A few minutes later, the user receives confirmation of the request along with information such as the estimated time of arrival of the assistance unit. The automated location data taken from the client's smartphone GPS coordinates eliminates the need for a phone call to an operator to initiate the assistance request, thereby further streamlining the Futura process.

It's hard to believe that Google Maps has been around only since 2004. In those short few years, geolocation applications have become a standard smartphone feature. As a leader in global auto insurance, MAPFRE is proud to lead the industry with location-based technology.

José Manuel Inchausti Pérez is Managing Director of Technology and Process at MAPFRE S.A.

DB Systel GmbH
Detlef Exner, Chairman of the Managing Board, DB Systel GmbH

Deutsche Bahn is the largest railway operator in Europe. We operate more than 30,000 train runs daily on our modern 34,000-kilometer rail network, and we deliver more than 2.7 billion passengers in trains and buses, 25,000 passenger trains per day (fiscal year 2012). We also ship more than 400 million tons of freight via rail each year.

Deutsche Bahn is tightly integrated into our customers' processes. For customers we coordinate multimodal logistics, and we can combine computer components made in Malaysia, manuals published in Ireland, and CDs created in Taiwan into a single product.

Given the nature of our industry, most of our nearly 300,000 employees are mobile. They utilize various modern technologies to scan barcodes on electronic tickets or to obtain maintenance tickets in rail yards.

With such a wide range of assets, employees, and customers, DB Systel, the captive technology subsidiary of Deutsche Bahn, has plenty of opportunities to innovate. Let me describe some of our recent digital innovations.

Rail-in-Motion
Rail-in-Motion is an information and communication platform that provides mobile employees with all of the information they need during their work day. It was developed to give Android users secure and comfortable offline and online access to all of the information generated and stored in the company's well-protected intranet. This information includes work assignments, shift schedules, and directives, as well as damage reports sent by the mobile staff to the company's maintenance systems. The objective is to ensure that information is always delivered as quickly as possible precisely where it is needed — to the employee.

Figure 4-2 displays a set of app classes for one type of employee — train drivers. By using the RiM-Broker middleware the drivers can connect those apps to different client-specific backend systems. The RiM-Broker acts as a kind of gatekeeper that determines whether a user has the appropriate authorizations for the system when he or she logs on. In addition, it checks which system elements he or she is allowed to access.

Selection of Rail-in-Motion app classes for loco-drivers

Documents Information Layers Use planning	ZRWD IRE	Instructions	Use plan	Forms
Access to document repositories (e.g. DMS) and local saving of selected documents.	• Access to third party applications. • Presentation and local provision of guidelines. • Access to internet fallback level of working schedule displaying timetable and speed restrictions.	Allows assignment and local saving of instructions for the user provided by the customer. With optional confirmation of transmission or receipt.	Provision of roster, registration at beginning of shift, registration and sending of actual roster.	Form generator for the design of registration forms by the special service.

Figure 4-2: Rail-in-Motion apps for locomotive drivers

Touch&Travel

Historically, passenger train travel in Europe has generated a very wide array of pricing structures and ticketing formats. Regarding pricing, one-way tickets, Eurail Passes, corporate discounts, concessionary discounts, BahnCard discounts, and reservation fees are just some of the variations that have emerged over the years. In ticketing, traditional formats are still used. For example, paper tickets are still common despite the fact that online booking channels have been available for more than a decade. Additionally, there is a full range of rules and restrictions associated with each ticket type; for example, some tickets allow passengers to change their minds and disembark before their final destination. Our ticketing systems and staff must accommodate all of these options.

Mobile ticketing in this complex environment must take these conditions into account. Since 2008, Deutsche Bahn has been rolling out a ticketing platform called Touch&Travel. Instead of the traditional method of purchasing tickets in advance, registered Touch&Travel users can make journeys on enabled public transport routes and pay the appropriate fares at the end of each month. Customers can touch their near field communication (NFC) smartphones at Touch&Travel's Touchpoints to "check in" before boarding and then "check out" at their destination stations. The Touch&Travel smartphone app reads the ID number encoded on the NFC tag inside each Touchpoint to identify the station where the customer is located. The app then sends this information to us, and we calculate the fare for each journey before sending the customer a monthly invoice.

In 2011, we expanded Touch&Travel to enable checking in and out through 2D barcodes using iPhone and Android apps. In addition, users can now enter the number of a Touchpoint manually on their smartphone keypads or locate their origin and destination stations using geographic locations identified through the Touch&Travel app.

WorldInsight

Systel has developed a 3D visualization tool, called "WorldInsight," that can represent geodata provided by Open Geospatial Consortium (OGC) compliant Web services, as well as data from planning and survey measurements and from customer-specific semantics, design data for technical objects, and status data (as in business events). WorldInsight is a real-time application that specializes in representing virtual copies of a real environment. It is based on a gaming technology that is extended by two major columns of functionality: a massive production line for 3D content (both fully and semi-automated production) and an online network layer for internet accessibility. WorldInsight is much more than just a "normal" visualization application; it is a technical tool that speeds up processes as well as communication. It helps customers achieve multiple objectives: planning mediation, technical simulation of processes, intuitive communication, smart data acquisition (3D search engine for technical entities and structures), operation and maintenance support, and so on.

Railroads have played a fundamental role in promoting economic growth since the First Industrial Revolution, and they remain a major force in the Fourth Industrial Revolution. Over the course of 150 years, however, the world has experienced breathtaking developments in science and technology. To remain relevant and productive, the railway industry, like so many other components of the service sector, has been forced to reinvent itself. Deutsche Bahn has navigated this process with great success. By introducing innovations such as Rail-in-Motion and Touch&Travel, we continue to provide a vital service to a new generation of digital customers.

Detlef Exner is Chairman of the Managing Board at DB Systel GmbH

The Museum's Digital Expansion
Max Hollein, Director, Städel Museum

Art museums are appealing because they are different. They are asynchronous with our times, and they must be understood that way. As symbolic locations with alternative concepts of time and reality, they are places to pause, slow down, and focus — places where we can experience a unique work of art or even an entire collection in person. Nonetheless, society is becoming increasingly digitized, and it is not stopping for seemingly analog cultural content. As a result, museums, like all institutions, are confronted by enormous changes in almost every area of life that are fundamentally redefining how we handle information, education, and culture.

Culture Creates Identity
The present crisis in the European Union highlights the reality that disputes about the future of our societies are being resolved on cultural grounds. Continued peaceful coexistence in Europe will depend largely on the extent to which the continent's cultural identities, history, traditions, and mentalities can be made transparent for its current residents while simultaneously making them appealing as a philosophy of life compared to others around the world. Cultural institutions therefore play a key role in maintaining a stable society and in encouraging people to identify with their local communities. Museums in particular play a vital role in society beyond just imparting art and aesthetics. They also function as places of learning, repositories of our cultural heritage, and centers of knowledge and insight. To continue to perform these roles in a digital world, museums must fundamentally transform they ways they interact with the public. One key strategy is to adopt more interactive and participatory forms of communication to accommodate cultural diversification and the increasingly heterogeneous levels of language competence and general education.

Every Visitor Is Unique — and So Is Every Visit

The Städel in Frankfurt is Germany's oldest private museum foundation. It has become nationally recognized for its expertise in serving all age groups and every segment of society. Its audience now includes a broad range of visitors, from children and school groups to adults, families, students, and senior citizens from all geographical origins and echelons of society, along with young artists and executives who are highly talented or are seeking work. The highly diverse needs of today's audience require us to provide an equally diverse spectrum of presentation and communication offerings that combine education and entertainment. Not only must museum activities draw on different interests and levels of knowledge as a starting point for individual access, but they also must draw on various occasions and motivations for visiting a museum. The Städel Museum's collection, which encompasses more than 700 years of art history (from 1300 to the present), provides a wonderful aesthetic experience. Moreover, its interdisciplinary approach to communication establishes a relationship between the art and its historical, literary, scientific, and political context. At the same time, it serves as the basis for topical debates concerning all social aspects of life.

Today it is becoming more and more common for everyone — not just young people — to obtain their information and education from sources other than traditional media and institutions. The digital world is transforming many areas of modern life, including entertainment and our personal lives. Cultural institutions must also accommodate these changes if they want to continue to fulfill their mission to teach and to be seen as culturally relevant. The challenge of the future will be to communicate again and again the relevance of museum collections — increasingly online and therefore to a broad international audience — and to enable unlimited access to the cultural content beyond the museum's walls.

Digital Expansion: Risks and Opportunities

The strengths of digital communication include its unlimited reach, the simultaneous dissemination of multimedia content, and the linking of content and institutions. These effects are facilitated by opportunities for active user participation, the cognitive effect of stronger connections between visual and tactile experiences, and the customization of digital communications to users' specific needs. Because the allure of the original is missing from the digital communication of culture, there is a danger of compensating for this shortcoming by trying to impress users with technology.

In fact, using technological features as the primary attraction of a digital application has proved to be rather short-lived. Initial attempts to simply transfer the real objects into the virtual museum space sometimes led to mistakes and dead-ends because this approach did not really serve users' interests. It has become apparent that offering quality content is the only effective strategy to build long-term user loyalty.

Digital Art Experience or Virtual Museum?

Whereas the value of visiting a museum in person is obvious, the digital museum experience is still evolving, with input from both the experts who are designing it and future visitors. The most important task for cultural institutions in the digital world — to provide orientation, explanatory models, and insight in the confusing jungle of available information — also represents an exciting opportunity. Intelligent and clear communication of cultural and interdisciplinary topics helps people to understand complex connections at their own pace, in a manner that works for them.

With a cluster of excellence comprised of partners from academia (Hochschule Darmstadt University of Applied Sciences, the Darmstadt University of Technology), business (Software AG), and the cultural world (the library at Darmstadt University), the Städel Museum developed a cloud-based exhibit platform for its collection, for this exact purpose. Our goal is to allow potential visitors from all around the world to take a "digital stroll" through our collection with links to multimedia content for individual artists and works of art. This self-guided path through our collection, which is oriented toward visitors' individualized interests and learning needs, will reconfirm the relevance of the collection, of producing and sharing art, and, ultimately, of the museum itself. At the same time, we are making the actual museum more physically attractive. In 2012, we opened a new underground gallery that was designed by the architects Schneider+Schumacher. We have devoted this gallery to our collection of contemporary art. The 3,000 square meters doubled the exhibition capacity at the Städel.

What Is the Städel Museum's Digital Potential?

In addition to our current offerings, the Städel is in the process of creating digital strategies for translating theoretical and practical communications into the specific options and requirements of a virtual experiential and learning environment. The result will be a wide range of access options for visitors to our digital collection. Another principle of our communication strategy that can be transferred to the digital world is developing offerings that reflect the latest findings of brain research and learning theory. In contrast to in-person communication, in a multimedia environment the user's attention cannot be held only through reading and listening. Rather, it is necessary to change from one medium to another and to alternate between passive consumption and active clicking, swiping, and so on. The multimedia approach can better portray topics from various perspectives, thus making it more suitable for complex content. The change in media makes users more active participants by allowing them to grapple more intensively with the content. At the same time, this method encourages cultural institutions to communicate with digital visitors as equals by transcending traditional barriers and promoting wide-ranging discussions of the content conducted in a much better way than when the museum acts as a town crier announcing an overarching and immutable truth.

What Makes the Digital Visit to the Museum a Sensual Experience?

The supposed drawback of digital communication is the absence of an emotional reaction that normally comes with viewing the original at a museum. Therefore, the value of visiting an online museum must be created on some other level. The appeal of communicating culture digitally lies in the degree of insight and understanding users can develop on their own via interactive technologies. In terms of methodology, this includes the following elements:

- Communicate complex topics using appealing examples

- Ensure small, easily understandable units

- Alternate between images, sound, text, and video

- Give greater regard to the storytelling element (arc of suspense, narrative structure, moments of surprise, continuous opportunities for users to recognize themselves in the topic being addressed)

- Select the right mix of topics

- Ask the right questions

- Awaken the desire to learn

- Allow sharing of thoughts

- Promote active thinking rather than passive consumption

- Put users into a discovery mode

What Are This Strategy's Key Success Factors?

An essential and unique selling proposition of this digitalization strategy lies in the customized, needs-driven provision of content for future users.

However, when extensive archives are simply made available digitally unfiltered and without any specific communication, the benefits are usually restricted to visitors who are already well versed in the topic. The majority of our visitors do not know where to begin with this information because they lack the necessary scholarly knowledge. Consequently, we must impart information to them through various means, similar to the experience of visiting a museum in person. This multifaceted approach provides digital visitors with a variety of options to access the collection. It is therefore the best method to link the nature of the experience with the museum's mission to educate and communicate. Especially for educational formats that build on one another and will need to be disseminated via our partners from the academic and educational worlds, the essential success factors will take the form of a variety of experiences and easy-access opportunities.

Max Hollein is Director of Städel Museum

5

Evolve Your Business Models Beyond Products and Services

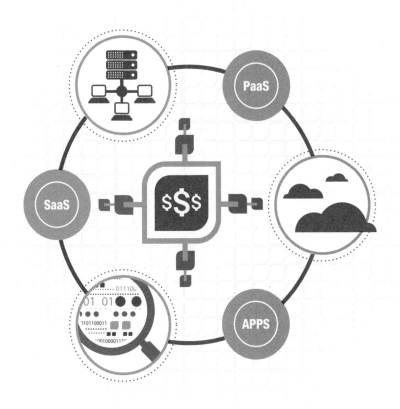

The evolution is obvious. Everything started with the products. Products are the prime vehicle for value generation. Especially during the early innovative cycle of a new product, companies can achieve high margins through selling products. However, successful products almost inevitably become commoditized, sometimes after the expiration of patent cycles, sometimes much earlier. One solution to this problem is to provide services along with the products. Businesses can employ this strategy to generate revenue, acquire customer insights, and deepen customer relationships. Unfortunately, people-oriented strategies to provide services don't really scale beyond human beings. For this reason, large-scale service organizations build up human resource volumes of 100,000 employees, and sometimes even 500,000 or more. The challenge, therefore, is to find a new model of scalability in providing offerings that does not commoditize, that provides high margins, and that develops unique offerings that the competition cannot copy, at least not easily.

One step towards achieving this goal is to develop smart services. Due to their proactive nature, smart services make it much easier for the supplier to predict — and therefore determine — their destiny, or at least their profitability and customer predictability. Smart services provide information not only for proactively fixing problems but also for proactively pursuing opportunities. Billions of users of social networks, in collaboration platforms and in other crowd-gathering platforms, are generating footprints, behavior patterns, patterns of likes and dislikes, and all kinds of data that, when correlated with certain user groups, create valuable insights into both crowd and individual behaviors.

In addition, modern organizations can rely on sensors to measure almost anything, anywhere, at any time. They can utilize these sensors to create correlations among myriad variables including temperature, consumption of liquids, time slots, locations, and popular events. This information enables suppliers to match supply with demand much more accurately than was previously possible. These new raw data, combined with the real-time analysis capabilities of today's systems, provide insights that were unavailable to earlier generations of business professionals. The value generated by the results of smart correlations can be significant for the right target group of suppliers or consumers, depending on the type of results. The key to success, then, is to evolve your business well beyond the classic model of product, people, or service-level provision. The maxim "Data is king" was never more true and relevant than it is today.

In the 1970s, airline reservation systems like American Airlines' Sabre evolved to support dynamic airfare pricing and what the industry called "yield management."[47] These systems fired up corporate imagination about how technology could help innovate business models in every industry.

The technology industry itself has functioned as a laboratory for a wide range of business models. One prominent example is cloud computing, which has transformed software and infrastructure pricing into a system based on consumption and time-based units. So, you can now purchase gigabytes of storage from Amazon by the hour at a predictable price using a credit card.[48] Amazon also offers its spare EC2 computing capacity using a much more dynamic, spot market-based pricing model. As another example, open-source software like Apache Hadoop is free and is supported by communities. However, tools and add-ons from vendors like Cloudera are available only as for-sale items.[49]

Many consumer tech business models, such as Google Search, are "one-sided," meaning they are free to consumers because they are paid for by advertisers. A growing number of services, however, are evolving into "multisided" models. An example is Evernote's "freemium" model: The base service for entry-level users is free, but customers can upgrade to a paid version that increases storage capacity significantly and also provides superior search and other features.[50] Evernote also offers the business buyer a more complex set of pricing options. When Inc. Magazine named Evernote its 2011 "Company of the Year," it praised the company for "rejecting industry trends, getting customers to pay for something that's free, and reinventing the way we remember."[51]

Going further, business process outsourcing is increasingly moving toward non-headcount, outcome-based pricing models — for example, based on the number of transactions processed. Telcos like Telefónica are packaging "insights" based on aggregated GPS coordinates of their customers.[52] Gogo, which provides airline Wi-Fi, offers its customers price plans both by the hour and by the year.[53] VoIP providers like Vonage have switched from metered calls to monthly fees.[54]

Let's examine how these and other business models have influenced several industries outside technology and telecommunications. Let's also consider how mobile and other technologies are reshaping business models in several industries, as Norm Fjeldheim, CIO of Qualcomm, describes in his executive contribution later in the chapter.

Media and Entertainment
The music industry is a vivid example of an industry that has experienced a dramatic technology-driven transformation. Albums and CDs and the record stores that sold them have given way to online music stores. Consumers buy many more "one-hit wonders" than they would if these songs were bundled. Apple and other stores next promoted premium versions of the MP3 — as in the 256 kbps AAC codec, whose audio quality they promised was indistinguishable from the original recording.[55] Apple, Amazon, and Google also introduced music in the cloud. Apple, for example, offers a "Match" feature for $25 a year that scans the music a user has previously ripped to the 18 million songs in its

music store and makes them available in the cloud in the higher-quality codec.[56] The model is now moving from single downloads to streaming subscriptions from players like Spotify, Pandora, and Rhapsody and even larger players like Apple with its iTunes Radio and Google with its YouTube music alternatives.

Netflix has similarly transitioned its movie subscription service from DVD by mail to a streaming model.[57] Its competitor Redbox continues to allow single-use rentals from more than 30,000 kiosks.[58] However, it also offers a streaming service on a monthly basis. Amazon bundles several movies into its Prime shipping service, while also allowing streaming on a single-use basis.[59]

Media companies like *The New York Times* have been transitioning from delivered paper subscriptions, single-copy news store sales, and related print advertising to digital subscriptions via their website, e-readers like the Kindle, and digital advertising.[60]

In his executive contribution, Dr. Paul-Bernhard Kallen, CEO of Hubert Burda Media, describes how the magazine publishing business model has evolved over the last couple of decades. Today, e-commerce sites, rather than traditional publishers, are the primary competition.

Insurance

The U.S. auto insurer Progressive allows its customers to plug their Snapshot telematics device into their car's electronic diagnostic port. This feature enables Progressive to analyze how far the motorist drove, what times of day he or she drove, and whether he or she engaged in activities such as hard braking. Progressive utilizes this information to provide more precise premium pricing based on the policyholder's driving patterns. Snapshot also provides feedback to customers to improve their driving behaviors.[61]

Of course, the insurance industry has never lacked for mountains of data — actuarial data, claims data, weather data, and so on, seemingly forever. Significantly, the industry is now utilizing advanced analytics to better understand risk and other scenarios, such as productivity levels and social media engagement. An interesting example comes from the specialized world of supplemental crop insurance. Climate Corp, a company founded by Google alums, prices its premiums using historic (30 years of daily data at a granular location level), simulated, and forecasted climate and weather data. Unlike other insurance processes, the company's loss calculations are determined by independently reported weather measurements, thus eliminating the need for a lengthy claims process.[62]

Retail

The retail industry is also moving to dynamic pricing. Amazon, for example, has pioneered "Lightning Deals" that are posted throughout the day, have limited quantities, last only a few hours, and offer discounts of as much as 50% off retail prices.[63] Another example is Groupon, which for a while was one of the fastest-growing companies in the world. Groupon's success stemmed from "daily deal" concepts promoted throughout the world such as CityDeal in Germany, Darberry in Russia, ClanDescuento in Chile, and Qpod in Japan.[64]

Mobile promotions promise to reshape retail as well. For example, Foursquare enables businesses to create deals and other promotions that users can see on their mobile devices when they are in the vicinity of a retailer.[65] Similarly, services like Pushpins allow customers to access digital grocery coupons on their mobile phones.[66]

As more retailers move to omni-channel models — buy online/pick up in store, buy online /get delivery at home, and other models — delivery costs have become a more significant factor in their business models. Amazon, for example, offers its U.S. customers two-day shipments for a flat annual fee as part of its Prime Membership. Prime also bundles other features such as streaming of selected videos and access to a lending library of eBooks.[67]

Automobiles

The U.S. electric vehicle manufacturer Tesla is innovating with a dealer-less sales model.[68] Most other car companies continue to offer complex pricing packages and rebates via their dealer network, though many dealers offer a limited, "no haggle" web sales channel. For example, CarWoo! offers a network of selected dealers who bid for a customer's preferred configuration.[69]

Most auto companies are adding subscription components for entertainment and service. GM's OnStar was arguably the first commercially successful venture in this field.[70] More recently, Mercedes and Acura added concierge services as well as roadside assistance.[71] Today, most automakers offer satellite radio and internet entertainment options like Pandora. They also package apps for these services — like the Mercedes mbrace2 in-car and mobile versions.[72]

Travel

Over time, as dynamic pricing, like yield management, progressed from airlines to hotels and rental cars, it was natural that other, more consumer-friendly models would evolve. Priceline's "Name your own price" was one example, although it did not allow users to pick their favorite airlines or hotels.[73] Services like Kayak and Expedia allowed customers to comparison-shop. In turn, most travel companies updated their pricing engines to compete with the shopping sites. Airlines like RyanAir broke down their pricing to offer cheap fares, but they then added fees for baggage, seat selection, check-in, and other features.[74]

Going further, the emergence of the "sharing" economy has given rise to other travel business models. For example, AirBnB allows people to share their houses and apartments with strangers for a night or a week.[75] ZipCar (now part of Avis) allows multiple members to share cars for as little as an hour at a time. NetJets sells fractional ownership units on its private jets.[76] None of these models would be possible without evolving technology. For example, ZipCar provides its members with access cards and mobile apps to unlock reserved cars.[77]

Summary

The technology industry has pioneered a series of new business models — as a service, freemium, and so on — that are influencing models in other industries. Additionally, mobile, analytical, and other technologies are helping industries to transition to insight, subscription, and other pricing models. The Digital Enterprise has plenty of opportunities to experiment with, and, in many cases, to respond to diverse business models.

Now let's look at two practitioner perspectives — first from Hubert Burda Media and then from Qualcomm.

Hubert Burda Media

Dr. Paul-Bernhard Kallen, Chief Executive Officer, Hubert Burda Media Holding

When people talk about publishing, they frequently focus on the digital disruption of printed media. The radical transformation of the media industry is being driven by the massive output of information across all kinds of digital platforms. Consider the newspaper industry, for example. The simple fact that information has become free and universally available has had a dramatic impact on the core functions of newspapers everywhere. In addition, new, digital performance-oriented advertising models like cost-per-click and cost-per-action have affected this section of the news industry.

Book publishing is also undergoing seismic shifts. The traditional business model of book publishing is increasingly being displaced by eBooks from providers like Amazon.

Hubert Burda Media is one of Germany's largest and oldest media companies. Our primary focus is neither books nor newspapers but magazines. In contrast to other print media, magazine publishing has witnessed much more of a digital/print coexistence model. Rather than compete with or displace analog, digital tends to complement it.

Burda's digital journey over the past 15 years has followed two parallel paths: (1) launching new digital-only properties and (2) digitizing the production of our popular print titles. Our opportunities and challenges, then, are very different from those facing the newspaper and book publishing industries. In this essay I describe examples of how Burda is simultaneously pursuing the two paths identified above. I also discuss how we have transformed our business and staffing models (Figure 5-1) to accommodate this digitization strategy.

Revenue

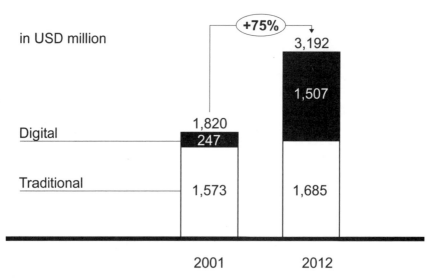

Figure 5-1: Digitization at Hubert Burda Media

Holidaycheck is an example of a new digital-only property. It draws on our experiences with a print magazine called *Holiday*, which we discontinued in 1996 due to a lack of interest among advertisers. *Holidaycheck* is enabled by new digital technologies. It relies on an open, crowdsourced model (as TripAdvisor does in the United States) to offer consumers a solution to plan their holidays without being disappointed. Visitors to various holiday locations relate their first-hand experiences to prospective vacationers. These individuals — who serve as our content "experts" — have contributed more than 3.5 million pieces to *Holidaycheck*, consisting of hotel reviews, photos, and videos. In contrast, our "journalists" — who are *Holidaycheck* employees — do not actually write anything. Instead, they offer guidance to our contributing experts, and they aggregate, authenticate, and accentuate the content. In other words, they perform a traditional editorial function.

Our business model has evolved from consumer subscriptions and page-based advertising to performance-based advertising revenues. At the same time, our staffing model has changed dramatically. We employ 75 technology staff members and 40 journalists. This ratio deviates considerably from a traditional magazine staff model, which included few, if any, technology staff. With more than 20 million visitors per month from Germany, Switzerland, Austria, Poland, and other European countries, we accumulate and publish content in 10 languages. Our technology staff performs a number of core functions including:

- Operating an elaborate content-management system to handle the wide range of rapidly changing textual and graphic materials, in multiple languages

- Navigating a highly optimized search tool

- Utilizing a price-comparison tool

Today these technologies are increasingly available off the shelf. In contrast, when we launched *Holidaycheck* in 2003, we had to develop robust functionalities for each area in-house. Clearly, then, both content and technology are essential to creating media products that reflect and satisfy consumers' needs.

Another example of a digital publication is *Focus,* a news magazine similar to *Time.* Launched in 1993, *Focus* quickly became one of the most successful weekly magazines in the world. What drove this astounding success was that the magazine anticipated some of the editorial techniques of the internet such as short text, infographics, and a highly intuitive navigation system. Then, in 1996 we went digital with the Focus Online news portal in collaboration with MSN Germany. For two decades, then, we have witnessed the digital impact on this market segment first-hand, and we learned a lot about how to differentiate the content on the two platforms. Specifically, the content in the printed magazine had to become more opinionated, more comprehensive, and more detailed. In contrast, digital content is much more dynamic and succinct. In addition, digital text is "fast," meaning it is published and updated much more quickly than printed text. Essentially, then, Focus Online, which is updated several times every day, serves as our digital complement to *Focus*, our weekly print magazine.

Today, Focus Online receives roughly 70 million visits every month. In addition, the portal offers various mobile apps, and it maintains a social media presence on Facebook, Twitter, and Google+. Thanks to mobile apps on smartphones, which account for 40% of our total web traffic, Focus Online is now closer to its customers than ever before. The business model for the portal continues to be advertising driven. Significantly, however, the portal generates considerable traffic for our specialty properties like *Holidaycheck*, which operate on a business model that is independent of traditional advertising.

Despite all of this digital innovation, however, magazines continue to offer readers a distinct and unique experience, regardless of whether their format is print or digital. Consumption, be it on paper or through a digital edition, is a "me-moment." Consumers indulge in a rich media experience, a lean-back moment. Magazines provide companies with the perfect platform for brand- and image-building advertisement. They are the only media where advertising is perceived as product enhancement; that is, as content. Even in the world of analog media, however, the production process has become intensively digitized. The content production is digital only, proofs are digital, and the transfer onto the impression cylinder or printing plate is digital as well. Controls of the paper and print quality are digital and real-time. And, with robotics, the entire production universe is becoming more automated every day. The coming years will undoubtedly witness increased reader contributions in content production as well, given that most magazines center around communities of passion.

Significantly, driven by the opportunities engendered by digitization, our competitive landscape has also evolved dramatically. Our traditional publishing competition is still increasing, because the overall number of magazines competing in the German market has doubled in the past 15 years. At the same time, however, technology-driven companies such as Google, Amazon, and Apple are steadily taking center stage in the media market. Finally, eCommerce players are entering the media landscape. Essentially, eCommerce becomes eMedia, and eMedia becomes eCommerce.

As an example, let's consider fashion, a market in which Burda publishing has traditionally been very successful. A decade ago, women would not buy designer clothes online. Having been inspired by fashion magazines, they had to physically purchase their wardrobe in shops and boutiques. Fast-forward to the present, where millions of women buy fashion clothing from online sites such as MyTheresa and Net-a-Porter. Interestingly, Natalie Massenet, the founder of Net-a-Porter, did not come from retail. Rather, her background was in fashion journalism. Massenet has been quoted as saying "I thought I'd abandoned my dream of being an editor; it was a couple of years until I realized that I was just doing the 21st century version with an interactive magazine that's entirely shoppable."[78]

Journalists sometimes claim that online retailers are not "independent" because they rely so heavily on revenues provided by advertisers of specific products. eCustomers respond that these fashion platforms offer a variety of brands and styles and they also encourage user reviews. Thus, eCustomers enjoy a range of choices similar to those of traditional in-store shoppers. Isn't this arrangement just as "independent" as any traditional fashion magazine?

I credit our digital transition to a series of conversations between our executives and several venture capitalists in the late 1990s. We discussed disruptive eBusiness models, and we concluded that we needed to work alongside disruptors instead of competing with them. Thus, we created a corporate venture capitalist. Back then we did not know exactly what a digital media landscape would look like. Our strategy was to focus on the consumer and to invest in companies that had a sound digital business, instead of limiting ourselves to what we already did. These watching posts helped us to acquire expertise concerning where the market was going and, as a result, to foster our businesses. By keeping the different businesses as independent entities, we created a healthy competition between start-ups and incumbents.

Making this decision when we did was a game-changing strategic move that has accelerated our digital journey considerably. Over the past two decades we have built Burda Media into an enterprise for entrepreneurs. The guiding principle was and is that our company can maneuver change and create growth only if we align ourselves with the most capable entrepreneurs in their respective fields. Following this approach, we transformed a German magazine and print company into an international digital media and magazine enterprise. Today, we maintain a presence in 14 countries. We created these businesses and markets by and with both start-up and established media entrepreneurs, who partnered with us to grow their business — be it digital or analog — and introduce it to new countries.

Dr. Paul-Bernhard Kallen is Chief Executive Officer at Hubert Burda Media Holding

Qualcomm: How Mobility Is Changing the Business Model

Norm Fjeldheim, Senior Vice President and Chief Information Officer, Qualcomm, Inc.

Qualcomm has always sought to push the boundaries of what is possible in wireless and mobile communication. The company was the leader in introducing a digital communications technique called code division multiple access, or CDMA, which is the dominant technology used in wireless networks today. Qualcomm also put internet Protocols on the first internet browser for a mobile phone. In addition, we built the first smartphone with the Palm operating system. And, although few people realize it, Qualcomm actually developed the first open application system, Binary Runtime Environment for Wireless (BREW).

Qualcomm began in 1985 as a radio communications company with a total of seven employees that supplied communications technology to the government. From that modest beginning we expanded to do the following:

- Develop a satellite-based data communications system for the transportation industry based on CDMA technology

- Help deploy CDMA networks worldwide

- Launch our own open application system

- Maintain a handset business

- Become a major global supplier of chipsets

As a result of these innovations, Qualcomm has evolved into a global enterprise with more than 26,600 employees worldwide at the end of fiscal year 2012 and is a recognized leader in the wireless communications field. The company continues to drive the industry forward and propel the evolution of business models, spurring new opportunities in the process.

Transforming Industries

Mobile technology is outpacing traditional computers as the leading computing platform of choice among consumers. In fact, there are now 5 billion mobile phones in the world, compared to only 1 billion personal computers. Going further, smartphone shipments are double those of PC shipments. Moreover, this trend gives no signs of abating. Just the opposite: Companies are investing more capital in mobile than in other computing platforms. According to Rutberg and Company, an investment bank that specializes in research, in 2012 venture capital investments in mobile technologies totaled nearly $7 billion. This sum represents 41% of all technology venture capital investments made that year, the highest percentage since 2001.[79]

What we are witnessing is an ever-expanding adoption of wireless technologies by users around the world. Countries are propelling the proliferation of wireless devices and driving smartphone shipments, which are estimated to grow at approximately 30% in these regions on a compound annual growth rate (CAGR) from 2012 to 2017, according to industry analysts. In addition, research firms like Strategy Analytics documented that in 2012 more than 1 million new smartphone users were added every day worldwide.[80] To put that number in perspective, it is about 3 times the number of babies born worldwide.

Consider the statistics: Most people look at their phones 150 times a day (Mary Meeker, May 2013), or equivalent to once every six and a half minutes. Further, in a mobility poll conducted by *Time*, 84% of all respondents conceded they couldn't go a single day without their mobile device in hand. Perhaps more significantly, 66% actually sleep with their mobile device right next to their bed.[81]

Clearly, mobile technology is central to many people's lives. More importantly and fundamentally, Qualcomm strongly believes that mobile technology has the ability to transform industries, such as healthcare and education, and improve people's lives. We look for and evaluate opportunities to fuel growth and spur innovation by ingraining wireless into traditional industries.

Mobile phones can be especially beneficial to the populations of developing countries because they are the most accessible technologies for people with limited access to basic resources. In fact, emerging regions have leapfrogged the rest of the world in becoming mobile-first societies, where mobile commerce has created entrepreneurial avenues that previously did not exist.

One critical area that is being transformed by mobile technology is patient care, particularly treatment regimens and preventive care. Patients in underserved or remote geographies can communicate with doctors and other medical specialists as needed, as well as be reminded of their treatments, thanks to mobile technologies. Plus, scientists are exploring even more advances daily. For instance, Qualcomm is collaborating with a researcher who is looking to put a tiny wireless sensor into a patient's bloodstream that could perform various medical functions. Perhaps someday, such a device could notify the patient ahead of time of an impending heart attack and trigger the individual's mobile phone to ring and prompt an immediate visit to the doctor. Such a technology literally would be life saving.

Not only has wireless technology transformed industries, it also has revolutionized traditional products and services both inside and outside the home. Consider, for example, that everyday products such as cameras, refrigerators, cars, and watches can be made even more functional by adding global positioning satellite (GPS) technology, connectivity, sensors, or microprocessor technologies that enable communications and graphics. As another example, security service providers and network operators can provide apps that enable users to remotely monitor and control their homes. For example, it's now possible to adjust your home thermostat while you're at work — simply by touching a button on your smartphone or tablet. In the foreseeable future these apps will be able to communicate data about individuals as well as status reports on appliances such as washing machines. In essence, they will be able to interact with the Internet of Things. The capacity for devices, both wireless and wireline, indoors and outdoors, to be connected and to be embedded with "smart" capabilities because of the network and services they connect to is creating an "Internet of Everything," personalizing the ways we interact with our environment and manage our lives.

Mobile technology also is transforming products into services. In addition, many services that used to be person-to-person can now be executed on a self-serve basis. Consider gym equipment, personal trainers, and nutritionists. Mobile technology is allowing people to bypass those products and services so they can monitor their physical activity, their weight, and their diet or caloric intake on their own.

Finally, mobile technology is changing the nature of the traditional gaming industry. Today Qualcomm is cooperating with companies like Gameloft to develop applications based on our augmented reality Qualcomm Vuforia technology that brings games to life through 3D graphics, touch, video, and audio on the user's mobile phone.

By driving wireless technologies into other verticals, like automotive, healthcare, and home appliances, Qualcomm is pushing industries to provide highly personalized and contextualized experiences that pro-vide their customers with better control of their lives — a driving factor in consumer adoption today. We are excited about the next wireless breakthrough and about further enabling a world where industries, people, and things are all interconnected.

Norm Fjeldheim is Senior Vice President and Chief Information Officer at Qualcomm, Inc.

6

Invent New Go-to-Market Models

"One size fits all." It worked for decades, if not for centuries. Large homogenous markets such as the United States created world market leaders for standard products, the so-called industry standards. In essence, the supplier that became biggest, became the standard. Today, circumstances have rendered this approach obsolete.

The digital way of doing business reflects the emergence of the mass production of goods that are individualized order by order. Enterprises can achieve this type of mass customization only through the digital factory, also called Industrie 4.0 or the Industrial Internet. We will address this subject in a later chapter, because it is based on the same technological drivers as the Digital Enterprise: mobile technology, collaboration platforms, cloud computing, and real-time analysis of Big Data.

In this chapter we focus on the primary requirement for successful mass customization: a go-to-market strategy of unprecedented efficiency. Put differently, mass customization requires a digital multichannel customer access to individualize the customers' products as efficiently as possible. Consequently, modern businesses need to rethink their go-to-market model completely. Today a successful model must provide 360° customer information in real time so that the organization knows everything about their customers' wishes, problems, complaints, likes, and dislikes. Significantly, businesses cannot obtain this information from a personal, human Q&A session. Instead, they need to collect vast amounts of data about their customers from social collaboration platforms, forums, events, and any other available sources of personal data.

Maintaining direct human contact with customers is one strategy to achieve customer intimacy. However, this policy will be the exception rather than the rule in the not-too-distant future. Instead, thousands of digital contacts will enable Big Data analytics technology to offer you the personalized products you want, at the same price as traditional standardized products.

Customized Products

There have long been rumors regarding how many thousands of combinations the average Starbucks coffee configurator can handle. It's a mystery no more. A customer's mobile app can display different components — the type of espresso beverages, cup size, type of coffee (regular, decaf), and so on. For the milk alone, you can choose nonfat, 1%, 2%, whole milk, soy, breve (half-and-half), or heavy cream. You can ask for the milk to be warm, regular, or extra hot. You can also specify whether the milky foam should be light, regular, or extra amount. You can similarly configure syrups, espresso shots, toppings, and additional ingredients like bananas. Further, after you have created your perfect concoction, you can ask the mobile app to calculate the nutritional value — calories, fat, etc.[82]

When we consider that the chain serves more than 2 billion cups a year, Starbucks clearly has created a highly profitable business model.[83] The fact that the most loyal 20% of its customers patronize its stores every two days is testimony to the remarkable success of the company's mass customization strategies.

Although Starbucks' customers can configure their beverages, the company's baristas actually make them. In contrast, consider the Coca-Cola Freestyle vending machines. Designed by the Italian design firm Pininfarina, which is better known for working with automakers such as Ferrari, Maserati, and Alfa Romeo, the Freestyle machine allows customers to blend more than 100 sparkling and non-carbonated flavors.[84] Customers select their drink — which can range from Coke and Diet Coke to lemonade to root beer to Dasani water — by pushing the appropriate button on a touch screen. The machine then uses a high-precision, micro-dosing technology to measure and mix the drinks. It also rinses the nozzle after it pours every drink. In addition to providing an impressive number of customer choices, the precision metering also supports more accurate and automated replenishment cycles. In his executive contribution, Esat Sezer, CIO of Coca-Cola Enterprises, explains how mobile, crowdsourcing, and other technologies are reshaping the company's Western European channel.

As sophisticated and popular as coffee and soft drinks are, they are relatively simple products compared to cars. Nevertheless, even products as complex and highly technical as automobiles are becoming increasingly customized. As one example, Audi's digital showroom located near Piccadilly Circus in London uses sensors, surface computing, and true-to-life scale panels to allow prospects to customize their cars. Specifically, customers can view the car from multiple angles, and they can select the colors and the trim. Choosing the sound of the specific engine configuration rounds off the experience. Customers can save their options on a USB drive, or they can order their custom car, which Audi will deliver within a few weeks.[85]

One-to-One Marketing
One-to-one marketing, like mass customization, has been around for many years. However, with so many social, email, phone, and other ways to communicate with an individual, the challenge to maintain a personalized marketing strategy has grown exponentially.

In 2012 U.S. President Barack Obama won his re-election campaign against his Republican opponent, Mitt Romney. A close analysis of Obama's victory reveals that his campaign dominated Romney's on many marketing metrics. Warner Jones, who served as the digital program manager for Romney's presidential bid, acknowledged it would have taken his campaign another two years to catch up with Obama's digital infrastructure, which included 23 million Twitter followers and more than 45 million Facebook likes.[86] Even though the voting took place by secret ballot, based on the social analytics and the information on campaign contributions gleaned from the digital channels — email, SMS, the web — observers contend that the Obama campaign could reasonably guess the identity of each of the nearly 66 million individuals who voted for him!

In general, the newer digital channels are allowing companies to measure their marketing campaigns much more closely and accurately than was previously possible. As one illustration, today many companies set up "command centers" during major one-time events like the Super Bowl and the Olympics and leveraging tools like Radian6 and Lithium for "social listening." Other companies go even further, using these centers year round to track customer feedback, generate product ideas, and acquire competitive intelligence. Additionally, these digital channels are often more affordable than traditional TV, and they allow for more spontaneous messaging. When the lights went out during the 2013 Super Bowl in New Orleans, Oreo cookies and other sponsors crafted humorous messages via Twitter and other social media.[87] Many of these impromptu ads turned out to be more effective and much less expensive than the companies' Super Bowl ads.

In his executive column, Heinz Kreuzer, CEO of TUI InfoTec, describes how Big Data, social media, and mobile technology are empowering the travel and hospitality industry to go to market using very different strategies than were possible just a few years ago.

Established brands are also digitizing more traditional marketing channels — print, billboard, TV — to make them both more appealing to customers and much more measurable. For example, IKEA, the Swedish furniture chain, encourages users to download a reality app to augment its catalog. Customers place their iPad on a page, and it automatically takes them to that section of its store.[88] This innovation dramatically enhances the user experience: It virtually fits the 400,000-square-foot store into a 300-page catalog. In addition to benefiting customers, this app enables IKEA to track user preferences much more precisely than they could using just the printed materials.

Omni Channel

Modern business markets are witnessing an explosion in delivery channels — shop at the store, order online and have delivered to your home, order online and pick up at the store, and so on. This diversity reflects several emerging trends in the logistics, retail, real estate, and other business sectors.

For an example of a successful in-store model, consider Apple. People questioned the company's sanity when it opened its first retail store in 2001. The tech industry was mired in a severe post-Y2K slump, and PC maker Gateway had struggled with its retail effort. Apple, of course, has since transitioned from strength to strength with its retail operations. In 2012 more than 300 million visitors entered one of Apple's global network of stores.[89] Apple generates almost US$600 per retail square meter, far better than even specialty, haute couture stores do.[90] Apple's success has led many industries to revisit the premise that brick-and-mortar is dying. Customers still want to touch and feel products and to experience helpful and friendly in-store service. A decade after the first Apple store opened in Virginia, the Genius Bar at its stores looks like a genius move.

Tesco's South Korean supermarket chain Home Plus provides an example of a next-gen delivery channel. Commuters can use a mobile phone app to take pictures of the products they want on a subway wall. The groceries are then delivered to their homes by the end of the work day.[91]

While a number of large retailers and grocery chains are looking to build their own same-day delivery competencies, a startup called Zipments has established a delivery service by utilizing modern technologies. Zipments provides an online platform that connects local retailers in New York City with its network of couriers at prices starting at $9 per package. Retailers can track deliveries online and receive real-time notifications that indicate the delivery status each step of the way. Customers receive visual confirmation of all delivery details (such as a photo of the courier) and direct access to the couriers. They can also select special features such as digital signatures and real-time notification. In addition, Zipments has developed a mobile app that enables the couriers to track current jobs and to collect clients' digital signatures.[92]

Customer service is also transitioning to multiple channels. Frontier, a regional U.S. airline, provides a good example. In July 2011 a hailstorm damaged 22 of its planes at Denver International Airport. As a result, thousands of their customers faced cancellations and lengthy delays. Customers were experiencing long lines at the Frontier service counters and even longer wait times on their toll-free reservation lines. Those are the traditional ways passengers rebook flights, even if they purchased their tickets on the web. Fortunately, Frontier's social media team was able to engage with more than 4,000 customers online over the seven-day period the flights were disrupted to answer questions and to move passengers to alternate flights. During that time more than 700,000 people visited Frontier's Facebook page.[93]

Summary
Today's customers are increasingly demanding customized products, personalized marketing, and choices for delivery options and customer service. These developments are the antidote to commoditization and, in some cases, they represent a road to premium pricing. Digital Enterprises are making all of these developments possible after years of promises and slow starts.

Now let's look at practitioner perspectives — from the CIO of Coca-Cola Enterprises and the CEO of TUI InfoTec.

Coca-Cola Enterprise's Digital Strategy
*Esat Sezer, Senior Vice President and Chief Information Officer,
Coca-Cola Enterprises, Inc.*

It is not unusual to hear the names "Borders" and "Blockbuster" in board meetings these days. Every company is terrified of being disrupted by digital competition as those companies were by Amazon and Netflix, respectively. In 2010 Coca-Cola held a board meeting in which we heard similar concerns. This feedback incentivized us to develop our Digital Strategy.

First a primer: Coca-Cola Enterprises (CCE) is one of the world's largest Coca-Cola bottlers. It operates locally in eight territories in Western Europe: Belgium, continental France, Great Britain, Luxembourg, Monaco, the Netherlands, Norway, and Sweden. With 2012 revenues in excess of $8 billion, we are independent of the Coca-Cola Company, and we are traded on the NYSE.

Our Digital Strategy is built on four cornerstones (Figure 6-1):

- Drive new growth

- Drive next-gen productivity

- Expand our engagement with our business constituents (stakeholders)

- Create new opportunities

CCE's Digital Strategy

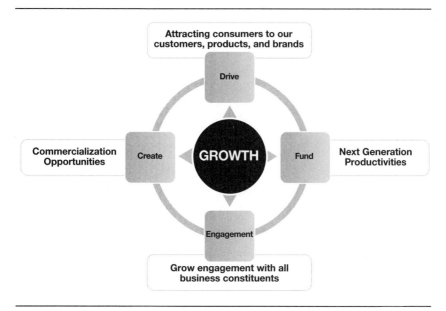

Figure 6-1: The four cornerstones of CCE's Digital Strategy

Drive New Growth

CCE has two major market channels. The first channel, which we call our Home channel, is comprised of Tesco, Carrefour, and other major grocers/retailers. Our Home channel products are "Take-Home." Our second channel — the Cold channel — includes mom-and-pop grocery stores, restaurants, and other places where our products are typically sold cold in coolers, soda machines, and so on.

In the Home channel, our digital strategy is to better align with the shopping trends that are affecting our customers like Tesco and Ocada. In 2012 nearly 20% of their growth came from new online models such as home delivery, drive-through, and pick-up. Going further, roughly 20% of these online orders came from mobile devices or tablets. Significantly, this number is expected to increase to 60% by 2016. Consequently, we are redesigning our promotional campaigns to emphasize this increasingly online, digital flavor.

In the Cold channel, we are helping to leverage the scale of our marketing sophistication to our smaller retailer customers. In a pilot program called "Pro Avec Vous" that we launched in France and are now rolling out across Europe, we help these retailers to plan meal deals along with our drinks, to reconfigure their mix of drinks, and to take advantage of our loyalty promotions. In this way we are helping these smaller businesses to increase their revenues. In addition, we are reaching via digital channels more of the 80% of remote and small stores our sales teams have not reached out to in the past. Finally, we are dramatically expanding our efforts to interact digitally with our customers.

Drive Next-Generation Productivity
Another goal of CCE is to deliver the next generation of productivities for our business. Put simply, we are striving to deliver more for less using a wide range of technologies.

Here's an example: In the past our salespeople and merchandisers visited stores in person to capture and analyze inventory and apply what we call the "look of success." Each visit lasted between 30 and 45 minutes. Today, we have equipped our salespeople with a mobile app that enables them to photograph the cooler, shelves, and backroom in the stores they service and forward this information to a cloud service. CCE then uses proprietary algorithms and crowdsourced resources to provide feedback within minutes on how best to reconfigure the store displays. Our photo-recognition technology can also estimate how much inventory is stored in the backroom. By correlating this statistic with past order information contained in our ERP system, we can advise the storeowner concerning product mix and future orders. Not only are our salespeople's visits now much more analytical, but we are shaving time off each visit. Consequently, our sales force can visit more stores in a day. We would never be able to achieve these productivities without applying a wide range of innovative technologies.

Expand Our Engagement with Our Business Constituents (Stakeholders)

CCE is currently employing social and collaborative technology to engage more directly with our employees, investors, and other relevant populations. Let's consider one example of an employee-related app that has produced impressive results.

Vending machines, soda fountains, and other physical stock are major CCE assets that are spread across our customer locations. In the past we relied on external audit agencies to track and report on these assets. Today, however, we provide our employees with a mobile app that can scan barcodes on these assets. Employees now voluntarily scan these assets in their local communities and send back asset identifier and location data. Not only has this process enabled CCE to reduce the involvement of external agencies, but our asset losses are down from previous years. Going further, our employees are using the photo-recognition app described above to provide competitive intelligence on outlets our sales force does not visit.

In addition to benefiting CCE financially, this system has generated a sense of pride in the employee base because they realize they are helping to protect company assets and contribute to company growth. CCE is exploring similar engagement and collaboration opportunities with other stakeholders; for example, engaging with Wall Street analysts using tools such as Twitter.

Create the Growth

Finally, CCE is planning to leverage the technologies we have invested into benefit peer companies. Consider, for example, our photo-recognition app. Why not do something similar to what we are doing around coolers in stores and supermarkets and provide that intelligence to other branded companies? These companies currently receive point-of-sale data from providers like Nielsen on a monthly basis. CCE can potentially provide much more timely data at various locations.

Similarly, we could make our cadre of technicians who service our equipment available to franchisers like fast-food chains and coffee chains. Providing data and related services would create new sources of revenue for CCE without significantly increasing our infrastructure investment.

Of course, to fuel this large-scale digital growth we have had to revisit our IT architecture. The traditional, on-premise ERP application foundation is not designed to enable rapid scale and ease-of-use that characterize digital systems. Just the opposite: It was actually slowing us down. Therefore, we started to build an agile architecture, layered on our ERP platform, which enabled us to make information transparent and to connect with both cloud service providers and our customers. As part of this process we have selectively been moving ERP components to cloud-based SaaS models: HR to SuccessFactors, CRM to salesforce.com, Procurement to Ariba, and T&E processing to SAP Cloud solution. Today, we are utilizing 30 SaaS applications, and that number is increasing.

The process of moving to SaaS has been deliberate, and we made several mistakes along the way. One critical lesson we learned is to invest heavily in security and integration skills. Security is driven by a guiding principle of utilizing only those data that can be safely uploaded to the cloud. Similarly, integration is driven by utilizing application programming interfaces (APIs) to expose data and services. In addition, we scaled the preservation and management of master data and other IT disciplines we had previously invested in.

For those applications we cannot move to the cloud we try to leverage infrastructure as a service (IaaS) from providers like Amazon. Finally, we are employing platform as a service (PaaS) using tools like Microsoft's Windows Azure and salesforce.com.

Our cloud footprint is significant at this stage. We believe it allows us to scale our Digital Strategy without too much fixed capital investment.

Esat Sezer is Senior Vice President and Chief Information Officer at Coca-Cola Enterprises, Inc.

TUI InfoTec GmbH

Heinz Kreuzer, Chief Executive Officer, TUI InfoTec GmbH

Few industries have experienced as much technology-driven change in recent decades as the travel business. From reservation systems in the 1960s to web-influenced business models in the 1990s, our industry has been "digital" for a long time.

TUI AG has undergone another layer of change. We were spun out of the industrial conglomerate Preussag AG in 2002, and we have since evolved into "Europe's leading travel group" with 74,000 employees and revenues of €18.3bn for 2012. Three sectors form the world of TUI: TUI Travel — which includes tour operating, online sales, high street outlets, airlines, and incoming agencies — TUI Hotels & Resorts, and TUI Cruises, the cruise ship business.

TUI has been well-trained for the new wave of social, mobile, analytical, and cloud technologies. Starting in the early 2000s we used the internet as an important sales and distribution channel along with the retail shops. Today, in many European countries this is the most important channel, accounting for more than 70% of overall sales.

In the last two years TUI has implemented new ways of commerce using these innovative technologies. The travel industry has traditionally penalized impulse travel. They impose penalties for changes in travel plans, and they charge very high prices for last-minute ticket purchases. TUI's approach is much more customer friendly. Using mobile messaging we can now offer our customers the opportunity to extend their stay or to take a side trip. If the guest clicks "yes" to an extension, then we extend the hotel reservation, cancel the Friday return flight, and reserve a flight for Sunday. Everybody benefits from this arrangement. The customer is delighted to stay longer. From our perspective the hotel is a lot easier to fill with someone who is already at the location.

Mobile technology will also allow us to provide all of the necessary guest information to our service people including the travel agent, the check-in service, and the guide at the destination. We will be able to serve our customers according to these specific profiles.

An even bigger opportunity is provided by the Big Data we maintain about customer travel profiles — preferred destinations, assistance from the hotel concierge, dining preferences — while, of course, being sensitive to European data privacy and protection guidelines. We also have extensive data on travel patterns such as popular destinations and popular activities in those destinations. This information is enabling us to significantly improve our seasonal planning and also to come up with better travel packages and products.

Instead of limiting our customers to "simple" search mechanisms based on destination, duration, and hotel classification, we now allow them to search by holiday categories such as Classic, Beach, Lifestyle, Nature, Scene, Premium, and Vital. Each category is aimed at a differ-ent consumer demographic. Christian Clemens, managing director of TUI Germany, announced: "We are developing from traditional travel producers into creative holiday designers. We offer our customers flexible and strongly individualized travel offers."[94]

Real-time analysis of social media in connection with Big Data will provide TUI with an early warning about "unhappy" customers. Our services at destinations and resorts can take immediate action to change them to "happy" customers enjoying a positive customer experience.

These examples demonstrate that a "digital company" is more than a company that uses the internet as a distribution channel. New technologies such as social media, real-time analytics, Big Data, and mobile devices help us to understand and serve our customers better, thereby creating a more enjoyable customer experience.

Heinz Kreuzer is Chief Executive Officer of TUI InfoTec GmbH

7

Outpace Your Industry and Your Competition

The digital paradigm enables new combinations and permutations of information.

We are no longer dealing with the classic analog knowledge that creates an entry barrier into new or foreign markets. In fact, it is the combinations of information that create new products.

As a prominent example, consider the iPhone. Prior to introducing its first mobile phone in 2007, Apple never had *any* experience building previous-generation analog phones. The digital world, however, gave Apple the opportunity to offer the entire value chain to the smartphone user, as the company had done so effectively with its iPod. Within a few years the iPhone had become the greatest mobile phone success in history. The keys to Apple's success:

- Focusing on customer usage rather than product features

- Focusing on software rather than hardware

- Focusing on the new combinations of all components of the value chain.

Significantly, this type of strategy is possible only in the digital world, the world of software.

Rethink your industry, because your business must become digital, no matter which industry you operate in. The basic rule of the digital world is simple: Become digital, or die as a company. There is no way to avoid this natural law in modern digital societies. Any analog company, regardless of its focus, must deal with two major threats:

1. Loss of competitiveness to any competitor that masters the transformation to the Digital Enterprise in its industry sector.

2. New entrants that can effectively manipulate the available data and provide a totally new, digital customer experience as a substitute for any services offered in the analog world.

The good news: Any company can master the challenge of reinventing itself as a Digital Enterprise, step by step. The first step in the right direction is the beginning of the transformation journey, as a Chinese proverb says within a slightly different context.

Thanks to today's technology, the small Chinese takeout restaurant can use a dual language printer to print tickets both in English for the customer and in a larger Chinese font for the cooks who are more comfortable reading and speaking their own dialect. Ethnic grocers and restaurants are examples of *micro-verticals*. Technology is making it possible for different segments of the food and beverage industry to satisfy their unique needs. Bakeries are more interested in shelf life management, breweries in the ability to trace their products. Companies that make athletic clothing employ very different supply chains than uniform makers do.

Further, as we saw earlier in the book, there are a few industries that are not making their products and services much "smarter" by embedding and leveraging technology. As a result, industry lines are being redrawn, and even more new micro-verticals are emerging. This redrawing of industry lines is also changing the competitive landscape in at least three fundamental ways:

a. Competition from "digital natives"

b. Competition from "digital babies"

c. Rebirth of "digital phoenixes"

Let's take a closer look at each one.

Competition from "Digital Natives"

In the past decade, a number of technology companies — like Google and Amazon — have transformed other industries. To cite one prominent example, Apple reshaped the music industry, transforming it from albums in record and CD formats to music and other digital content delivered over the web. In addition, along with Google, Apple has reshaped the telecom industry, where buyer decisions are increasingly influenced more by the device than by the choice of the carrier service. Netflix has similarly reconfigured the video and TV markets.

From a slightly different perspective, Google's search function and other services have redefined the media and advertising markets. In addition, with its fiber-optic service, Google is emerging as a broadband provider.[95] Finally, it is beginning to influence the auto market with its experimental autonomous car.[96]

Meanwhile, Amazon has reshaped the retail industry. It is also looking to transform the grocery market with AmazonFresh, a system in which Amazon provides customers with mobile apps that enable them to purchase food products from local stores and restaurants and have them delivered to their home.[97] Also, its cloud services have reshaped data center infrastructure markets. Meanwhile, eBay's PayPal is reshaping mobile commerce and payments markets.

Online brokers like eTrade have reshaped the stock brokerage industry. Travel sites like Expedia have transformed travel. Skype revolutionized global communications. Samsung and LG, better known for their TVs and mobile phones, are poised to take over leadership of home appliances from traditional providers like Whirlpool and Electrolux.

Competition from "Digital Babies"

New startups that take advantage of technological changes are emerging as another form of competition in every sector. We refer to these companies as "digital babies."

Consider Virgin America, which made an impressive entry into the U.S. aviation market by designing a technology-enabled cabin. Mood lighting, streaming TV, on-demand movies and music, Wi-Fi on all planes, ordering meals via a seat display, and online shopping all contribute to a digital experience that is winning a number of loyal customers.[98]

As technology evolves, the new generation of digital babies often challenges the previous one. For example, GPS devices from Garmin and other manufacturers are experiencing competition from mobile navigation apps on smartphones, live traffic, and other enhancements offered by the auto companies. As mobile devices outstrip laptops, VoIP services like Viber are challenging Skype for international calls and messaging. Gaming companies like Supercell from Finland are supplanting previous-generation successes like Zynga.

Rebirth of "Digital Phoenixes"

Technology is also allowing many incumbent enterprises to redefine themselves. In some cases it even enables them to emerge from oblivion. As Reinhard Clemens of Deutsche Telekom T-Systems describes in his guest column in this chapter, established industries like airlines and luggage makers are also using technology to collaborate and create new products and services.

Consider the case of Marvel Comics, which entered into bankruptcy in the late 1990s. The company effectively resurrected itself by creating highly successful TV and movie franchises around its superhero characters including Spider-Man, the X-Men, and the Avengers. Additionally, in 2007 the company launched a digital archive of more than 2,500 back issues of its comic books. Marvel's stunning turnaround is evidenced by the fact that comics have inspired some of the most popular apps in Apple and other mobile stores. Marvel itself ended up being acquired by Disney for $4 billion in 2009.[99]

Another "phoenix," Deutsche Post, has transformed itself from a national mail carrier into one of the largest global logistics companies. Deutsche Post supported this process by acquiring DHL, Van Gend & Loos, Exel, Airborne Express, and other delivery services and by making massive investments in technologies.[100]

Today most in-flight Wi-Fi offered by global airlines relies on air-to-satellite communication. Gogo, the most widely available Wi-Fi service in the United States, is one of the few providers to leverage air-to-ground frequencies. Gogo is reusing 92 cell towers that its company, Aircell, employed in the 1990s when air phones were available on many planes. Gogo's strategy is an excellent example of redeploying an asset for commercial advantage that appeared to be obsolete.[101]

Finally, railroads, an old-school industry by most definitions, have experienced a stunning comeback in many freight markets. CSX, a major transportation company, emphasizes that railroads can move 3 times as much freight as trucks using the same amount of fuel.[102] This fact highlights the operational efficiencies railroads derive from technology like GE's Trip Optimizer. Trip Optimizer calculates the most efficient operational systems by considering such factors as train length, weight, grade, track conditions, weather, and locomotive performance.[103] Most rail cars use RFID to track their rolling assets. Union Pacific deploys track-side sensors that support predictive maintenance.[104] Norfolk Southern uses automated dispatching. Technology has been a vital element in the railroad renewal story.[105]

Summary

Technology is increasingly redrawing industry boundaries, leading Digital Enterprises to explore new industries or even micro-verticals. Within this environment, competition is rapidly changing. Digital natives, startups, and even former incumbents that are being reborn are all threats to the major players in most markets.

Now let's look at a practitioner perspective — from an executive at Deutsche Telekom T-Systems on how technology is reshaping industries.

Telcos: Drivers of Digital Transformation
Reinhard Clemens, Chief Executive Officer of T-Systems and
Member of the Board of Management at Deutsche Telekom AG

Despite its remarkably fast-paced development and innovative creativity, the telecommunications industry must contend with declining revenues and margins, not to mention the extreme competitive pressures that characterize today's markets. Global internet enterprises and newcomers from other industries may even be gearing up to overtake classical network providers. That's why telcos are frantically searching for new sources of revenue. The age of the digital transformation in other industries offers telcos an opportunity to reinvent themselves by creating new business models, expanding their focus beyond the network business to become catalysts and platforms for the development of cross-industry innovations, services, and products.

"For Lisa! Lots of love from Robbie Williams." With a broad and friendly smile, the superstar autographs his photo and presents it to Tom. "Have fun at my concert tomorrow night in Munich." Tom is really thrilled that he can fulfill his daughter's wish, not just by purchasing a concert ticket, but by giving her a personal autograph from the king of entertainment as a special surprise. Robbie Williams gave his last solo performances six years ago, and now he is in Germany for a limited tour of only four concerts. Tickets were completely sold out on the internet — within minutes. Although Tom was in his car on the way to a business appointment, he was still able to get two VIP tickets — and an opportunity to get an autograph from Robbie Williams.

Just a few years ago, accomplishing this would have been absolutely impossible for someone like Tom. Back then, thousands of fans huddled in front of their PCs at home or in the office, anxiously waiting for tickets to go on sale. Anyone driving his or her car at that moment didn't have any chance to purchase a ticket. In recent years, however, carmakers and telecommunications providers have collaborated on cross-industry projects, pushing innovations that have transformed automobiles into "connected hotspots." That was the final hurdle — today the internet is truly ubiquitous. Children can enjoy movies in the car thanks to video streaming, while their parents listen to their favorite music via internet radio. In fact, the front passenger can even reply to emails using a display integrated into the vehicle's interior.

Tom used the features of his new "connected car" to garner those prized Robbie Williams tickets while he was on his way to a meeting with a customer. As the internet radio played his favorite song, "Let Me Entertain You," the display signaled the exact moment when tickets for the concerts went on sale. One click on "Munich, August 7, 2013" took Tom to the reservation portal, where two VIP tickets for the concert were still available. One more click, and the tickets were his. All of the ticket reservation processes run autonomously in the background: payment, the QR code for the admission ticket, and even a reserved parking space. As a VIP ticket holder, Tom can listen to a special music-streaming program that offers exclusive live recordings of Robbie Williams's concerts — at home, or with his smartphone or tablet — in advance of the performance in Munich.

Interdisciplinary Synchronization of ICT Competencies

This connected car scenario illustrates how traditional network providers can — and must — develop new business models. Today more and more enterprises with core competencies in various branches of industry must deal with information and communication technology in one form or another, and they need support from competent partners. Telcos like Deutsche Telekom T-Systems, which has its own expert IT service provider in T-Systems, can synchronize their competencies as they interact with enterprises in completely different business segments. This interactive collaboration leads to the joint development of innovative products and services that each partner alone would not have been able to realize. This approach goes far beyond providing broadband network infrastructures that never cease to grow. Sooner or later, traditional providers with an exclusive focus on networks will face a serious problem: They will be forced to continuously invest in mobile and fixed networks that demand more and more speed. In effect, these network providers will be trapped. At the same time, their revenues and profit will suffer due to the enormous competitive pressures they will face. In turn, the declining revenues will restrict the freedom they need to make the necessary investments.

Deutsche Telekom T-Systems recognized this trend early on, and it embarked on a new path. The company decided to supplement its classical communications business with internet-based services and products. By employing this strategy the company has transformed itself from a purely classical telecommunications provider into a new, future-centric business with innovative offerings. At Deutsche Telekom T-Systems we refer to this transformation as "from telco to telco plus." The core of our business is centered around high-performance networks and very efficient customer service. This focus differentiates Deutsche Telekom T-Systems from its competitors. The extras in terms of inno-vation originate through cooperative alliances with other enterprises. These special features enhance our developments, partnerships, acquisitions, and business holdings. Efficient, high-performance fiber-optic and mobile telecommunications networks are the prerequisite for offering new premium services. They are also the basis for potential business growth.

Market analysts suggest that telecommunications enterprises should be active in vertical markets. They perceive growth potential in cloud solutions for all industries: fleet management, building automation, telemedicine, intelligent power grids, and connected cars. For all of these business segments, enterprises need more than the pure know-how of a network provider.

Innovation Driver — the ICT Industry

Information and communication technologies (ICTs) are among the most innovative industries in Germany, with an innovation intensity rating of 6.7 percent (2011). In 2011 nearly 25% of all ICT revenue in Germany was generated by product innovations. Further, with its classical inter-disciplinary technologies, the ICT industry catalyzes innovation in other business segments. The Center for European Economic Research (ZEW) recently conducted a study to identify the factors that make ICT so significant in terms of innovation and growth. According to the study, in 2011 roughly 40% of the innovative enterprises in Germany introduced innovations that were based on ICTs.[106]

Thanks to technologies and trends such as mobile internet, cloud computing, and Big Data, we can expect even more increases. In light of these developments, Deutsche Telekom T-Systems has assumed the role of a trusted partner for customers in a complete ecosystem. Telekom acts as a broker for IT-driven business models, bringing together business ideas and enterprises from diverse branches of industry so that these new business models can be developed successfully.

To accomplish this task, Telekom provides much more than simply services for establishing and operating communication networks. In a digital society, new products and services cannot be realized without comprehensive security know-how as well as additional services like billing, payment, and data management. "Telcos are changing, from providers of vertical integration to providers of multi-layer network architectures," claim strategic consultants at Booz & Company.[107] In addition to typical services like access to broadband networks and bit-pipe infrastructures, telcos today must develop and deliver apps, provide service platforms, and offer complete operating and support systems. In addition, they must be in a position to support customers as they migrate from proprietary to open systems.

There are many examples of cross-industrial cooperation — and they have become quite competitive even among the powerhouses of the New Economy. In Germany, for example, Telekom formed an alliance with publishers and booksellers to launch the Tolino eBook reader as a competitor to the Kindle. The success of the device proves that Telekom had the right idea: Tolino is popular because — unlike Kindle — it is an open system that gives customers more freedom and flexibility. Tolino users have access to many booksellers like Weltbild and Hugendubel, where they can store books in the cloud, and they can even read eBooks borrowed from the public library. This open-source approach is attracting more and more customers.

One Team: Aircraft Manufacturer, Luggage Maker, and ICT Provider

In June 2013, Deutsche Telekom T-Systems announced it was launching a cross-industry innovation project together with aircraft manufacturer Airbus and RIMOWA, which makes travel luggage. Passengers will soon be able to send off an intelligent suitcase on its own, without having to carry heavy luggage when checking in at the airport. The intelligent suitcase is fitted with a radio and software module that contains a display. The airline passenger inputs all of the necessary flight data via a smartphone app and transmits it to the airline. In turn the airline generates a bar code and sends it to the display on the unit on the suitcase. This bar code assigns the baggage a unique identifier linked to the passenger. The airline uses this identifier to check in the baggage and forward it to its destination.

The airline creates a separate bar code for each flight that contains information such as the owner and the weight of the suitcase, along with all of the flight details. These data enable the suitcase to travel independently of its owner, right to the destination — even if flights are changed or canceled on short notice, or a connecting flight is missed. Thanks to the intelligence of the smart suitcase, both the owner and the airline can locate the baggage at any time with the touch of a button. Finally, this "smart baggage" solution also registers whether a suitcase was opened during its journey, and, if it was, it informs the owner as to when and where this occurred.

Connected Car with App Store

Tom, who spends a great deal of time behind the wheel, soon may also enjoy the benefits of a cross-industry innovation. Telekom has been collaborating with car manufacturers for several years. Initial projects focused on connectivity. In the meantime, however, Telekom, auto-makers, and other service providers have been developing innovative services for drivers. As automobiles increasingly become equipped with integrated SIM cards, drivers will soon be able to download apps into the car from special App stores. They will also be able to take advantage of many solutions and subscription services when they are on the road.

This is just perfect for people like Tom. While on his way to meet with a customer, he heard that Robbie Williams was signing autographs for fans. "New Message" appeared on the display, and his connected car read the text aloud: "Robbie Williams is giving autographs to his fans — only three kilometers from your current location. As a VIP ticket holder, you have exclusive access — without waiting." One click for navigation and ten minutes later, Tom was face to face with a superstar — a thrill for him, and, of course, a surprise for his family.

Reinhard Clemens is Chief Executive Officer of T-Systems and Member of the Board of Management at Deutsche Telekom AG

8

Rethink Speed

What is speed? Put simply, speed is a relative concept. Whenever the word "speed" is used, however, the perception is that things are going faster than expected, faster than we previously experienced. This is exactly what digital business is all about: Things are going faster. Consider the following examples:

a. We can connect more people faster than we ever anticipated through the proliferation of mobile devices such as smartphones and social collaboration platforms such as Facebook, LinkedIn, and similar technologies.

b. We can expect results faster than ever before because processes can be automated — they are no longer dependent on human interaction. One prominent example is business process management (BPM). Human interaction frequently becomes a bottleneck, a source of malfunction that slows down the process. (Fortunately this is not true of every process: There are still valuable human processes that we all appreciate very much, such as in the service industries.)

c. We implement digital solutions faster than equivalent non-digital projects because "ease of" is the common denominator for all digital projects. Ease of planning, ease of deployment, and ease of use are key drivers for the success of cloud applications. They are the new benchmarks for all on-premise IT systems.

d. We fix systems faster, because we know, very often in advance, that something can go wrong, or that it went wrong, or what went wrong and which countermeasures we should implement. Through the Internet of Things, or Industrie 4.0 technology, hundreds, thousands, or even millions of sensors can proactively alert us if something is about to go wrong. Predictive maintenance is the concept behind this innovation ("prepare" instead of "repair").

e. We can analyze a situation much faster, because data analysis is no longer restricted to historical data as was true of classic business intelligence (BI). In today's digital environment we can analyze data quickly on the move, even massive Big Data. Real-time business analytics is the focus here. The in-memory computing speed of analysis, even for massive amounts of data, is up to 1,000 times faster than was possible with classic IT systems such as disks and databases.

f. We know earlier what might happen. Predictive systems can forecast potential problems much earlier and much more precisely than ever before, and for much more complex circumstances. Sensors connected with multiple additional information resources through computational intelligence can provide insights that no human being can. Digital technologies can combine hundreds or even thousands of information sources; for example, to predict the weather much more accurately than was previously possible.

g. We know much better. Human beings generally can take into account two or three variables. Some exceptionally intelligent people can manage four, five, six, or even seven parameters in a complex setting. However, no human being can take into account a thousand or more algorithms to calculate in a second what could go wrong or whether something already has gone wrong, as is possible in fraud-detection algorithms in payment systems.

In recent decades China has come to represent speed with every aspect of its economy and society. As China modernizes its agricultural sector, it will need to house 300 million people who will migrate from the countryside to the urban areas.[108] That is the equivalent of rebuilding all of the cities and towns in the United States — and doing it in only a quarter of a century.

In the last couple of decades, China has built a nationwide network of high-speed trains including the world's longest high-speed stretch of 2,300 kilometers between Beijing and Guangzhou.[109] Further, whereas new airports or even extensions to existing ones in the West take years to be approved, China has been opening 10–15 new civilian airports *each* year.[110] Its capacity of container terminals is expected to increase by the equivalent of 100 million 20-foot containers in this decade alone. In general it is also the acceptance of speed that expedites the development of societies, enabled through digital technologies.

Developments like these are redefining the concept of speed across all types of projects — construction, technology implementation, and product releases. In this essay we explore several cases in which Digital Enterprises successfully met the modern, accelerated expectations concerning speed.

Speed in Product Cycles

In 2013 Samsung launched its newest smartphone, the Galaxy S4, to compete with mobile devices like the Apple iPhone 5. Samsung introduced the phone into the market with a global promotional campaign that labeled the Galaxy S4 "The Next Big Thing."[111] Samsung also introduced the original Galaxy S in 2010 with a 400 x 800 resolution screen and a 5 megapixel camera. Every year since then Samsung has produced a new generation of Galaxy phones with improved specs. The S4 clocks in with 1080 x 1920 resolution and a 13 megapixel camera. In every other dimension including CPU speed, memory, battery life, and number of sensors, each generation has exhibited impressive improvements over its predecessors.[112]

In terms of user features, the S4 is several steps ahead of the first generation S phones. These features include the following:[113]

- The Dual Camera mode, which allows you to use the front- and rear-facing cameras at the same time

- The S Translator, which can translate nine languages even if you are not on the mobile network

- The S Health, which tracks various exercise and diet metrics

- The camera's infrared capabilities, which allow you to use it as a universal remote to control multiple TVs in your household.

In enterprise software, Workday and other SaaS vendors are similarly redefining the speed of their product releases. Workday issues a new release every six months, compared to the two- to three-year cycles that used to be normal in that sector. More impressively, because the upgrades are performed in the background, the entire customer base is migrated to each new release. This contrasts with the release horizons of three to five years that were common in traditional enterprise software.[114]

Workday claims that these accelerated release cycles also make their customer community much more vibrant. Their competitors' customers use different product versions and different database platforms, with different customizations, maintenance schedules, and national regulations. Consequently, it is a major challenge for these companies to assemble a representative group of customers in a single room to conduct an effective discussion that touches everyone. Workday markets its advantage as the "Power of One." When the company innovates a product to help one of their largest customers, say, Flextronics, that same innovation might benefit a smaller customer, such as Illumina, as well.[115]

At the end of this chapter, two banks — BBVA and Standard Chartered — provide executive perspectives on speed. BBVA is striving to build a world-class investment banking service. Standard Chartered has been delivering new features for its Breeze mobile banking, which it has been rolling out rapidly across continents that have very different regulatory environments.

Supply Chain Velocity

Apple raised the bar for global supply chain coordination when it launched the 3G version of the iPhone in 22 countries in 2008. Over the next few months Apple introduced the phone in more than 50 additional countries. Among the carriers with which Apple coordinated the rollout were VimpelCom in Russia, three companies in Hong Kong, Etisalat in Dubai, and Telia in Sweden — not exactly the household names Apple was used to dealing with.[116] The coordination took place across the physical supply chain, with the goal of ensuring that the 7 million phones sold in the first quarter were available not only in local stores but also across the digital supply chain, because many customers purchased their phones from home via the iTunes store.

The consumer electronics industry has also demonstrated that traditional supply chain planning based on historic demand forecasting techniques is no longer sufficient. As with other industries, consumer electronics can plan on increased demand for established products during back-to-school campaigns, Black Friday (the day following Thanksgiving Day in the United States, often regarded as the beginning of the Christmas shopping season[117]), promotions, and regional holidays like the Chinese New Year. Predicting the demand for a brand new product category like a smartphone, a tablet, or an eBook reader, however, is much more difficult. For some of those products first-quarter demand can total millions of units; for less successful products demand won't exceed a few thousand units. There is little history to go by.

What options are available to companies in these circumstances? The best strategy is to implement a combination of long-term and short-term planning. Companies secure critical long-lead components through purchasing agreements in which capacity and flexibility needs are negotiated in a long-term planning window. Procurement teams continuously manage the overall supply flow based on both dynamic production schedules and continuous information obtained from product demand channels. It is a compliment to many of these companies that the 2010 Eyjafjallajökull volcanic explosion in Iceland, which shut down several European airports for weeks, and the 2011 tsunami in northern Japan, where many electronic components are manufactured, did not significantly disrupt their supply chains.

The short-term component involves a network of contract manufacturers like Flextronics that assemble, package, and ship the final product.[118] Companies like this have invested in high-volume production capabilities that include the ability to quickly "flex" up or down in response to changes in market demand. They are legendary for their flexibility — it's not uncommon for them to incorporate last-minute product changes. They are even more valued for their discretion — leaks of product features can lead to a loss of competitive advantage.

The dynamic planning, the security, and the other business aspects described above are highly dependent on modern technologies. Significantly, very little of this technology could be delivered without digital supply chain tools. Such dynamic supply chains are gradually appearing in other industries. As products become digitized, similar component contracting and assembly models will become more common.

Going further, even when supply chains slow down, the need for information does not. As an example, the ocean freight business has been struggling for several years due to weak demand and increasing fuel prices. One coping strategy the industry has implemented is a practice called "slow steaming" — running ships considerably below their maximum speeds to save on fuel. However, seaports have fixed and other costs, which require them to optimize the use of their berths and other facilities. The challenge is to accommodate these needs to the slow steaming policies. To meet this challenge, Royal Dirkzwager — a maritime information and nautical service provider based in the Netherlands — has developed the Automated Identification System (AIS). AIS continuously analyzes real-time signals from a variety of sources, such as from a ship's onboard systems, that provide information such as location, speed, and direction. Rather than send the same list of static information to all customers on a daily basis, Royal Dirkzwager forwards only the most current updates indicating changes in status that are customized for each client. These updates allow a port, for example, to re-plan its activities, such as putting another ship into a berth in place of a delayed vessel.[119]

Summary

The future comes faster in most industries. The Digital Enterprise thrives on its speed — in product release cycles, in the velocity of supply chains, and in other operational areas — as a competitive asset.

Now let's look at two practitioner perspectives at two banks — Standard Chartered and BBVA — that are rapidly rolling out investment banking and mobile banking products.

Standard Chartered PLC

Jan Verplancke, Chief Information Officer and Group Head of Group Technology and Operations, Standard Chartered PLC

Standard Chartered PLC is a London-based financial services company with more than 85,000 staff based in more than 70 countries. The financial services sector has traditionally invested more resources in IT than in any other sector. Like other global banks, Standard Chartered invests heavily in IT — even though we are considered a "traditional" bank because our roots go back to the 19th century and we are well represented in emerging economies in Asia and Africa. My team (globally, even though I am based in Singapore) is always working on cutting-edge projects.

Despite the industry's large-scale IT investments, the retail banking consumer is a conservative adopter of new technology. That's understandable, because people want their money to be safe, and they view banks as trusted intermediaries. For this reason consumers of all ages continue to use paper checks in U.S. retail stores, even as technology has transformed their music, reading, and communication behaviors. One of the most popular technology features of mobile banking is the SMS alert we send to customers whenever they complete an ATM transaction.

So, even though Standard Chartered has conducted "digitization campaigns" for several years, we have to keep our customers well informed across all of our channels — branch, ATM, web, mobile, and so on. Many of our business processes and event management technologies operate behind the scenes across our global network of more than 1,700 branches and 5,800 ATM machines.

There are signs, however, that we may be at a tipping point when it comes to retail banking consumer behavior. Consider, for example, how the mobile phone-based money transfer and microfinancing service called M-Pesa has flourished in Kenya and Tanzania. Similarly, consider how Malaysia's Central Bank is pioneering funds transfers using beneficiaries' mobile phone numbers instead of their bank account numbers.

Our launch of Breeze mobile banking and its subsequent rollout across several continents has also been pioneering in three ways:

a. Rollout of features

b. Social marketing as a component of launches

c. Global rollout

Let's take a closer look at each one.

Rollout of Features

We launched the Breeze mobile app in Singapore in the summer of 2010 using fairly basic features on iOS devices. We digitized transactions that consumers already completed in person in branches or via ATMs. We focused on simplicity, and the menu was driven by two high-level paths — see your money and move your money.

Since its launch, Breeze has become more feature rich. In addition, we have enhanced the service by extending mobile web technologies to other platforms including Android, Windows mobile, and Blackberry. We introduced Breeze Good Life, which provides location-based services across three views: Augmented Reality, Map, and List. Further, we offer customers coupons based on their past consumption patterns and their geo-locations.

An even more interesting feature is our Wish List. Customers can identify the specific items or trips they are saving for. They can also track their savings progress towards that goal. Consider what the bank can do with that knowledge. We can inform product makers and retailers how many hundreds of our customers are in the market for specific products. In turn, these companies can share reduced marketing costs in the form of lower prices for customers and banks. In addition, we can utilize this information to offer customers loans or other financing to help them achieve their goals more quickly.

Phase 1 of Breeze focused on offering transaction convenience to customers. Phase 2 involves finding contextually relevant methods to engage and sell to customers. Again, we have to be respectful of our customers' cautious approach to banking relationships.

Social Interaction

Breeze has leveraged social marketing and crowdsourcing far more than other banking products. With the initial launch we ran a "World's Coolest Intern" contest, and we received close to 1,200 applications from more than 65 countries (in addition to valuable social media coverage). The goal of the six-month internship was to help us develop and implement a social media communication strategy for Breeze.

Another popular feature of Breeze is its "intelligent" wallpapers, which change not only based on the time of the day but also for events such as the Chinese New Year and Christmas. Working with the global innovation firm frog[120], we also used a crowdsourcing contest — InMode — to design Breeze background screens for other world events.

Social media also helped to publicize the fact that mountaineers on their way to the top of Mt. Everest had successfully traded shares and conducted fund transfers with Breeze Trade and Breeze Banking at record heights of 6,500 and 8,000 meters.

Going further, customers are sharing their Wish Lists described above with their Facebook friends, who can cheer them on and perhaps help them achieve their goals. This social angle reflects the increasing technical sophistication of banking consumers and the ways in which banking product launches and communities are evolving along with them.

Standard Chartered views the online social media space with great enthusiasm. We use dedicated tools to monitor what is resonating with our fans. Social media also helps us to stay on top of conversations and questions. This is how we know that we average 224 "Likes" per post on our Facebook page and that "Breeze" was mentioned close to 400,000 times across social media platforms in June and July of 2013 alone.

Global Rollout

Utilizing the lessons we learned from our Singapore launch, Standard Chartered has subsequently launched Breeze in India, Malaysia, Indonesia, Hong Kong, Korea, China, United Arab Emirates, Pakistan, and Nigeria, with more countries to follow. Although banking regulations vary considerably by country, there is a growing "cosmopolitan" customer in every country who is tech savvy, well traveled, and an ideal customer for Breeze. Breeze currently averages close to 2 million logins per month. When we recently launched in Pakistan, we reached 22,000 active users in the very first month.

Jan Verplancke is Chief Information Officer and Group Head of Group Technology and Operations at Standard Chartered PLC

BBVA

Ramón Laguna García, Chief Technology Officer of the IT Corporate Investment Banking, BBVA S.A.

BBVA is one of the largest banks of Spain, with more than €600 billion in assets. We also enjoy a dominant position in Spanish-speaking Latin American countries, and we have expanded to other regions; for example, we acquired Compass Bank in the United States. Overall we now have locations in more than 30 countries.

For 150 years BBVA has focused on retail-and consumer-oriented banking (we have more than 20,000 ATMs worldwide). In 2010 we decided to make a sizable push in corporate investment banking (CIB). As Francisco González, Chairman and CEO of BBVA, explained to the magazine *Euromoney,* "Post crisis, we need more fee earnings to boost returns on the capital tied up in lending to fewer key accounts. We're trying to price our provision of capital properly and partly that comes down to providing more services to key clients."[121]

In investment banking, particularly in trading services, it is a commonly known fact that the global giants enjoy a significant cost advantage — they are frequently 2 to 5 times more efficient per trade — because of their larger scale. So, to support that dynamic, BBVA is improving the skills of our staffing rapidly and significantly. It is also introducing new IT architecture and infrastructure.

Let me share the story of our rapid digital journey, which we have undertaken without compromising our exemplary quality and economic standards. In our digitization process we have pursued four clearly articulated goals:

- Offer a holistic solution to our internal customers, as conveyed in the elements discussed below

- Construct speedily — we have evaluated and adopted many best-of-breed technologies from a wide range of vendors

- Maintain standards and consistency across our offerings

- Enable our customers to build with speed — so different groups, like M&A and traders, can provide infrastructure and build specific applications quickly

Our Holistic Coverage

Four components are particularly important:

- The front-end architecture, which we internally call Blue-Spring, supports portals, profiling, personalization, security levels, and widgets that can be customized.

- The back-end architecture, which we call Elara, supports banking transactions using a vendor-neutral model based on standards established by OSGi, an open standards organization. This architecture can be scaled rapidly.

- Case management centrally manages unstructured processes, across multiple roles in multiple formats.

- Low Latency enables banks to respond quickly to market events to increase trade profitability.

Construct Speedily

BBVA has assembled a small research group that investigates new technologies, compares competing products and their economics, and conducts early testing of concept pilots on the products. This team has allowed us to rapidly assemble a portfolio comprised of both commercial and open-source technologies in multiple areas including:

- Complex event processing — to quickly evaluate data from multiple sources to detect patterns

- Grid memory — to allocate objects in memory to share the best performance between applications

- Streaming — to share large volumes of real-time data with our customers and partners

- Portals — to make it easier to create websites and web-based apps

- Enterprise Service Bus — to support both low-latency and real-time messaging

- Private Cloud — to manage servers and storage as infrastructure-as-a-service (IaaS) and lifecycle-management tools as platform-as-a-service (PaaS). We currently support 62 applications in the "as-a-service" model — for example, databases, web and applications servers, grid software monitoring agents — for rapid provisioning.

Maintain Standards
Given the regulatory environment in our industry, we are particularly committed to high standards of governance and transparency. As an example, consider our guidelines for infrastructure usage:

- Use traditional infrastructure for nonstandard and low-latency services

- Use our private cloud for standard services

- Use public cloud providers for non-core services with low security requirements and to manage overloads of punctual service (for processing without relevant data sharing)

Allow Our Business to Build Functionality Rapidly
We have designed our Elara architecture for back-end transactional applications with high elasticity. Consequently, we can rapidly provision

nodes across a wide range of infrastructure: virtual or physical, private or public cloud, etc. Going further, we can ensure that each node has a copy of relevant transactions and is able to execute and be productive quickly; for example, to comply with the U.S. Dodd-Frank legislation.

The mandate our team received in 2010 was to rapidly scale a technology infrastructure to implement our ambitious goal to become a Tier 1 global investment bank. As a testimonial to our success in realizing this goal, *The Banker* recognized BBVA with an "Innovation in Dealing Technology" award in 2012.[122] In addition, several of our vendor partners provided feedback affirming that we are innovating in many areas. As a final acknowledgment of our accomplishments, several of our largest competitors are raiding our IT staff!

Ultimately, the most satisfying aspect is that we have several staffing, project completion, and other benchmarks to demonstrate that we have made an excellent start in assisting our CIB colleagues with their rapid growth plans.

Ramón Laguna García is Chief Technology Officer of the IT Corporate Investment Banking at BBVA S.A.

9

Digitize Your Factory

Product packaging intelligence driving the production process, agile robots, urban factories, augmented reality training, 3D printing, predictive maintenance, products that instruct the machines how to form them: These are all elements of one common theme known as Industrie 4.0, also known as the Fourth Industrial Revolution or the Industrial Internet.

The goal of Industrie 4.0 is to enable the mass production of individual goods, or an individualized, customized product that costs the same as a standard, uniform product. Are we talking about some far-off utopia? By no means: In fact, it is already happening. Going further, product lifecycle management now expands far beyond the production lifecycle. For example, car manufacturers can monitor the status of any part not only during the production process but throughout its product lifecycle, which might span one, two, or three decades, or even longer. Imagine what insights any goods manufacturer can acquire if they know virtually everything about their products throughout their lifecycle. Parts can be optimized much more rapidly, systems can be monitored more precisely, countermeasures can be taken before parts break, and safety measures can be taken before risks develop into problems.

In his 2013 State of the Union speech, U.S. President Obama announced something few recent presidents have been able to. "After shedding jobs for more than 10 years, our manufacturers have added about 500,000 jobs over the past 3. Caterpillar is bringing jobs back from Japan. Ford is bringing jobs back from Mexico. And this year, Apple will start making Macs in America again."[123]

The United States has offshored manufacturing for years. Now, the country is poised for a stunning turnaround, for multiple reasons. Differences in labor rates compared to developing countries like China are rapidly shrinking. Industrial strife and intellectual property theft in certain regions and cultures have become major business impediments. Shipping costs from overseas plants have been rising. Finally, the U.S. energy outlook is increasingly bright, at least in terms of carbon-based fuel reserves, due to new shale explorations. These factors are combining to create a much healthier manufacturing environment in the United States.

In the meantime, the National Science Foundation has been investing in research on advanced manufacturing technologies. Its 2013 budget request to Congress includes funding in "cyber-physical systems and advanced robotics research; materials processing and manufacturing; and advanced semiconductor and optical device design."[124] As a result, the new U.S. factories will look nothing like those from previous eras.

Germany, Japan, and other industrialized nations have not experienced the same manufacturing losses as the United States. They are facing other challenges like ageing workforces, however, and they understand the need to continuously innovate their products or risk being displaced by competition from China and other emerging economies. For several years now German Chancellor Angela Merkel has assembled a group of advisers — including Prof. Dr. Wolfgang Wahlster and Prof. Dr. Siegfried Russwurm, who contributed guest columns for this chapter — who have been developing a vision for the Fourth Industrial Revolution. A working group report predicted this concept:

> "In the future, businesses will establish global networks that incorporate their machinery, warehousing systems, and production facilities in the shape of cyber-physical systems (CPS). In the manufacturing environment, these cyber-physical systems comprise smart machines, storage systems, and production facilities capable of autonomously exchanging information, triggering actions, and controlling each other independently."[125]

Below we discuss some of the most promising technologies for the next generation of factories.

Agile Robots

Industrial robots invariably evoke the image of massive, noisy pieces of equipment. They are intimidating enough to be locked away in cages. In contrast, the next-gen robots are more human-like, and they perform much better as junior assistants, which means they work in a quieter, more flexible environment.

Japan is pioneering the use of service robots in the home, especially to take care of its aging population. In addition, many of these "gentler" robots are making their way into the new, redefined factory. For example, Hitachi is using robots from NextAge (which look like the animated character Wall-E) in its disk drive production plant located outside Tokyo.[126] These robots install covers and tighten screws.

Walk into a Zappos shoe warehouse, and you see R2D2-sized Kiva robots (both Zappos and Kiva are now part of Amazon) zipping around. Instead of having workers walking around and looking for ordered items, the robots do the running around, and they bring the items to the workers, who check the orders and seal them in shipping boxes.[127]

Similarly, Daimler is using lightweight KUKA robots to work alongside human employees. These robots have sensitive motorized grippers that give them a delicate touch. Consequently they can handle objects gently, and they can perform difficult tasks precisely; for example, installing panels on cars. Significantly, these robots function as companions rather than as competitors to the human workers.[128]

Additive Printing

3D printers have been around since 1976, when the inkjet paper printer was invented.[129] Instead of ink, 3D printers deposit plastic and other materials in successive layers to create a physical object. The cost/quality quotient of such printing is improving to a point where the term "additive manufacturing" is entering the business vernacular. Companies such EOS of Germany, 3D Systems in the United States, and the U.S.-Israeli company Stratasys are among the leading providers of 3D printers. Significantly, in his State of the Union speech mentioned above, President Obama highlighted the National Additive Manufacturing Innovation Institute (NAMII) in Youngstown, Ohio: "A once-shuttered warehouse is now a state-of-the art lab where new workers are mastering the 3-D printing that has the potential to revolutionize the way we make almost everything."[130]

Hobbyists have established a cottage industry of products created from 3D printers that ranges from cars to planes. In addition, one of the leading commercial applications today is to transform digital design to physical prototypes. For example, the athletic shoe industry has aggressively employed this technology to rapidly create and reshape prototypes and to obtain customer feedback.

One major consequence of 3D printing will be to enable the manufacturing of smaller parts and components to become increasingly decentralized, away from large factories. For example, a home repair rep could make a replacement part in his or her service truck rather than carry large inventories. Similarly, hospitals could print custom-designed implants for patients.

Of course, 3D printing would also allow consumers to print out replacement parts at home. This technology clearly raises intellectual property and print quality issues that need to be resolved. Nevertheless, 3D printing promises to reshape the manufacturing world.

Augmented Reality
Industries with complex assets such as aviation have long used simulators for training. In contrast, on-the-job training has been transformed

at consumer website companies such as Amazon and eBay, who pride themselves for being so easy to navigate that users require very little training.

Modern manufacturing is increasingly making use of interactive and situation-aware training. For example, wearable computers are enabling context-sensitive, on-the-job training. Škoda, the Czech automaker, has been pioneering this practice since 2004 for its assembly line workers. Škoda provides its trainees with information digitally to help them perform individual production tasks. Their work is then tracked via mobile sensors mounted on the worker's body and on the car. This system provides the trainees with instant feedback.[131]

Metaio, whose augmented reality tools are being used by a number of companies in mobile marketing and sales apps, has long positioned its Engineer brand of software and hardware solutions in the industrial field. These solutions are especially useful for precision engineering, design, and training tasks.[132]

Green Manufacturing
Influenced by seminal works like the 2002 Michael Braungart and William McDonough book *Cradle to Cradle: Remaking the Way We Make Things*, manufacturing is increasingly focused on reducing resource usage, waste, and pollution. One of the concepts that underlie this movement is the idea that "waste is food." This concept encourages manufacturers to make and use components that can either be reused and returned to the manufacturing cycle or be broken down organically for use as food for the natural environment.

As one example, Wittenstein AG, a German manufacturer of "mechana-tronic" — drives, actuators, and gears and related software — is build-ing a next-gen factory based on the Industrie 4.0 concepts mentioned above near its headquarters in Igersheim-Harthausen. The building is designed to provide "spacious, light, and clean office and production areas with short lines of communication, transparent to both the inside and outside, low-noise and low-emission."[133] The goal is for such "urban factories" to be more attractive from a work-life perspective. Being "clean" allows them to be closer to where employees live. This new factory follows the path of the VW Gläserne Manufaktur (The Transparent Factory) in Dresden, which opened at the turn of the 21st century. This building showcases its clean manufacturing processes through the transparency of its walls.[134]

Summary

Inspired by thinking such as Industrie 4.0 concepts as well as by technology such as adaptive printing and augmented reality training, the Digital Enterprise is shaping the factory of the future — a greener version that is driven more by software and sensors than its predecessors were. Now let's look at two practitioner perspectives — Prof. Dr. Wolfgang Wahlster on the promise of semantic product memories and how that technology can reshape product manufacturing, logistics, and commerce, and Prof. Dr. Siegfried Russwurm of Siemens AG on the Industrie 4.0 vision.

DFKI GmbH

Prof. Dr. Wolfgang Wahlster, Director and CEO, German Research Center for Artificial Intelligence (DFKI GmbH) and Professor of Computer Science at Saarland University

Smart products are everywhere — smartphones, smart appliances, smart cars. Several building blocks have been evolving over the past few years that enable conversations between such products and humans. IT specialists call this network the "Internet of Things."

As an example, the Object Memory Model (OMM) language with embedded Ontology Web Language (OWL) expressions was designed for use by applications to process the content of information stored by these products instead of simply presenting the information to humans. By building actuators, sensors, and radio modules for web connectivity directly into products or their packaging, we can create "event recorders" that record the life histories of products — similar in concept to the black box that records flight data on airplanes and that can be retrieved and analyzed.

The SemProM (short for Semantic Product Memory) consortium has been evaluating how the Internet of Things affects various production and supply chain processes. The consortium is one component of the IKT-2020 research program of the German Federal Ministry of Education and Research.

Based on all these pioneering efforts, it is not futuristic to envision a digital journal that various products "write" and to use that journal to facilitate a wide range of consumer decisions, commerce, logistics, safety recalls, and other traceable actions.

To illustrate this concept I have outlined below and in Figure 9-1 the "diary" of an order of chocolates. With minor changes, you could apply the same concepts to a box of frozen pizza or a tub of ice cream. Later I will apply similar concepts to other groceries and to pharmaceutical products.

In the Smart Factory

The chocolate factory receives an order for assorted luxury pralines from a chocolate store I will call Althaus. The factory order management system initializes the semantic memories of the boxes in which the pralines will be packaged. On the shop floor, the memories guide each filling station as to the kind of pralines to put in each box and how to position them in the box.

This digital system is fundamentally different from the traditional manufacturing flow where the bill of material drives most of the production, and customization is usually one of the last steps. Here the semantic product memory guides the flow across conveyor belts and filling stations in the factory.

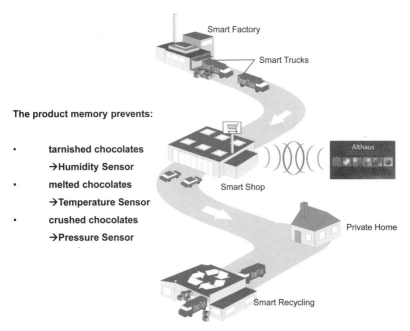

The product memory prevents:

* **tarnished chocolates**
  →Humidity Sensor
* **melted chocolates**
  →Temperature Sensor
* **crushed chocolates**
  →Pressure Sensor

Figure 9-1: The digital diary of an order of chocolates

In the Smart Delivery Truck

These expensive pralines justify the costs of shipping via temperature-controlled trucks that logistics providers increasingly provide. DHL, for example, offers its Smart Sensor packages that combine a sensor with a passive ultra-high frequency (UHF) radio frequency identification (RFID) transponder, which allows authorized personnel to read the temperature data without having to open the shipment. DHL also offers services like COLDCHAIN, which provides temperature control, security, and handling for life sciences and healthcare products.

In addition, the chocolate package contains a "black box" that frequently has its own temperature sensors. If the truck were to get too hot, these sensors can "complain" via machine-to-machine communication to the truck's refrigeration system to increase the cooling.

When the shipment arrives, the Althaus storeowner opens the secure delivery box with the PIN/TAN authentication he or she has been provided by the factory. He or she may find that the pressure sensor of the boxes in the order has been triggered. In that case, instead of accepting crushed chocolates, the storeowner can decide to return that box to the factory.

In the Smart Retail Store

The semantic product memory on the boxes allows a consumer to perform a side-by-side comparison on digital signage in the Althaus store. Specifically, it allows her to compare calories, freshness, and other product features.

Once the consumer decides on a product, its box updates the electronic shopping list on her smartphone. The cashier-less checkout station then reads the relevant contents of the semantic product memory. BMW and DFKI have developed a car key fob that also doubles as an electronic payment device in our innovative retail lab (IRL).

In the Consumer's Smart Car

BMW and other automakers increasingly offer temperature-controlled storage space in the central console or glove compartment. The car's indoor sensors detect the praline box and read its semantic product memory. They then help recommend the ideal air conditioning setting and the best navigation route home to avoid a temperature violation for the pralines.

At the Consumer's Smart Home

In the customer's home, smartphones enabled by NFC can continue to monitor the humidity, temperature, and pressure sensors of the praline box. As an added benefit for customers with diabetes, medical devices like the Medivox system from Kohl Pharma Group can read the semantic product memory and warn them to take their medication before eating a praline. NFC readers and health apps on smartphones can also warn patients with food allergies that there are traces of nuts in the pralines.

In the Smart Recycling Plant

The consumer discards the box in the garbage, and the waste pickup service brings it to the recycling plant. At the plant the automatic sorting module recognizes the embedded black box, and a robotic gripper communicates with the product memory to locate its position. It then separates the black box from the rest of the box so the electronics can be recycled.

Now let's look at two other products — one with somewhat less elaborate packaging, and one with more — and see how they can tell their "life stories."

A black box like the one we just described would not be feasible for a pack of frozen spinach or a bag of lettuce. However, take a look at Iglo's packages of its creamed spinach, Rahm-Spinat. (Iglo, formerly a division of the giant corporation Unilever, is one of Europe's leading frozen food makers.) Below the expiration date is a uniquely engraved set of codes. Enter those codes on Iglo's website, and you receive information about the farmer who grew the spinach, the region where the farm is located, the date it was packed, and other pertinent details. Not only is this information important for traceability during recalls, it also provides transparency to the consumer on the Iglo supply chain. Indeed, search social media sites, and you can find consumer compliments and complaints about the spinach with the specific codes included.

In another industry — pharmaceuticals — opportunities for smart packaging are even greater. Smart blister packs with printed electronics embedded in a thin plastic foil can monitor when a pill is taken out of its packaging. Not only can this help with dosage management, it also helps in monitoring for tampering. Worldwide sales of counterfeit medicines could exceed US$75 billion in 2013, a 90% rise in five years.[135] Going further, smart tags on packs permit reverse audits, known as "pedigree" in the industry. They also enable precise tracking, so the origin and destination of even the smallest package can be known at all times.

There are also packages that can verbally convey prescription instructions to patients. The City University in London has found that 25% of fully sighted consumers either cannot read or have difficulty reading these instructions. That number jumps dramatically to almost 75% for partially sighted people.[136] To address this problem, the German company Wipak Walsrode came out with a "TalkPack" that includes a pen reader that can speak aloud instructions encoded on the packaging. Along these same lines, some packages are embedded with NFC tags that can be read by mobile phones and played back orally. Also available is packaging with large scrolling instructions in glowing images.

As you can see, semantic product memories promise to reshape how products are manufactured, shipped, sold, consumed, traced, and recycled. Each product leads an interesting life, and if we listen carefully to it, it can help us to redefine our businesses and our lives in many fascinating ways.

Prof. Dr. Wolfgang Wahlster is Director and CEO of the German Research Center for Artificial Intelligence (DFKI GmbH) and Professor of Computer Science at Saarland University

Siemens AG Digital Enterprise

Prof. Dr. Siegfried Russwurm, Member of the Managing Board,
Siemens AG

Digitalization is a fact of life in modern societies. It also affects innovation in industrial products and processes, which is driven largely by information technology and software. As a result of the continuing transformation of the internet into a network that even lets objects, devices, machines, and systems communicate with one another, we are now experiencing fundamental change. In Germany, the concept "Industrie 4.0" has been coined to describe this change, which will lead to the integration of the digital and real worlds on a Digital Enterprise Platform.[137]

For decades, the manufacturing industry has optimized the processes involved in developing and producing its products. One of the most important aids has been the use of industry software. Today, instead of building hardware models and prototypes, development and testing frequently take place virtually, and the data related to the digital product models provide the basis for manufacturing. Value chain structures have also changed radically. Companies whose future was formerly decided primarily in their production halls have been replaced by a global network of manufacturers, partners, and suppliers.

Software such as NX and Solid Edge from Siemens PLM Software supports the process of designing and developing products. In fact, even the calculation and simulation of future properties and functions are managed using IT tools. However, the existing systems still rely primarily on individual technical disciplines to generate and test models. The next step, then, is to link these systems with the models they generate. Modern systems have to be understood in their functional interplay. That is why Siemens recently acquired the Belgian company LMS and others.

Software also supports production planning and engineering. At Siemens, we offer Tecnomatix for the digital factory and the TIA Portal for production. With "Totally Integrated Automation (TIA)" we sent out a message many years ago that highlighted the direction in which we think industry is developing. Today the portal demonstrates just how much more quickly and productively manufacturing can be developed, planned, and controlled if a single interface handles everything that was formerly managed by multiple systems.

Data that are generated in engineering or tests need to be available for the entire value chain. By the same token, modern companies must be able to use data from production and service for modifications and new developments. For example, in our electronics plant in Amberg we coupled the manufacturing execution system (MES) with product lifecycle management (PLM) so efficiently that error rates fell from 24 per million in 2007 to just 15 in 2011.

Products have also changed — and they continue to change at an ever-faster pace. In this arena, too, software is the driving force. Embedded software enables the development and construction of "intelligent" technical systems whose sensor and actor technology, networked wirelessly via the internet and other services with standard protocols, increasingly allows autonomous actions and communication without operator control. These are called cyber-physical systems (CPS). Of course, these innovations also involve the production and automation systems that bring these products to market.

Industrial companies nowadays are facing a paradigm shift: the merging of the real and virtual worlds of product development and production processes through industry software and IT. This development brings with it the promise of such immense productivity gains that future-looking companies are giving it top priority.

Nevertheless, we still have a lot of work to do. To create parallel digital companies that can truly be integrated with the real companies, all of the involved tools have to be networked on a common platform. This Digital Enterprise Platform requires far-reaching standardization and open tools. It also calls for an ease of operation that parallels today's mobile devices. The challenge faced by modern industry can be compared to open-heart surgery. Although existing models serve as the basis for running production, new models have to be created that meet the needs of the future.

The Vision and Development of Industrie 4.0

The future-oriented project Industrie 4.0 addresses this evolutionary change, which is reflected in the convergence of modern information and software technologies, with traditional industrial processes as well as its revolutionary impact on industry. It seems reasonable to assume that a broad-based penetration of industries by these technologies will take a certain amount of time — despite their revolutionary consequences. We must therefore distinguish between the vision of Industrie 4.0 and the steps required to realize that vision.

In the vision, the product itself is an active element of the production process. In "smart" factories, the digital and physical worlds merge seamlessly. Products carry all of the necessary information for their own production. In their interaction with the cyber-physical systems they can be identified and localized. In addition, they know their history, their current status, and alternative paths to the planned status. The result is a self-organizing network of machines, inventory systems, and other resources that autonomously exchange information in real time and control one another. CPS identify permissible scenarios, compare and evaluate these scenarios according to predefined optimization criteria, and then determine the best possible combinations.

The production systems are then networked along two dimensions: (1) vertically, with business processes in factories and organizations, and (2) horizontally, with distributed value creation networks — from order to delivery. Both networks enable and require end-to-end engineering over the product's entire lifecycle. "Cyber-physical systems are going to revolutionize production, mobility, and healthcare delivery," predicts Germany's National Academy of Science and Engineering (acatech) in a position paper. The academy forecasts that the new production processes will generate productivity increases of 30 to 50 percent.[138]

There's quite a way to go, however, before we can realize such ambitious goals. The core element is the Digital Enterprise Platform, the previously described link between the virtual and real worlds of manufacturing in a uniform development environment, as well as an IT-based, bidirectional and end-to-end concept with data harmonization from the shop floor to the top floor. Only with such comprehensive integration can the Industrie 4.0 vision become a reality.

In Germany, the development of Industrie 4.0 is receiving strong government support, including financial support. As part of its high-tech strategy, the German government is earmarking up to €200 million for the project. Nevertheless, the segment will not experience a technological eruption. Instead, it will be developed through a process that is expected to take decades and that will pose myriad questions that have to be answered. The major challenges include suitable migration paths, the definition of standards, the continued development of sensor technology, and the development of security measures, concepts, and strategies, to name just a few. Only by looking back a few decades from now will we be able to evaluate whether the term the "Fourth Industrial Revolution" is justified. This same observation applied, however, to the previous industrial revolutions.

Siemens is both a supplier and a user in this context. The naturally holistic view of the entire value process of a company that develops and manufactures products has a decisive influence on the definition and development of the software products we offer to our customers. We are doubly interested in seeing the Digital Enterprise develop quickly into a practical reality.

The Human Factor of Industrie 4.0

In contrast to what some people fear, the role of humans in Industrie 4.0 will *not* be less important than it is now. People will design the products, systems, and production facilities, and they will engineer them intelligently — something CPS could never do. People will also define production rules and targets, such as energy efficiency, as the most important optimization criterion at some point. Only then will CPS come into the picture, first to identify production options within the framework of the parameters defined by people and subsequently to assess the various options and select the most viable one.

Of course, a more strongly networked world will place different demands on the people involved. That is true in the virtual world for the creative planning process as a part of requirements analysis, product design, and production planning, as well as for the operations-related work process in the real world of production and logistics. More than ever before the new form of development and production will require people to master increasingly complex matters, independent work, decentralized forms of management and control, and a new, multidisciplinary work structure.

In the "smart" factory, the worker's function will evolve from an operator to someone who controls and regulates. Industrie 4.0 will create a vital need for workers to actively make decisions and optimize processes. So, it will certainly not lead to factories without people. Workers will carry out central functions in designing, installing, retrofitting, maintaining, and repairing complex cyber-physical production systems and new network components. And, increasingly, they will model production facilities, describe boundary values, and define and weight optimization algorithms that enable adaptive IT systems to independently run simulations and evaluate alternatives. After all, the product does not decide how it is to be produced — at most it selects the best production options from the various ones available.

Ultimately, then, the Fourth Industrial Revolution will create a paradigm shift in workforce qualifications. Specifically, as products and production methods become increasingly technical and demanding, the necessary level of workforce expertise will increase accordingly. Just as the virtual and real worlds are increasingly merging in the production process, knowledge work and production will grow closer as well. The workplaces of the future will be characterized by on-the-job training and by work that is much more flexible and less easily planned. This is a demanding task for companies' HR departments. However, it is also a challenge for societies and their educational systems — from primary school to training and post-secondary education and on to further training and continuing education.

Prof. Dr. Siegfried Russwurm is Member of the Managing Board at Siemens AG

10

Transform Your Value Chain

Digital businesses are redefining the concept of consumer access. The direct link to the end-user is a major element of the disruptive element of digital businesses. Shortening the value chain can generate lower costs, faster deliveries, and direct customer feedback. A company's value chain partners are frequently its business-to-business (B2B) partners. Eliminating partners from the value chains in the value-generation cycle has already disrupted several industries. The music industry is a great example. Today, artists are posting their songs directly onto internet-based music platforms, and in the process avoiding consolidators, distributors, and intermediaries of any kind. That this new system creates a value chain that is faster, less expensive, and generates fewer failures is obvious.

So, when you revisit your value chain, consider the following elements:

- Simplification
- Direct consumer contact through digital channels
- Faster time-to-market
- Reduced market preparation times and costs

Last — but certainly not least — think globally from the start.

Be aware of the disruptive elements for your business, from classic competitors within your industry as well as from new competitors who are applying the reduced digital value chain to reach your customers with competing products. The disruptive threat is real, and it happens in all industries. So, no matter what industry you are in, your business must become digital to survive.

As an example, consider logistics value chains, an area where disruption is most obvious. Classic logistics companies provide motion services for goods. They have direct contact with the goods owner on one side and with the distribution channel on the other side. In the classic logistics game the stakeholders are:

- Manufacturers

- Logistics carriers

- Manufacturer's channel partners

- End consumer

In contrast, the stakeholders in the new digital world are:

- Goods manufacturers, who tag their products with sensors for all kinds of environmental parameters including temperature and humidity as well as location parameters including inclination, altitude, latitude, and shock

- Carriers, who provide logistics systems with GPS-based location and routing information in addition to radio/video/phone connections for general information

- Agents, who manage the material flows for goods manufacturers and distributors to optimize the "goods on the roads" process

- Mediators, who function as managing agents for logistics business creation

In sum, then, the core targets of digital logistics management are traffic optimization, improved treatment of individual goods, and overall reductions in the costs and timeframes associated with value chains.

In the 1920s, Ford Motor Company was a model of *vertical integration*. The company operated coal mines, rubber plantations, a railroad, and plenty more — and, of course, its automobile factories. This structure gave Ford a great deal of control over its entire supply chain. A century later Ford and many of its competitors have moved in the opposite direction. They now receive roughly 70% of their car value from an elaborate ecosystem of suppliers.[139]

The auto industry (and many others) has been influenced by the seminal work on value chain analysis by Michael Porter of the Harvard Business School.[140] Companies decomposed key aspects of their operations into what Porter called primary activities, such as purchasing and production, and support activities, such as HR. They made varying decisions on what to build versus what to buy.

In recent years, technology, globalization, and other influencers have allowed companies to fine-tune these buy-versus-build decisions and to quickly reverse them when necessary. For some businesses this process has lead to vertical integration; for others — such as the auto industry discussed above — the result has been *vertical disintegration*. Let's examine some value chain scenarios across industries.

Apple's Vertical Disintegration

In the late 1990s, Apple made a strategic decision to deemphasize its manufacturing sector. Metrics such as its inventory turnover did not look impressive, especially when compared to Dell, which at the time was a model of supply chain efficiency. So, Apple shut down its plants in Ireland, Singapore, and the United States, and it outsourced the manufacturing of its products.[141]

Moving beyond Apple, the contract manufacturing model with providers like Flextronics and Jabil Circuit has become the accepted model for the consumer electronics industry. The design sharing, the production scheduling, and the physical and information security that inevitably accompany highly competitive consumer electronics all would be impossible without advances in a variety of visualization, collaboration, and related technologies. Let's consider an example of integration in a fragmented industry; specifically, U.S. healthcare.

Kaiser Permanente's Vertical Integration

Healthcare in the United Sates is a highly fragmented system replete with hospitals, clinics, medical staffing, and health insurance, often provided by separate entities. A major exception is Kaiser Permanente, a vertically integrated healthcare system headquartered in Oakland, California. The company's 180,000 employees service more than 9 million members in 500 hospitals and other healthcare sites.[142] In addition, they own laboratories, pharmacies, and imaging centers, and they offer health insurance plans.

The technology glue for this vast system is Kaiser Permanente HealthConnect — a system for electronically sharing medical information, in which Kaiser has invested billions of dollars. HealthConnect enables health providers to share notes, lab test results, and digital images with their patients across the system. Voice-recognition software and other technologies facilitate data entry into the system.[143]

HealthConnect's greatest benefit is the analytics available from the patient and treatment database. As Kaiser Chairman and CEO George Halvorson, explained in an interview:

> "We take care of the entire patient and can focus on things like preventing broken bones. We have one of the lowest stroke rates. We focus on early detection, best care, and we do the right follow-up care. We have the lowest sepsis death rate. Sepsis kills more patients than cancer, stroke, or heart disease. Pressure ulcers generate a lot of revenue in a lot of care settings. We make sure people don't get pressure ulcers. Because we are prepaid, we don't make our money by having care go wrong."[144]

The Oil-Refining Supply Chain

An interesting anomaly has been playing out in energy trading markets since 2010. The spread between Brent and West Texas Intermediate (WTI) — two prominent crude oil trading categories — has been unusually high, averaging US$17 per barrel during 2012. As we will see in the Statoil column in Chapter 11, significant new oil reserves have been found in U.S. shale deposits and in Canadian oil sands.

The majority of global oil supplies are transported via tankers and pipelines. The new North American reserves are landlocked, so a new infrastructure is needed to move the crude to shipping ports and to refineries on the coasts.

These developments have opened the door for a significant new trade route — crude oil by rail. BNSF, a prominent U.S. railroad company, has seen oil shipments out of the Bakken shale reserves in North Dakota grow exponentially, from 1.3 million barrels in 2008 to nearly 90 million barrels in 2012.[145] The typical railcar carries 600–700 barrels of crude, and trains can have as many as 120 cars, using multiple locomotives to haul that load.

The boom in transporting crude by rail may be short-lived, however, especially as the number of alternatives to pipelines increases. By July 2013, the Brent/WTI spread had collapsed to an average of $3. In addition, a series of accidents in Canada spurred popular concerns concerning the safety of trains carrying vast quantities of crude.[146] Nevertheless, this scenario provides a clear example of how value chains can rapidly evolve. Refineries have been furiously calculating whether they should agree to long-term leases on railcars and make other logistical investments to accommodate the rail trafficking of crude.

Banking Disintegration

Most large banks have spent decades becoming one-stop shops — loans, credit cards, retirement accounts, currency trading, etc. It's interesting how many startups are picking off specific bank services and going after those niche markets. For example, Kickstarter, a funding platform launched in 2009, has helped a number of entrepreneurs use crowdfunding to finance their ideas.[147] Another example is Square, which provides credit card services to small businesses with a mobile card reader and pay-as-you-go fees.[148] Transferwise, founded by Skype alumnae, focuses on cross-border currency transfers for individuals.[149] Iwoca brings working capital to internet retailers, especially those in the eBay and Amazon ecosystems.[150]

Each of these entities is promising better or less-expensive services than the large banks. In their own small way they are precipitating a disintegration of the traditional banking sector.

Brazil's Natural Resource Value Chain

Brazil is blessed with massive amounts of natural resources. The Chinamax class of ships with 400,000 of deadweight tonnage, coupled with technology installed at new superports such as Acu and the widened Panama Canal, are enabling the country to export iron ore, soybeans, and other commodities to China and other Asian markets.

In the 1970s, Brazil's "gasahol" — a blend of sugar cane-sourced ethanol and gasoline — was a curiosity to the rest of the world. However, this new fuel has improved refining yields while reducing the corrosion of fuel tanks. Most of the gasoline sold in Brazil contains 25% anhydrous ethanol. In addition, some "neat ethanol" vehicles run entirely on ethanol. The rest of the world has noticed. Blends of 10% or less ethanol are used in more than 20 countries, led by the United States (which derives its ethanol from corn). With significant land resources,

Brazil is poised to expand its sugar cane production and become a major biofuel exporter. Indeed, the country has been labeled the "Saudi Arabia of biofuels."[151]

Another Brazilian enterprise, Cutrale, the world's largest orange juice producer, uses satellites to monitor ideal picking conditions in Brazil's many orange groves.[152]

Significantly, Brazil's value chain will adopt more of an internal focus as construction related to the 2016 Olympics and the country's PAC 2 infrastructure program creates a growing domestic demand for its iron ore and other resources.[153]

Summary

Enterprises have long vacillated between build-versus-buy decisions and vertical integration versus disintegration. Digital technologies are making such swings easier and quicker.

Now let's look at a practitioner perspective. William Ruh of GE describes the Industrial Internet, in which digital applications are transforming several key sectors of the economy.

General Electric

*William Ruh, Vice President and Global Technology Director,
General Electric*

William Ruh, Vice President and Global Technology Director at GE, is comparing the consumer internet to a new productivity revolution that GE is leading. Ruh refers to this revolution as the Industrial Internet, the place where "operational technology meets information technology."

"Imagine if companies had a crystal ball in the late 1990s — or even a McKinsey report — that guaranteed that 3 billion people would be interconnected by 2013. Suppose that it also predicted that entertainment would be digitized, social marketing would occur in real time, and retail would be less dependent on brick-and-mortar. Now, consider how many media and retail companies would have had made a totally different set of strategic decisions based on that foresight. Many, of course, did not, which is why the digital natives — Google, Amazon, etc. — emerged."

"Fast-forward to today's digital world. Within a few years roughly 50 billion machines will be interconnected. We can remotely monitor these machines, and we can conduct predictive analytics based on the signals they transmit. Going further, these machines can "heal" themselves. Finally, by helping professionals become better connected, they will improve the overall quality of services. Given these developments, the question becomes: Are utilities, hospitals, airlines, and railroads making decisions based on these new capabilities? Or, will a new wave of digital natives emerge to take advantage of these technologies, as Google and Amazon did in previous iterations?"

Ruh continues,

> "The payback will be massive. Seriously, we see US$15 tril-
> lion in added global GDP over the next decade and a half.
> I know that sounds hyperbolic, so let's put it in bite size,
> operational terms. 1% of aviation fuel savings is US$30 bil-
> lion over 15 years. 1% in better optimization of healthcare
> facilities adds US$63 billion over 15 years. 1% reduction
> in oil and gas CAPEX adds another US$90 billion. And so
> on. At GE, we call it the power of 1%, and our economists
> have looked at granular industry-specific processes and
> modeled the payback opportunities."

Paul Maritz, former CEO of VMWare and now CEO of Pivotal, a GE
partner, echoes Ruh's sentiments:

> "Historically much of the innovation in information technol-
> ogy has originated in the financial services industry. In the
> last decade it has moved to 'consumer internet giants.'
> Now, we are seeing it move to the industrial space, which
> is taking data to a whole new level."

The point was illustrated by Jeff Immelt, CEO of GE, in a presentation
on the Industrial Internet he delivered in San Francisco in October 2012.
Immelt was dwarfed on stage by the prop of one of his 12-foot-tall GEnx
aircraft engines. As he admired the precision machining in its blades,
he focused on its 20 sensors that capture real-time continuous data —
temperature, engine performance, etc. These sensors generate 5,000
data points per second to optimize the flight.

Below I investigate five sectors — energy, health, aviation, railroads, and oil and gas — that are being innovated by the Industrial Internet.

Brilliant Energy

GE's vice president for renewable energy, Vic Abate, explains their 2.5-120 wind turbine (2.5 refers to the 2.5 MW platform, 120 refers to the 120-meter rotor):

> "Analyzing tens of thousands of data points every second, the 2.5-120 integrates energy storage and advanced forecasting algorithms while communicating seamlessly with neighboring turbines, service technicians, and customers."[154]

The implications are significant. The turbine's storage capability offsets traditional concerns about the intermittent and frequently unpredictable nature of wind. The giant 120-meter rotor of the 2.5-120 makes it productive even in low-wind terrains. The ability to communicate with nearby turbines allows each turbine to "learn" from the others and to pitch blades accordingly. The turbine farm-to-farm communication allows for balancing of voltage to the grid. The remote monitoring of each turbine reduces manual maintenance costs. Other dimensions of the next-gen turbine are depicted in Figure 10-1.

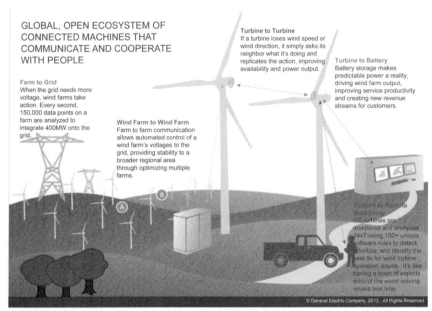

Figure 10-1: Industrial Internet of GE wind turbines

Ruh adds: "We don't call these new turbines smart. We call them brilliant!"

The Industrial Internet is creating other optimization opportunities for the utility industry. As one example, Michael Niggli, president and COO of San Diego Gas and Electric, maintains that thanks to smart meters and other innovations the company now has 1000 times more data on consumer usage than it did just three years ago. The company is also deploying "smart transformers" that will enable more efficient scheduling of nighttime charging of electric vehicles across the customer base.[155]

Brilliant Healthcare

The Industrial Internet is also making significant contributions to the healthcare industry. One example involves what Ruh refers to as a "care traffic control system" for hospitals. Hospitals carry thousands of pieces of critical equipment, many of which are mobile. Tracking these expensive assets and implementing a system that can alert doctors, nurses, and technicians to changes in their status provides hospitals with the metrics to improve both resource utilization and patient and business outcomes.

GE's Healthcare unit offers a solution called AgileTrac, which allows medical personnel to track and manage key patient flow functions like discharge scheduling, transport requests, and bed requests. These data will enable healthcare practitioners to improve the quality of their operations. Going further, AgileTrac provides smart tags for mobile assets like wheelchairs and IV pumps. This technology enables hospital staff to track the location and status of these assets from any web-enabled device. In turn, this capability helps ensure that the right equipment — clean and in working order — is in the right place at the right time.

New Jersey-based Virtua Health,[156] a GE customer, is also using smart tags to track bed availability. Hospitals utilize these data to efficiently allocate beds as patients are transferred from emergency rooms.

GE's Healthcare unit estimates that such innovations can reduce hospital equipment costs by 15–30% and enable healthcare workers to gain an additional hour of productivity on each shift. GE Healthcare CEO John Dineen maintains: "Healthcare has always relied on 'Big Data,' and the need to understand data is even greater now. What is important is how we use data, providing the right technology that allows physicians to pinpoint the right diagnosis, match it to the right treatment, and make more informed decisions."[157]

Brilliant Aviation

Most airline carriers around the world are customers of GE Aviation. Fuel is one of their major costs. Better flight planning and operational changes can make a significant impact, according to Ruh. A GE subsidiary, Naverus, pioneered what the industry refers to as Required

Navigation Performance (RNP). RNP was designed to build flight paths around the mountains in Alaska so that aircraft could safely descend through the clouds.

That safety emphasis has morphed into a focus on more efficient performance. As airports start to adopt RNP procedures, aircraft will line up miles away and glide at idle almost all the way to ground. Today they descend in much less fuel-efficient stair-steps by powering up engines to level off.

Figure 10-2 illustrates several aviation optimization opportunities beyond fuel savings made possible by the Industrial Internet.

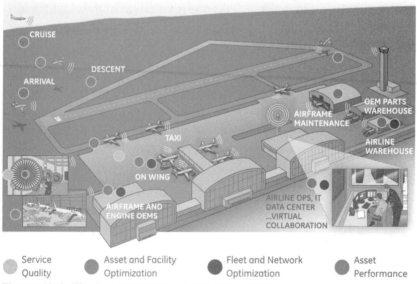

Figure 10-2: The Industrial Internet in the aviation industry

Taleris, a joint venture with Accenture, leverages GE Aviation's predictive analytics technology to analyze data from "tip-to-tail" sensors for multiple aircraft parts, components, and systems, and to make recommendations based on this analysis to optimize aircraft maintenance and flight operations.

Gary Beck, Vice President of Flight Operations of Alaska Airlines, forecasts other uses of the massive data that aircraft already create — performance, g-forces related to turbulence, and similar elements. [158] These data could be communicated directly to pilots across the air grid rather than being summarized and communicated via air traffic controllers as they are today.

Ruh continues: "While we work with individual carriers to optimize performance, GE recently ran a crowdsourced competition via the site Kaggle. Kaggle's community of data scientists worked on models of when flights would land and arrive at the gate using data provided by our customer Alaska Airlines. It included data on weather, flight plans, air traffic control, and past flight performance. It provided a glimpse about how Big Data analytics will reshape aviation performance."

Brilliant Railroads

GE Transportation sells locomotives to a number of railroad companies around the world. For example, Norfolk Southern Railway displays optimization opportunities at the network level. It uses GE's RailEdge Movement Planner[159] to integrate railroad logistics with traffic control systems. This software can deliver real-time overviews of network operations from a single display. Rail operators can monitor trains using GPS, track-circuits, equipment identification readers, and time-based tracking. In addition, built-in traffic management applications enable operators to manage train schedules and to respond to exceptions. These applications also help operators to manage their crews more efficiently. Norfolk Southern estimates that every 1 mph increase in the average speed throughout the network saves an estimated US$200 million in annual capital and operating expenses.

At the individual train level, GE's Trip Optimizer is designed to fine-tune locomotive performance. As Ruh explains, "Think of cruise control in your car. Now add to that terrain-based adjustments. So, based on GPS data, it can slow down for downward slopes. It optimizes speed as an example for cutouts based on data of other rail traffic." The Optimizer calculates — and continuously recalculates — the most efficient way of running by factoring train length, weight, grade, track conditions, the weather, and locomotive performance.

Brilliant Oil and Gas

Upstream oil and gas CAPEX, estimated at more than US$600 billion per year, is particularly attractive for digital enhancement. New fuel reserves increasingly are located in remote and expensive-to-reach areas, while safety and regulatory oversight continues to increase globally. As a result, annual exploration CAPEX is steadily increasing. GE estimates that a 1% reduction in CAPEX could save US$90 billion over a 15-year period.

Extending the Industrial Internet to the oil and gas industries could create multiple opportunities including:

- "Intelligent completions," which use sensors to read downhole pressure and temperature data in real time to identify problems without costly well intervention

- Wireless systems that link subsurface with above-ground information networks and enable technicians to monitor both networks from remote sites

- Time-series analysis of fluid migration and reservoir changes as a result of production efforts using 4D seismic and other technologies

Downstream there are opportunities for tags and GPS to track all kinds of expensive assets such as tankers, sensors to enhance predictive maintenance and safety planning in refineries, drones to monitor thousands of miles of pipelines, point-of-sales, and other technologies in the retail chains.

Horizontal Apps and the GE Ecosystem

Beyond industry-specific applications, GE is also upgrading horizontal applications as part of its "Predictivity" suite of tools. One of these tools is the Proficy Historian HD, which is designed to conduct time-series analysis across massive data sets. Comparing years of historical data to real-time data opens up a new set of analytics. The current iteration of Historian is built on the open-source Hadoop platform, which increasingly is the choice for Big Data projects.

GE has also purchased a 10% stake in Pivotal (mentioned above), a recent spinoff of VMWare and EMC, its parent company. Pivotal is positioned as a cloud PaaS player. Finally, GE has also partnered with Amazon Web Services for IaaS to store these massive data streams.[160]

Software is increasingly important to GE. In the company's 2012 Annual Report, CEO Immelt wrote: "A GE annual report has never fully featured software and Africa. Today, we feel they are essential, and we can lead."

GE's tools and its partner ecosystem position the company as an IT player. Historically, GE has embedded technology in its various products and industry solutions. That is unlikely to change. As Ruh notes: "The greatest software companies in the world don't sell software."

William Ruh is Vice President and Global Technology Director at General Electric

11

Reconsider Your Physical Assets

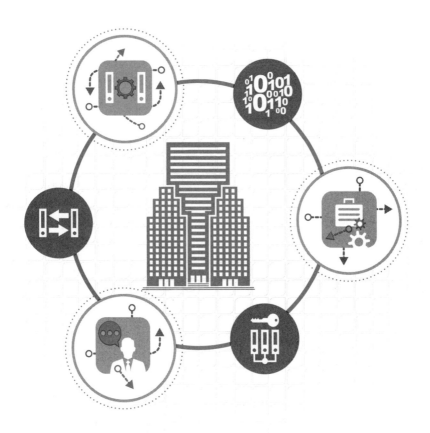

Think of your physical assets as data-capture tools — for predictive maintenance, for capturing data for revenue purposes, as input for alarm systems, and as sensors — wherever you are, whenever you need this information. Next, imagine sensor data as publicly available knowledge regarding temperature and humidity, noise levels, heat limits, and any other predefined emergency sensory data. Finally, imagine that anyone can use this information to predict and to prepare a system for more serious potential future problems. Open data from open governments is just one area in which digital technology will benefit society tremendously. Open sensors available to anyone are simply another version of open data.

But, why stop there? Now, imagine that every car has the capability to detect problems while on the road and to alert other cars using that same road. Imagine that any person who is out for a walk can monitor his or her surroundings with sensors that can inform him or her of any potential security problems. Imagine that you can locate any child, regardless of where he or she is. Imagine also that the child can send out alarm signals to anyone in the vicinity if he or she is in trouble.

Imagine that every smartphone informs the user as to what is happening in the immediate surroundings, sending predictable content to cloud infrastructures that will be able to paint a crystal-clear picture of potential hazards, threats, or events that might occur due to a certain constellation of elements. Utopia? By no means. This technology already exists, although in many cases it has not been fully adopted due to concerns about data privacy and integrity. However, a controlled proliferation of environmental information will be to the public's benefit. Therefore, such a policy might have to take priority over individual sensitivities. However, the positive example of Estonia (discussed in Chapter 1) illustrates that public acceptance and digital societies must evolve along parallel lines so that the public perceives the benefits and therefore trusts the system. Realizing this goal is essential if digital societies are to achieve further advancements that will benefit humanity.

Examine the job descriptions of the asset management staff, and you will see terms like "impairment" and "planned maintenance downtime." Examine the features of asset management software, and you will see terms like "disposals" and "book and tax depreciation."

For the longest time, the discipline of physical asset management has seemed frozen in time and in accounting language. Behind the scenes, however, assets are actually becoming more intelligent, and the discipline of asset management is becoming much more tech savvy. Let's explore some areas where assets need to be reevaluated.

Assets Live Longer

Although it has been a common practice with technology assets for many years, most other asset vendors are now embedding software and firmware that can be upgraded far more easily than hardware components. One prominent example is the auto industry. Ford owners can now use a USB drive to install upgrades to the car's Sync infotainment software.[161] Daimler, in collaboration with Hughes Telematics, is taking this feature to the next level by offering "over-the-air" (OTA) upgrades to its mbrace2 safety, navigation, and other applications.[162] Car stereo, Bluetooth, and GPS navigation device makers have similarly allowed owners to upgrade firmware and other features. The vision is that other components in the car could similarly be made smarter. The laws of physics support the fact that software lifecycles can be extended much more easily than those of hard components.

During his 2013 State of the Union address, U.S. President Barack Obama invoked the concept of "self-healing power grids."[163] Although he did not elaborate on this technology, these grids are not a futuristic concept. In fact, they can already utilize sensors and software to detect and isolate faults and to reconfigure the distribution network to minimize the impacts of any malfunctions on customers. Similarly, Intucell's software (part of Cisco) enables mobile networks to automatically adjust their activity based on demand to minimize network congestion and also minimize risk by making outages far less severe.[164]

Speaking of risk, in his executive contribution at the end of this chapter, Magne Frantsen of Statoil describes the massive exploration platforms currently employed in the energy business and the process-management disciplines needed to manage safety and other risks in that industry.

Assets Have Become Social

Again invoking the auto industry, Toyota is interconnecting its electric cars like the Prius into a network called "Friend" using Salesforce Chatter. How does this feature work? Imagine that the tires on a Prius are out of alignment. The car can actually tweet this information. The Toyota Friend hub then provides the driver with a map of nearby mechanics, and it enables him or her to make an appointment online. iPhone users can also initiate a FaceTime video chat with service agents.[165]

Coca-Cola has integrated screens and Kinect sensors into their vending machines in malls in South Korea. These machines encourage passersby to mimic the dance moves displayed on the screen. Using basic artificial intelligence apps, they then reward selected participants with free drinks. The marketing payback comes from the large crowds that form to watch this "show."[166]

Finally, the Dutch company Lelyhas introduced a robotic milking system that takes "social" to a new level. The Astronaut A4 actually feeds and cleans the cows. Going further, it customizes each cow's feed based on historical data. As the machine is milking the cows, it monitors for mastitis (inflamed breast tissue), fat/protein, and lactose content to ensure both the quality of the milk and the cow's health. If a cow misses a couple of feeds or if the quality of the milk is substandard, then the robot alerts the farmer.[167]

Assets Have Become More Impactful on Income Statements

Historically, IT projects and assets have accounted for a significant portion of capital expenditure in many industries. Today, the advent of cloud computing models — SaaS, PaaS, and IaaS — is transforming a significant amount of the IT CAPEX into an operating expense. That consumption-based pricing model is likely to move into other capital asset-intensive areas.

To cite a classic example, consider the copying industry. A growing number of services now charge by the copy, sparing the buyer the capital expenditure of purchasing a new printer and the operating expense of the consumables.

Assets increasingly provide a flow of data that can lead to newer, insight-based revenue streams. Consider GE's GEnx aircraft engine. The engine has 20 sensors that capture real-time continuous data — temperature, performance, etc. They generate 5,000 data points per second — almost a terabyte of data every day.[168] Implementing this technology currently requires GE to charge a premium for its engines. However, this system could easily evolve into a model in which GE (1) analyzes and sells the data as a service, (2) licenses the IP to airlines as a separate pricing line item, or (3) sells engine availability and security rather than simply the engine itself. In his column in Chapter 10, William Ruh of GE discusses similar opportunities involving wind turbines, hospital machinery, and assets in many other industries.

Summary

Companies have a love-hate relationship with their physical assets. These assets tend to be capital intensive, they frequently break down, and they become obsolete too quickly. Today, technology and emerging business models are helping Digital Enterprises to address many of those issues, thereby changing physical assets back to what they are supposed to be — assets to an enterprise. Because a product's software component is easier to update than its hardware component, shifting the balance in favor of software can help to keep the product up to date, thereby increasing its lifecycle significantly.

Now let's look at a practitioner perspective. Magne Frantsen describes the Statoil Management System the company uses to manage safety and promote operational excellence across its massive exploration efforts and other assets in the oil and gas industry.

Statoil Management System

Magne Frantsen, Vice President, Corporate Management System, Statoil ASA

Statoil, headquartered in Norway, is a global energy company with 23,000 employees. We are the leading operator on the Norwegian Continental Shelf, we are one of the world's largest net sellers of crude oil and condensate, and we are the second-largest supplier of natural gas to Europe.

The Norwegian Continental Shelf, where we initially focused our exploration and drilling activities, is considered one of the harshest areas in which to operate, due to extreme temperatures and storms that create waves of 10–15 meters. Our Troll A production platform in those waters was among the largest and most complex engineering projects in history. It has an overall height of 472 meters — on land its four concrete pillars would each be taller than the Eiffel Tower — and it weighs more than a million tons with the ballast. It holds the distinction of being "the largest object ever moved by man."

Figure 11-1 illustrates some of our growth objectives from our current level of 2 million barrels of oil equivalent per day (boe/d).

Statoil

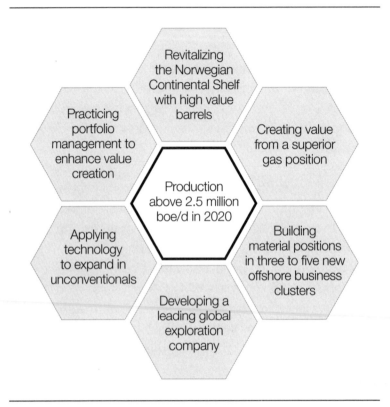

Figure 11-1: Statoil's growth objectives

Easy-to-access energy sources around the globe have been depleted for years. Consequently, modern oil companies need to explore in other, less-accessible regions in a responsible manner, applying the most current technologies and processes. These new endeavors include exploring U.S. shale and Canadian oil sands. Statoil has pioneered innovative technologies in several of the most exciting shale and tight oil formations in the United States. In Canada, Statoil uses the most environmentally friendly and commercially successful technology, called steam-assisted gravity drainage, or SAGD, to recover bitumen from the oil sands.

Statoil is active in regions besides North America. Some of our ongoing projects include a platform in the Peregrino field off Brazil and a CO_2 injection project located at the In Salah gas field in the central Sahara region of Algeria. We anticipate that by 2020 nearly 70% of our global production will come from outside the Norwegian Continental Shelf.

Safety is Job 1

A strong commitment to safety has been a cornerstone of Statoil's policies from the beginning. Given the conditions under which we operate, that has always been a demanding goal. Since the BP Gulf Oil Spill in 2010, the oil industry has redoubled its safety efforts. Authorities have issued stricter requirements, and organizations like the American Petroleum Institute have recommended that companies modify their practices for operating blowout prevention equipment and other technologies.

In addition to safety, Statoil has long had a commitment to sustainability. As an example, we have developed our first full-scale commercial offshore wind plant, Sheringham Shoal, located off the Norfolk Coast of southeast England. This project is one component of Statoil's renewable energy strategy that focuses on establishing market positions where we have competitive advantages. As the world's largest offshore oil and gas operator, we naturally lean towards offshore wind power.

Statoil has implemented a management system to ensure that our operations are safe, reliable, and efficient and to enable us to comply with external and internal requirements and regulations. The core of the system is the Statoil Book, which articulates our guiding principles:

- Our values and what they mean: Courageous, open, hands-on, and caring

- People and leadership: What we expect of our employees and our leaders

- Our operating model: Who our organizational leaders are, what their responsibilities are, and so on

- Corporate policies: Key policies pertaining to health, safety, and the environment (HSE); ethics; social responsibility; etc.

Every employee has to take a mandatory e-learning course on the concepts contained in the Statoil Book.

In addition to the Statoil Book, our management system consists of functional requirements, work processes, work requirements, and technical requirements. Figure 11-2 diagrams our high-level processes.

Statoil's high-level processes

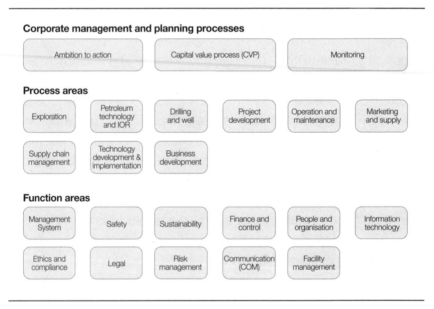

Corporate management and planning processes

| Ambition to action | Capital value process (CVP) | Monitoring |

Process areas

| Exploration | Petroleum technology and IOR | Drilling and well | Project development | Operation and maintenance | Marketing and supply |

| Supply chain management | Technology development & implementation | Business development |

Function areas

| Management System | Safety | Sustainability | Finance and control | People and organisation | Information technology |

| Ethics and compliance | Legal | Risk management | Communication (COM) | Facility management |

Figure 11-2: Statoil's high-level processes

Each of the process and function areas is further broken down into process flows. As an example, a user can drill down from the Operation and Maintenance process area to the workflow that explains how to apply for a work permit. The lowest level describes how tasks are performed. This description is illustrated with involved roles and activities including all of the relevant requirements.

Statoil's work processes and requirements are modeled and presented to all users via Software AG's ARIS software. ARIS is the repository for all requirements, and it is used throughout the company, by both employees and contractors. All work performed at our plants and production facilities is based on work processes from ARIS.

Process management documentation is by no means unique to Statoil. However, the scale of our implementation is extremely large. As of May 2013 ARIS contained more than 1,400 workflows and nearly 8,000 activities, supported by more than 15,000 requirements across the organization. When ARIS was implemented in May 2012, we had migrated documents and processes from three previous tools. Today, 36,000 employees and contractors are registered users.

Ongoing Challenges
Despite our successful adoption of modern technologies, we continue to face challenges. Two of our greatest challenges are:

- How to keep our large data repository useful to every user

- How to keep the content fresh while minimizing change

We address the first challenge through personalization. User views are context driven, and we filter the data to select and present the relevant information to each user. For the second challenge, change management follows a rigid governance process. Statoil employs a risk-based approach to decide which content needs to change. We implement these changes on a quarterly schedule to ensure predictability and to give the business sufficient time to prepare and train personnel.

One important lesson we have learned is that leadership is the most efficient and effective improvement and simplification tool. Surveys reveal that when leaders are engaged in understanding and using the management system, teams find it easier to embrace the required work processes. This leadership approach enables our employees to work more safely and efficiently.

Magne Frantsen is Vice President, Corporate Management System at Statoil ASA

12

See Human Capital in a New Light

As the number of digital products and Digital Enterprises grows, more jobs will require skills in science, technology, engineering, and math (STEM, called MINT in Germany). The median age by country varies widely, resulting in both young and ageing workforces. Both scenarios create recruiting and training challenges. Technologies such as social recruiting, augmented reality training, wearable computers, personal robots, massive online open courses (MOOCs), telepresence, and mobile computing are all revolutionizing policies and practices regarding human resources development.

For example, there is no natural law mandating that job markets can be managed only by public agencies, private companies, or other institutions. Today, many job seekers use platforms like LinkedIn to find new employment opportunities themselves.

The same concept applies to learning. Lifelong learning has evolved into a global theme, particularly in societies with ageing populations. User interfaces have become so intuitive, and training materials so easy to comprehend, that self-initiated learning conducted one-on-one with a computer will challenge overcrowded universities and other training institutes as the most common venue for learning. However, the speed of disruption will vary from country to country, for several reasons. Perhaps the key variable will be the costs of a higher education. In countries where education is almost free — as in Germany, for example — it will take longer to build a business case for MOOCs. Even in those countries, however, the total costs associated with a university education will cast MOOCs in a more favorable light. Ultimately, MOOCs will be the disruption challenge for universities throughout the digital world.

The underlying concept here is that human beings increasingly want to be self-determinate, self-sufficient masters of their destinies. This reality drives the new methods of educating students, hiring workers, engaging with freelancers, and teaming up with relevant communities, both real and virtual. The basic rule is to think the unthinkable regarding human freedom, human interaction, and human behavior in crowd circumstances.

A pressing need — and opportunity — is to bring seniors into the digital workforce. A related challenge is to integrate disadvantaged populations, people with disabilities, and anyone who did not or does not have real opportunities in the analog world to explore his or her potential. Digital tools and digital policies to support human needs and realize human potential will be essential features of future demographic environments. The digital world opens up new opportunities for disadvantaged groups in the analog world — what a great prospect for those groups and society in total.

The human brain is so complex that scientists have not yet found a way to record the activity of more than a tiny portion of its estimated 100 billion neurons. Further, technicians historically have monitored brain activity invasively using physical probes. Today, however, digital technologies are creating capabilities that were unimaginable just a few generations ago. Specifically, the explosion in computing power, the increasing resolution of imaging technologies, the growing fields of materials, chemistry and other physical sciences, nanotechnology, and synthetic DNA research are all helping scientists to map the brain.

Hopefully, this research will help us to better understand and treat serious medical conditions like Parkinson's disease. Moving beyond medical considerations, however, our enhanced knowledge of the brain will also make humans much more imaginative and productive. Ideally, as technology continues to take over repetitive tasks in every field, humans can increasingly focus on business functions that emphasize critical thinking and creativity.

As progress on brain research continues, several other trends are helping the human element in enterprises to evolve. Let's discuss a few of them.

From Universities to MOOCs

The introduction to this chapter argued that MOOCs will be the disruptive force in the world of higher education. Already, online educational programs like Coursera, Udacity, and edX are attracting venture capital as well as funding and intellectual property from well-respected U.S. universities. Coursera, for example, offers nearly 400 courses, and it has enrolled more than 9 million participants from around the world.[169] Its algebra course is based on contributions from the University of California, Irvine, and its genetics course from Duke University in North Carolina. The objective — and also the challenge — is to blend the best thinking from a variety of schools.

The MOOC phenomenon is spreading globally. Examples are the OpenHPI, associated with the Hasso Plattner Institute (an SAP co-founder) in Germany; FutureLearn in the United Kingdom; and EducateMe360 in India.

From On the Job Training (OJT) to Augmented Reality (AR) Training

Employee training is another significant area of human capital development. The aviation industry, for example, historically has employed bulky simulators to train pilots. In today's high-tech world, however, this process is increasingly becoming digitized. As one example, the U.S. Navy has been developing augmented reality (AR) training in which software algorithms and sensors present scenarios from the trainee's perspective. This system inserts virtual aircraft and targets through wearable technology like goggles and visors.[170]

From "Office" to "The Future of Work"

The TV show *The Office* (both the U.S. version and its British predecessor) today appears so quaint with its long-obsolete cubicles, water coolers, and fax machines. The reality, of course, is that the workplace — where, when, and how we work — has undergone seismic shifts, almost all of them enabled by digital technologies.

Jonathan Olivares, a respected furniture designer, envisions office work as an outdoor, rather than an indoor activity. Working indoors goes back to the paperwork explosion and related filing cabinets that characterized the office environment of the 20th century. Paper and all that heavy metal were not conducive to working outdoors. Today, however, with a laptop or tablet, you can perform many tasks outside as well as inside. This type of thinking is poised to revolutionize building and workflow design in the next few years.[171]

Overall, according to the U.S. Census Bureau, home-based work in computer, engineering, and science occupations increased by nearly 70% between 2000 and 2010.[172] Video conferences, improved broadband connections, and more-affordable home-based scanners and other devices have made home offices a viable — and often a very attractive — alternative for many occupations.

Few people realize that UPS delivery personnel have been using their mobile delivery information acquisition devices (DIADs) for more than 20 years. Data collected from the DIADs has helped transform their truck into a mobile office. The data also enable drivers to minimize left turns and to schedule "on-the-fly" pickups.[173]

From Resumé to Social Profile

With the rapid growth of social networks like LinkedIn and Facebook, recruiting, especially for midlevel executives, has increasingly become a social function. Consider the case of GE, whose internal recruiters have filled 25,000 openings in the past few years using such networks. By circumventing outside recruiting firms, the company claims to save more than US$100 million every year.[174] Although many companies can-not enjoy these kinds of savings, for a growing number of employers the LinkedIn profile is replacing the traditional resumé or CV.

The interview process is also evolving with technology. HireVue's Digital Interview Platform allows companies to pre-record interview questions and then invite candidates to respond via webcam. Not only does this process eliminate the travel time and expenses associated with pre-liminary interviews, but it enables the recruiters to watch, score, and share the streaming videos wherever and whenever it is convenient.[175] HireVue claims that its technology can make the interview process almost 10 times faster because recruiters can avoid small talk and fast-forward through "poor-fit" interview recordings.[176]

From Overalls to Wearable Computers

Google Glass, which offers a smartphone-like display, natural language voice command support, and Bluetooth and Wi-Fi connectivity, is gen-erating plenty of excitement about "wearable computers."[177] For many years already companies have been experimenting with embedding wearable computers in clothing.

As one example, the Golden-I headset was developed for police, fire-fighters, paramedics, and maintenance workers, who can use its natural voice recognition, its nine axis-motion sensing features, and its 14MP camera to take still images and record HD video that can be stored on the device and shared remotely via Bluetooth and Wi-Fi.[178] Also, over the past decade the European Community has funded a project called WearIT@work that is piloting the use of wearable computer devices in four areas: emergency rescue, healthcare, aircraft maintenance, and production management and training.[179]

Summary

Technology on its own continues to commoditize the human element in many processes and tasks. On another note, however, companies going digital are leveraging employee talent by assigning projects that are more complex and can't be replaced by technology. The balance between technology and employee talent becomes more efficient for the company and also drives up value and encourages growth.

Now, let's look at a practitioner perspective. Frank Riemensperger, senior managing director of Accenture, explores several areas in which the digital revolution is redefining the global business environment, including digital consumers, intelligent devices, and relationships of scale. Accenture's global staff has to stay even further ahead of its clients by acquiring rapidly changing digital skills.

Accenture

Frank Riemensperger, Geographic Unit Senior Managing Director for Austria, Switzerland, and Germany, Accenture

Accenture is a global management consulting, technology services, and outsourcing company that employs approximately 275,000 people who service clients in more than 120 countries. We collaborate with our clients on a wide range of leading-edge technology projects, and every year we summarize the significant trends we observe in a "Technology Vision" report. This year, the theme of the report appropriately is "Every Business Is a Digital Business."

With digitization progressing at a rapid rate — a trend that is being spurred on by the ever-increasing fusion of intelligent products, mobility, cloud computing, analytics, and social media — businesses will have to systematically transform themselves if they wish to take the lead and enjoy a competitive edge in the race toward digital business. The businesses that will enjoy success are those that think digitally and make use of the available promising technologies to apply new business models and venture into new business areas. After all, technology is now at the heart of the vast majority of business processes. This means that all companies are in the process of becoming digital businesses. Consequently, a company's entire executive board — not just the CIO — needs to understand, internalize, and help shape the influence that new technologies are exerting on existing business models. Below I consider some of the major trends and their implications for the business world.

The next wave of digital consumers — In the West we have experienced the social and mobile impact of the digital consumer. Now, as incomes in emerging economies cross the threshold of US$15,000 a year, we are witnessing an explosion of new digital commerce opportunities.

The next wave of intelligent devices — The digital revolution is reshaping myriad sectors of the business and professional world, including utilities that operate via smart grids comprised of billions of connected nodes, healthcare that can be provided at home, and education with personalized offerings.

Relationships at scale — The time is right for technology strategies to move beyond e-commerce and marketing and to strive for the kinds of personal relationships that were typical years ago.

Two client projects illustrate these trends. The first project involved digital transformation at a Swiss health insurance company. The company had been losing clients for 10 years. To reverse this trend, it decided to use a different sales channel to attract new clients while reducing finder's fees. A quick piloting of an online adviser was crucial for the company to introduce an optimized release of the offering onto the market in September 2013. Coincidently the launch date corresponds with the season (late summer/autumn) in which Swiss health insurers can obtain the biggest share of their new business given calendar-year contracts and termination periods that enable clients to switch their provider. Accenture supported the first phase of the company's transformation into a digital business by analyzing and optimizing its search engine marketing concept. The goal of creating a more direct digital client channel was to help fill the gap left by the traditional channels like insurance brokers. Accenture also defined the target group, and we drafted a universal online advice approach, including a link to offline advice. In addition, we personalized our website to make it more attractive and user friendly. To accomplish these tasks, Accenture used predictive analytics and business intelligence to generate customer insights.

The second project involved translating analytics into a managed-services approach at a global telecommunications company. In a rapidly changing market with low margins such as the telecommunications sector, the development cycles for new customer knowledge have to be short in order to provide customers with a unique experience. The time-to-market and the capacity to develop new customer analyses are limited due to fixed analysis capacity. However, analytics is different in the various national subsidiaries, where it needs to be customer based. This requirement results in higher specific costs.

To address these issues, Accenture developed a pilot project to integrate an analytics service for the client, based on the innovative Accenture Analytical Subscription Environment (AASE) approach. The project was implemented by an international, interdisciplinary team over a period of six months. The team first developed an analytical blueprint and defined a pilot case. It then utilized these elements to identify the necessary data volume. The next step was to convince the company to invest in churn models for B2B and B2C. Finally, the team created an analytics portal with both a web and a mobile interface.

Design for analytics — To compete successfully in the digital world, software providers need to rethink their products, not so much for their features and functions as for their ability to generate data-rich answers. An example is Bosch Software. Bosch collaborated with one of the world's leading mechanical engineering companies to implement a solution for the early identification of machine failure. This technology helps companies to avoid production downtimes as well as the concomitant costs. The solution is available to all interested customers via a practical service portal.

Adjust to data velocity — Modern businesses must improve their rate of response, despite having to manage unprecedented volumes of data and the proliferation of data sources.

An example is a pay-as-you-drive functionality for an auto insurance company. Accenture is able to run a managed-services environment that allows insurance companies to offer their customers pay-as-you-drive fees. The system focuses on the megatrend of mobility/telematics (mobile connected devices). It offers real-time driver coaching and additional services (e.g., accident reports), the logging of risk data, and a service platform for insurers. It also provides real-time logging and analysis of acceleration and deceleration behavior, the number of instances of exceeding the speed limit and the degree to which it was exceeded, and variables such as nighttime drives, weather, and so on. The system also provides direct feedback to the drivers, incentivizing them to modify their driving behaviors to reduce their premiums. Experience has demonstrated that solutions of this kind can reduce claims expenses by one-third. This concept has already proved to be very successful in the UK market in the form of young driver insurance. Significantly, this system also benefits the insurance companies by providing them with a unique selling point (USP).

Seamless collaboration — Users' new social behaviors, coupled with their increasing expectations that every app will be "social," are pushing companies to create new user experiences. An example is Procter & Gamble. In an effort to speed up and simplify external innovation connections, P&G's Connect+Develop program launched a new website (pgconnectdevelop.com) that links innovators directly to business priorities and P&G executives directly to innovation proposals submitted by external parties. In the spirit of Connect+Develop, the website was developed in collaboration with several external partners. This arrangement brought new innovative technology to the back-end of the site. This technology feeds user submissions directly to the business category leaders. This system will allow P&G to review proposals more quickly and more efficiently for strategic fit and for scalability across the business.

Software-defined networking — Companies can reconfigure the connectivity of their systems without modifying their physical characteristics. An example is Smart Grid Alliance / Siemens IT solutions for advanced metering infrastructure (AMI) and meter data management (MDM). These systems provide energy utilities with more information on the activity within their networks, enabling them to make their operations more efficient and to respond more quickly to outages and other problems.

Active defense — Companies must increasingly move beyond perimeter protection to proactive probing, and beyond isolation to integration.

Beyond the cloud — A major challenge confronting digital businesses is devising strategies to exploit cloud computing to become more responsive, flexible, and scalable.

An example of a successful implementation is the online Deutsche Telekom travel portal Tripdiscover.de. Deutsche Telekom developed this portal as a PaaS. With this type of cloud computing, a service provider supplies the platform needed to develop applications. The provider also operates and maintains the hardware, databases, and other components on behalf of the company. Costs for development and operation are incurred on a usage basis: A higher degree of activity translates into greater capacities and higher costs, and vice versa.

The primary benefit of PaaS, however, is not reducing costs but accelerating the development cycle. PaaS makes this possible because a cloud-based platform does not require any major outlays for making available the infrastructure for application development. In addition, developers dispersed throughout the world can work on an application simultaneously. Thanks to these advantages, and with Accenture's assistance, the online travel portal was launched within just 12 weeks.

How impressive was this accomplishment? Consider that it normally takes a business this long just to purchase the hardware and software it needs for an internal project

Each of these opportunities offers massive opportunities to enterprises in different industries. Consequently, consumer product goods are being reshaped by digital consumers, most capital-intensive industries by sensory data from their assets, and banking by much better security. The greatest opportunities Accenture perceives is when two or three of these trends converge.

Consider, for example, Accenture's joint venture with GE, called Taleris, which is focused on aircraft parts and systems to help manage preventive maintenance. Taleris leverages the convergence of device data from aircrafts, advanced analytics, and cloud computing resources. Etihad Airways — the national carrier of the United Arab Emirates (UAE) — will utilize this system's web-based prognostics service to monitor its fleet of Airbus and Boeing aircraft. The expected benefits include a reduction of unscheduled maintenance, fewer delays and cancellations, increased aircraft availability, enhanced on-time performance, improved maintenance efficiency, and reductions in both maintenance costs and lost revenues.

We are similarly working with the Infrastructure & Cities group of Siemens to provide smart metering solutions to help utility companies improve the automation, planning, monitoring, and diagnosis of their electric grid infrastructures. The goal is to increase operational efficiencies; for example, improving the response time to an outage. One of our joint customers is SaskPower, a leading Canadian company. SaskPower is currently implementing an advanced metering infrastructure that will help the company provide more reliable energy and better customer service.

Finally, Accenture is collaborating with other partners to bring to life the "smart factory" that utilizes cutting-edge technologies such as 3D printing and next-gen robotics.

The CEO needs a "digital vision" — The digitization of the business world is occurring on an immense scale. Sooner or later, every business will have to consider how this process is affecting its business model. To retain their customers, businesses need to adopt a digital vision using intelligent products for their supply chains, for the services they provide, and for the ways in which they convert data into information that is crucial to their decision-making process.

The changes I envision involve not so much creating new technologies as using technologies that have already been developed. The company's business side needs to appreciate just how IT-based the modern-day world is — in particular, how people and data are interlinked. This reality has an impact on the interplay between a CIO and the specialist divisions and on the role of the individuals who are responsible for IT. I predict that in 10 years a two-tier system will emerge among CIOs: highly strategic, innovative managers on the one hand and regimented IT managers on the other. At some companies, the CIO will continue to play the part of an administrator. Only a proportion of businesses will succeed in making the CIO a strategic head without experiencing substantial opposition. The crucial and differentiating factor is that the best businesses will develop a "digital vision" — a digital business with digital customer retention, a digital supply chain, and digital business intelligence based on coherent data and equipped with well-developed analytics. I forecast that CEOs who delegate this task to someone at the second or third level will be the first to miss the boat in terms of the digital revolution. In the future, IT expertise will be an executive priority.

Frank Riemensperger is Geographic Unit Senior Managing Director for Austria, Switzerland, and Germany at Accenture

13

Take Another Look at Interfaces

Ease of use is the key to success in the digital world. No one wants to read manuals before he or she starts to use a new system or gadget. So, what is the ultimate human-machine interface for maximum ease of use? It is definitely something close to the human senses, such as voice recognition, gesture-based control, eye tracking, and any other form of natural human interpersonal interaction.

Why is this concept so critical? The answer is that current and past machine interfaces have been driven by bells and whistles, with push buttons, knobs, wheels, lamps, and other classic machine-to-human communication interfaces.

The acceptance of machine interfaces will increase proportionately with the ability to develop interfaces that look, feel, and sound human. This observation holds true for customers, trainers, employees, suppliers, and any other individuals who are seeking advice or an action that can be provided by a system, anytime, anywhere, in a mode that is less expensive and more efficient.

In sum, then, efficiency, speed, availability, flexibility, and agility are possible not only from machine to machine (M2M) but also from machine to human being, and the other way around. This capability offers major benefits for special populations such as individuals with disabilities and groups with limited resources who don't have the benefit of operating a complex machine interface. It can also benefit the occasional user by making the system more intuitive and easy to use at the point of operation.

After decades of keyboard- and mouse-based interfaces, the last few years have witnessed an explosion in interfaces that utilize touch screens, voice recognition, and eye tracking. Apple's devices understand our "swipes" and "pinches," Microsoft's Kinect understands more of our gestures and other movements, Android devices have improved capacities for understanding our voices, and Hollywood movies like *Ironman* display working 3D holographic interfaces.[180]

These technologies are clearly signs of progress. Nevertheless, the reality is that we are still too connected to the keyboard, whose dysfunctional design goes back to early days of typewriters and the need to space frequently used character keys so they did not jam. However, a few industries and product categories have been aggressively experimenting with a variety of interfaces. Let's explore some of them.

Automotive Industry

Automakers today are challenged to achieve the seemingly contradictory goals of keeping drivers informed and entertained without distracting them. To realize these goals they are innovating interfaces in a variety of ways. For example, GM's Cadillac cars provide haptic alerts via vibrating seats.[181] Ford offers lasers and proximity sensors that recognize your leg (and the key in your pocket) as a gesture to open the rear tailgate.[182] BMW offers a heads-up display on the front windshield in many of its models.[183] The Mercedes mbrace apps enable drivers to send navigation data from their laptop or mobile phone. They also offer navigation in 3D layouts.[184] Toyota is leveraging the Nuance Dragon's natural language capabilities for voice commands.[185] Finally, VIA radar cars are helping drivers with assistive cruise control, VIA sonar is assisting them with parking, VIA cameras improve drivers' rearview and blind-spot vision, and VIA sensors alert drivers to low tire pressure.

BMW's Connected Drive allows drivers to read and send emails in voice format.[186] Hyundai is developing eye-tracking and gestural interfaces that will likely make knobs redundant on car radios, air conditioning, and other features.[187] Meanwhile, Tesla is replacing knobs with its 17-inch touch-screen display.[188] Nissan and other automakers offer mobile apps to remotely open doors, honk horns, and perform other basic actions.[189] Most cars support making phone calls and playing

MP3 music via Bluetooth. Many models also support satellite radio and streaming music options like Pandora.

Quick Response (QR) codes are finding their way into cars to enable first responders to quickly scan for safety information for the specific model.[190] They are also being integrated into car manuals to allow owners to watch training and other videos. Finally, they are found on the Monroney labels on cars to help buyers compare fuel efficiency and other features.

In the executive column, Dr. Michael Gorriz, CIO of Daimler, and Dr. Kai Holzweißig, Information Technologist at Information Technology Management of Daimler, describe how M2M interfaces are evolving utilizing Linked Data concepts.

Healthcare Industry

There are a growing number of fitness bracelets on the market like Fitbit Flex and Jawbone Up that people can use to track calories, exercise, sleep, and other personal information.[191] These bracelets were originally developed by NASA to monitor astronauts' body heat. Another innovative technology, ingestible thermometer pills, is increasingly being used to wirelessly monitor athletes for overheating.

In another healthcare sector, user interfaces (UIs) implanted just under the skin hopefully can improve the maintenance of larger implanted devices like pacemakers. In addition, brain machine interfaces that help translate electrical brain activity are proving promising for paralyzed patients.[192]

For many years healthcare facilities have used barcodes on nurses' badges, patients' wristbands, medications, IV bags, and other objects to ensure that the right caregiver administers the right medication to the right patient. In addition, audible alarms to alert caregivers of problems have become so common that international standards for these devices have been instituted. As one example, the IEC 60601-1-8 standard specifies the pitch of the alarms and the burst of pulses — a distinctive sequence of sounds — depending on the priority assigned to the medical condition. Basically, the more dangerous the condition, the higher the priority it is assigned.[193]

As discussed by Prof. Dr. Wolfgang Wahlster in his column in Chapter 9, the pharmaceutical sector is experimenting with a variety of "smart" blister packs and other packaging that communicates with devices, delivery trucks, and other equipment.

Retail Industry

The grocery industry has never been the same since 1974, when a cashier scanned a 10-pack of Wrigley's gum.[194] Although point-of-sales (POS) terminals and UPC codes continue to be a staple of the retail industry, this sector is experimenting with a whole new set of interfaces.

For example, the app FaceDeals allows retailers to use facial recognition to identify individuals (subject to their privacy settings) and provide them with a deal based on their preferences and location.[195] Shopkick allows retailers to send a unique audio signal that can be detected by smartphones on which its app is installed.[196] Shopperception provides depth sensors that storeowners place in the aisles to analyze shoppers' reactions toward various products. These sensors monitor real-time events and generate metrics to help retailers reorganize their shelf space to increase sales.[197] Me-Ality offers a full-body scanner for the clothing section of a store to take measurements of customers from more than 200,000 points.[198]

Even traditional POS and payment functionality is now software-driven. Consequently, sales employees are not tied down by bulky terminals. Instead, they can use a mobile device to process transactions anywhere in the store.

Home Devices

As appliances and devices for the home become "smarter," the range of their interfaces with users is expanding dramatically. For example, in the kitchen the Gaggenau brand of ovens now comes with thin film transistor (TFT) displays.[199] De Dietrich offers "smart" induction hobs. Should the user move the pan anywhere in the cooking zone, the hob's automatic pan detectors ensure that the temperature of the pan remains constant. Thus, the user no longer has to guess where the hot spots are.[200]

Another innovation, the Nest thermostat, glows orange when it's heating and blue when it's cooling. In addition, it turns on when you approach it, and it discreetly goes dark when nobody is nearby. It "learns" from the user's manual adjustments and then begins to automatically set its own schedule based on the user's patterns.[201]

ADT and other home security providers are developing mobile apps to arm or disarm home alarms, view live video via security cameras, adjust lights and temperature for comfort or energy efficiency, and perform other useful functions.[202]

Finally, as home theaters grow in popularity, providers like Hulu, the over-the-top streaming service, offer their "living room experience" UI that viewers can use to easily search through hundreds of channels and to control features such as fast forward and rewind.[203]

Summary

Although keyboards continue to dominate computing, Digital Enterprises are exploring a wide variety of interfaces that communicate with all of our senses. The automotive, retail, healthcare, and domestic appliance industries are prime examples.

Now let's look at a practitioner perspective. Dr. Michael Gorriz and Dr. Kai Holzweißig of Daimler discuss Linked Data and explain how this phenomenon is helping to define machine-to-machine interfaces.

Daimler: Driving the Digital Enterprise with Linked Data

Dr. Michael Gorriz, Chief Information Officer and Head of Information Technology Management, Daimler AG

Dr. Kai Holzweißig, Information Technologist at Information Technology Management, Daimler AG

Daimler AG is one of the world's most successful automotive companies. With its multiple divisions — Mercedes-Benz Cars, Daimler Trucks, Mercedes-Benz Vans, Daimler Buses, and Daimler Financial Services — the Daimler Group is one of the major producers of premium cars and the world's largest manufacturer of commercial vehicles with a global reach.

For us at Daimler AG these are exciting and challenging times. The automotive industry is currently experiencing deep structural changes. More and more, information technology (IT) is determining our everyday professional life, especially our products and the processes for building them. We are faced with an increasing digitization of vehicles. The product side has experienced major innovations including new driver assistance systems, vehicle connectivity, and new mobility services such as Car2Go[204] and Moovel.[205] New car features benefit both the auto companies and our customers by making our products safer and easier to navigate while keeping drivers more connected to the outside world than ever before. On the process side, the industry is becoming more productive and efficient thanks to information technologies such as digital product data management, computer aided construction, and enterprise resource planning systems, just to name a few.

IT is everywhere nowadays, and it has become a transformative force driving our enterprise. As such, IT functions as "*deep infrastructure* capable of producing the vital *information capability* necessary for transformation."[206] The pervasiveness of IT in every aspect of modern businesses has led to the creation of the Digital Enterprise. This trend is also reflected in the increasing digitization of the whole product development process itself. The proliferation of digital business enterprises and processes is the foundation of "Industrie 4.0;" that is, the idea of a Fourth Industrial Revolution based on the convergence of IT, intelligent products, and manufacturing processes.[207]

The trend toward digitization, which will accelerate in the future, has serious implications for the work of corporate IT, not only in the automotive sector, but in other traditional, manufacturing-focused industries as well. Classic in-house IT business processes and the core business processes of automotive companies are gradually moving closer together. A vital element in meeting the new demands of the Digital Enterprise is new technologies that add value by supporting our core processes in an effective and cost-efficient manner. Daimler has identified one such technology, Linked Data, as a driver for using the innovative power of the data economy to sustainably support the structural changes described above. As such, we propose that Linked Data can support the implementation of Industrie 4.0. In the following sections we consider several business cases that illustrate the potential of Linked Data and its business value. We conclude with a brief synopsis that summarizes our key findings.

Use Cases in the Automotive Industry
Linked Data is all about semantics. It is about explicating the meaning of entities and their relationships in a machine-readable format. To accomplish this task, Linked Data utilizes graphs, called "semantic networks," that consist of concepts (= vertices) and the edges between the vertices, which represent the relationships between and among the concepts. In addition to semantic networks, the core elements of Linked Data include several other principles and technologies. Particularly important are common W3C standards like the Resource Description Framework (RDF), which is used to *represent* semantic information, and the SPARQL Protocol and RDF Query Language (SPARQL), which

is used to *request* semantic information.[208] Standards such as these elevate the quality of data representations and data networking to a new level. Information objects "receive" a certain meaning, and they can be processed correspondingly by machines. The Linked Open Data (LOD) Cloud[209] has demonstrated how this technology can work. The primary business benefits of Linked Data can be summarized as follows:

- Cost-efficiency arising from the fact that Linked Data is an open and free technology

- Sustainability in terms of employing open standards that are supported by a large internet community

- Flexible usage in terms of application neutrality; that is, Linked Data does not depend on the underlying technologies of the systems to be linked

- Innovation in terms of creating the possibility for new business cases

In order to explicate these benefits, we want to discuss several exemplary use case scenarios for Linked Data in the automotive industry. In particular, we focus on the following applications:

- Conceptual tagging in content lifecycle processes using controlled vocabularies

- Systems integration in the product development process, with a particular emphasis on the following:

  - Remote maintenance of manufacturing execution systems

  - Synchronization of supplier data and service catalogues

Because Daimler's core business functions, such as product engineering and manufacturing and sales, are highly information intensive, content lifecycle processes play a vital role. For information to be effective, it must be properly stored and easily retrieved. Consequently, it must contain meaningful and precise metadata. The basis is an underlying semantic network of knowledge that captures a conceptual structure of the content domain in question. By using such a knowledge network, it is possible to employ a semi-automated process to sustainably improve the tagging of contents based on predefined concepts, which is illustrated in Figure 13-1. Specifically, controlled vocabularies can be applied while content is being created. Direct access to the knowledge network during content creation allows an editor to use and to further develop this standardized vocabulary.

Linked Data in the content lifecycle

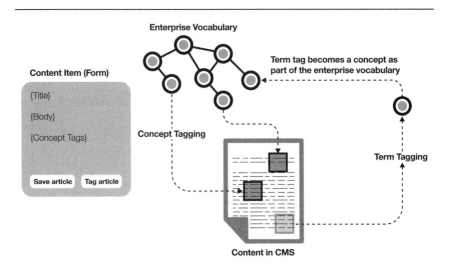

Figure 13-1: Linked Data in the content lifecycle

How does conceptual tagging benefit Daimler? Consider that under the traditional system, we experienced several problems, including a lack of precise data, intensive manual efforts in tagging contents, and difficulties in applying controlled vocabularies. Conceptual tagging and the use of controlled vocabularies address these problems in a number of ways. First, they make the contents easier to access because they utilize more precise metadata. They also generate substantial time savings during the creation of the contents because the existing contents and terms can be reused. Finally, they make the process of implementing standardized terms more efficient by taking advantage of semi-automatic term proposals.

Another application scenario is the use of Linked Data in systems integration along controlled vocabularies within the product development process. This scenario is depicted in Figure 13-2:

Systems integration along controlled vocabularies

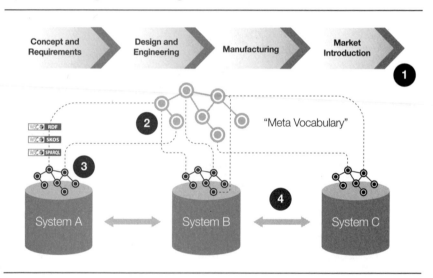

Figure 13-2: Systems integration along controlled vocabularies in the product development process

Product development is the foremost core process in the automotive industry. It consists of several phases: concept and requirements engineering, product design and engineering, product manufacturing, and

product sales and after sales ❶. Product development is a highly infor-
mation-intensive process that relies heavily on the distribution of labor. For
product development to be successful, it is essential that all participants
in the process create shared understandings of the product itself as well
as of its creation process. To achieve this goal, data from various source
systems need to be integrated. For example, illustration data from CAD
systems have to be linked with data from parts lists and production planning. Human work becomes more efficient when the underlying systems
are connected to one another without media discontinuity.

For systems to be successfully integrated they must possess a common vocabulary, or a meta-model, that enables them to communicate
effectively ❷. Put simply, terms used in one system are matched via
concepts contained in the meta vocabulary to terms used for the same
thing/concept in other systems. After creating this common vocabulary, the next step is to ensure that the data contained in the individual
systems, or data silos, are accessible so they can be linked ❸.[210] When
both processes have been completed, then communication between
the linked systems can take place ❹.

This arrangement builds a sound basis for implementing Industrie 4.0
use cases, which rely on these types of communication mechanisms
to function. The resulting business benefits include the following:

- Nearly seamless integration of systems along the product development process

- Elimination of communication breakdowns between and among
  systems

- Effective linking of data, which allows for new queries to be carried out that otherwise would be impossible

- More rapid integration of information from different systems

- More efficiency and effectiveness in the product development process as a whole

The use of Linked Data for purposes of systems integration, especially in terms of Industrie 4.0, can be further clarified using the following use case. This case involves the interplay between an execution system at a manufacturing plant and the maintenance database at the supplier's location, as depicted in Figure 13-3.

Systems integration in supplier-consumer settings

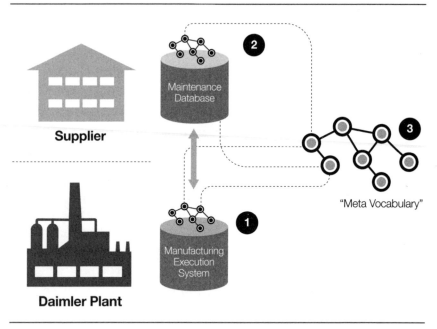

Figure 13-3: Systems integration in supplier-consumer settings

In a Daimler plant a manufacturing execution is responsible for controlling the plant's production flow ❶. The machines in the production flow are maintained by a supplier from a remote location. Daimler transmits distinct machine parameters to the supplier on a regular basis ❷. The supplier then uses these data for purposes of analysis and optimization.

In terms of the mechanisms described above, after both parties have agreed on a standardized controlled vocabulary (meta vocabulary), data can be exchanged in a fully automated fashion ❸. This scenario can be generalized to all supplier-consumer settings; for example, to external suppliers that deliver parts or services for manufacturing processes.

The example described above illustrates several of the myriad benefits that systems integration utilizing Linked Data offers to Daimler. To begin with, automating the update and analysis cycles saves the company both time and money by making manual transmitting and updating obsolete. In addition, because the cycles are fully automated, no manual updates and synchronization of master data are necessary. Another benefit is that the supplier can respond instantly to potential problems by accessing the transmitted machine data. Finally, the availability of open and free Linked Data technologies renders expensive proprietary technologies obsolete.

Clearly, then, applying Linked Data technologies provides Daimler with numerous benefits. This observation can be generalized to other automobile companies and to modern businesses in general. However, every company must carefully evaluate the feasibility of such enterprise applications for Linked Data before it undertakes any such initiatives.

This case study has demonstrated that Linked Data can perform a vital role in transforming automotive companies into truly Digital Enterprises. In addition, it has explained how Linked Data can support the implementation of Industrie 4.0.

Dr. Michael Gorriz is Chief Information Officer and Head of Information Technology Management (ITM) at Daimler AG.

Dr. Kai Holzweißig is an Information Technologist at Information Technology Management (ITM) at Daimler AG.

14

Scrutinize Analytics

Decision making in the analog world fluctuates between two extremes: relying on the "gut feelings" of long-tenured executives and relying on actual data contained in spreadsheets, historical financial statements, and budgets. This behavior might have been adequate for the analog, non-real-time information world where a company could survive with single-digit growth. In contrast, in the high-speed digital world intuition can be a valuable asset, but by itself it is insufficient to explore the potential that Digital Enterprises provide. Decision-support systems must reflect the real-time nature of Digital Enterprises, particularly their capacity to respond instantly to changes and challenges in both their internal and external environments.

There are two major enterprise levels where decisions have to be made immediately: the management level and the operational level. Classic management decision-support systems — the so-called *business intelligence systems* — focus on the aggregation of historical data. These systems are no longer adequate in the digital world. Making strategic decisions by focusing on historical data is like driving a car by looking into the rearview mirror. Today, businesses need to know what is happening *now*, in real time, for static data as well as for data — even mass data — in motion.

On the operational level, employees need ongoing support, also in real time, and not just based on historic reasons. On this level, as well as on the managerial level, you can't make forward-looking decisions by looking backwards. For example, a customer comes into the shop, and the clerk has the necessary information to provide individual treatment as though the shopper were a long-term customer.

The next step after real-time decision making is *predictive* decision making; that is, anticipating what will come rather than simply assessing what just happened. Big Data analytics helps modern executives to take into account hundreds of parameters to predict with reasonable accuracy what will happen. For example, car drivers receive information concerning possible consequences if they turn right at the next crossing, based on current weather conditions, accident history, traffic information, general road conditions, and other parameters. Or, factory workers can anticipate what will happen with their machines, based on a myriad of sensor information regarding the condition of any machine part that can be measured. Factories can utilize this information to proactively manage entire manufacturing systems. Finally, imagine the value of intelligent energy grids that predict energy consumption and manage the delivery of both renewable and classic energy sources just in time.

The global recession starting in 2008 was a wake-up call for most enterprises. The realization sank in that after investing tens of billions of dollars in past analytical tools, their business forecasts were not just off, they were off by huge margins.

Since that time, enterprises in every industry have come to acknowledge that the spreadsheets and data warehouses they have traditionally relied on are filled with historical data and that plenty of external data and much more real-time data are available to be analyzed. In this column we discuss some developments in business applications of analytics.

Advanced Analytics

Facebook has more than 250 billion photos on its site, and it receives 350 million new photos every day from its 1 billion users.[211] These volumes of data are totally unprecedented. To manage these vast data collections, Facebook leverages open-source tools like Hadoop in tandem with myriad custom-developed tools and a highly customized and optimized data center infrastructure.

While you might expect a technology leader like Facebook to implement a sophisticated analytics infrastructure, how do you explain advanced analytics in sectors like water utilities and farming? TaKaDu, an Israeli company, helps water companies around the world monitor leakage. The water industry routinely mislays 25–30% of its product in the process of delivering it. Theft and an outdated infrastructure are common leakage culprits. Unfortunately, neither problem is easy or inexpensive to monitor. Not surprisingly, then, the industry focuses on analytics that pinpoint the best payback areas.[212]

Moving to the agriculture industry, Climate Corp, a company started by Google alumni, provides crop insurance for farmers by analyzing 22 data sets for weather at a sub-zip code level (every couple of miles) every few hours, calculating roughly 10,000 scenarios that a grower could experience over the next two years. The company is leveraging 30 years of daily weather data and crop yields, among other data.[213]

In his executive column in this chapter, Ralf Schneider, Group CIO of Allianz, describes how real-time analytics is reshaping the broader insurance market.

Another sector that has come to embrace analytics is professional sports. *Moneyball*, a bestselling book and popular movie, told the story of how the Oakland Athletics applied analytics to baseball players' performance relative to their compensation to acquire productive but affordable players.[214] A decade later, every sport is applying analytics to every operational area. For example, in the National Basketball Association (NBA) the team doctors for the Dallas Mavericks are trying to match anti-inflammatory medications to players' DNA markers.[215] The San Francisco Giants and other baseball clubs have experimented with secondary ticketing markets.[216] This approach is leading to a pricing revolution for both single games and seasons tickets.

Analytics has become so deeply embedded in modern sports that the 2012 London Olympics could easily be renamed the "Data Olympics."

Not only did teams use high-speed cameras, lasers, and other high-tech instruments to improve athletes' performance, but they meticulously benchmarked the data.[217] Sponsors used social analytics from tweets, Instagram, and other platforms to measure the responses to their commercials and also to evaluate potential athletic spokespersons for their products. Transport for London (TfL), the government body that oversees transportation in the city, used technologies from the Bartlett Centre for Advanced Spatial Analysis (CASA) at University College London (UCL) to analyze patterns for the time of day people were traveling and the locations of the most heavily trafficked stations to better prepare for the tourist rush.[218]

Complex Event Processing

The advanced analytics described above provide a valuable snapshot of all kinds of business scenarios. A different technology, called complex event processing (CEP), provides the equivalent of video for greater clarity. Dr. John Bates, founder of Apama, a leading CEP product, explains the concept:

> "CEP enables real-time analytics to be performed on streaming data to show, for example, impending trends; it also allows patterns to be correlated across events in diverse data streams that can represent occurrences the business needs to know about and/or proactively respond to. Inputs to a CEP system can include sensor data (e.g., SCADA sensors on an oil pipeline), data feeds (stocks, news, etc.), application data (e.g., CRM, ERP, credit card transactions, etc.), location data (GPS, RFID, etc.), and any other kind of feed. CEP can shut down fraud while it is happening, push a marketing offer to a customer while they are in the right place at the right time, or detect and place an algorithmic trade in microseconds, before a competitor spots the opportunity."[219]

The financial services industry was an early adopter of CEP for the technology's trading algorithms and its capacity to identify patterns in fast-flowing data feeds. The industry now also utilizes CEP for pattern recognition to detect insider trading — for example, by correlating business events like earnings announcements with stock trades. In addition, many banks, including DBS, Singapore's largest bank, are adopting CEP on the consumer side of financial services for fraud detection. The more DBS knows about each customer and his or her habits, the more easily the bank can spot a deviation from the norm — which may be a fraudulent transaction. These transactions can have temporal and spatial dimensions; for example, a scenario where two ATM withdrawals using the same card are carried out a hundred miles apart within half an hour.[220]

Another industry that is benefiting from CEP is healthcare. Consider, for example, the "Four-Day March," an annual fitness event held in the Netherlands in which participants walk 140 kilometers over four days. The march attracts 40,000 people from around the world. The event was marred in 2006 when, due to extremely hot weather, 2 people died, and 70 others collapsed. Dealing with this crisis was difficult due to the lack of real-time visibility of what was happening where, who was in trouble among the vast numbers of participants, and the extensive distances involved.[221]

This disaster led Radboud University in the Netherlands to conduct an experiment with the aim of proactively identifying potential dangers to the participants. The university developed an ingestible RFID pill that, when swallowed, continuously monitored the body's core temperature and communicated that information to a smartphone carried by the walker. The phone also tracked the walker's GPS location. The locations and temperature events for all walkers were fed into a CEP system, which was configured with rules to detect a number of temporal and logistical scenarios that indicated current or potential danger to a walker.

One example is detecting a significant change in a walker's core temperature, combined with the walker's being stationary for longer than a specified period of time — indicating a potential collapse. Another example is using real-time analytics to identify a problem proactively, such as when a walker's core temperature is rising and his or her pace is slowing at a rate that indicates an impending problem. This information can be used to trigger a text message to the walker, suggesting that he or she take a break.[222]

Social Analytics

Marketing executives have long used analytics — for example, Nielsen ratings for TV viewership, retail point-of-sales data, email campaign data, and Google search optimization. With social networks expanding dramatically, social listening and analytics have become essential tools for most marketers.

The Salesforce Marketing Cloud showcases the many nuances its partners have developed. Clarabridge offers multilingual sentiment analysis.[223] Klout Scores calculate people's influence on social networks.[224] Lithium specializes in natural language processing for a more accurate understanding of comments.[225] OpenAmplify specializes in identifying and classifying brand and product mentions for customer service purposes.[226] Several other platforms that provide similar capabilities are now on the market.

Marketers are also taking advantage of the capabilities offered by CEP. Turkcell — the largest Turkish mobile phone operator, with 35 million subscribers — is able to provide personalized offers to each of its subscribers based on 150 criteria including the subscriber's location. Thus, a customer who is interested in designer shoes and is walking past a mall in Istanbul during her lunch break may receive a mobile coupon offering "10% off designer shoes if you come into the store within the next 30 minutes." The time required to execute a campaign is reduced to just minutes. Turkcell also utilizes CEP to continuously monitor customer responses to different marketing scenarios. Those scenarios that generate low response rates are retired, and the more effective ones are enhanced. In the first year alone, Turkcell experienced a tenfold increase in offer uptake and a US$10-million increase in revenue.[227]

Summary

Big Data technology and a growing base of primary data, both structured and unstructured, are empowering the Digital Enterprise to move to more fact-based decisions and away from "gut calls."

Now let's look at a practitioner perspective. Dr. Ralf Schneider, Group CIO of Allianz, describes how real-time analytics is reshaping the broader insurance market.

Allianz

Dr. Ralf Schneider, Group Chief Information Officer, Allianz Group

Allianz, founded in 1890, is one of the world's largest insurance and asset management service providers. Our 144,000 employees and thousands of agents service more than 78 million consumers and corporate customers in more than 70 countries.

The Allianz workforce includes nearly 10,000 IT employees. As I describe below, we are working on a number of leading-edge cloud computing and global network initiatives. However, our "game changer" projects revolve around the next generation of business analytics and intelligence.

The insurance and risk management industry has always involved extensive data analysis — actuarial, weather, traffic, etc. We believe that the next wave of insurance companies will be even more sophisticated in their use of data. In addition, because our industry is a trusted custodian of so much proprietary data, we will place an even greater emphasis on security.

Advanced Analytics

An example of our use of advanced analytics is our real-time Fuzion Travel Insurance program. Customers enter personal information — destination, travel dates, etc. — on a partner travel site, and our algorithms present a personalized offer in less than a second (the average response is 125 milliseconds!). We have made more than 1 billion offers to customers in 38 countries, and we have sold more than 18 million policies. In addition to making the purchasing process much easier for our customers, we are finding that digital commerce is more profitable for us because it reduces both our loss ratio and our operating costs. In addition, it helps us to continually fine-tune our analytics.

Another example is our "Fast Quote" for automobile insurance that we offer through our GeniaLloyd subsidiary in Italy. We ask customers (via the web, mobile, etc.) for only two personal data items — their license plate number and date of birth. We then generate a quote based on that information. In the first ten months of the pilot phase we acquired 40,000 new customers. Additional benefits created by Fast Quote include a high conversion rate from competitors, greater trust in our local agents, and an increased Net Promoter Score.

Allianz is also exploring the use of customer-facing analytics across most of our products and geographies. In addition, we are using advanced analytics for real-time customer management. For example, we are using sophisticated data techniques for customer retention analysis — early warnings on customer issues, patterns across products and countries. Of course, this type of analysis has been done before. With more advanced analytics, however, it can be executed much more quickly and on a global scale.

Consider another application: Instead of relying on human detection of fraud as in the past, Allianz is employing algorithms to make the initial detection, after which we subject the identified items to further human scrutiny. We are also translating the expert knowledge on fraud into business rules that will then feed models that will recognize patterns and forecast the probability that a certain case involves wrongdoing. Going further, network analysis within the claims database will alert us if known fraudsters are involved in the examined case. In the future, we will expand these mechanisms to unstructured data such as textual descriptions of claims.

Allianz is developing these capabilities as a shared solution across our global operating entities. This arrangement will enable us to implement common practices while also accommodating unique nuances on a cross-country basis. Currently we are speaking about gigabytes or even terabytes of primarily structured data that we utilize for analytics. The real challenge awaits us in the future when petabytes of unstructured data become available from newsfeeds, social media posts, videos, and similar sources. Combining these vast data stores in real time will help us to create a new level of insurance experience for our customers.

One innovative and exciting application involves social media analytics, sentiment analysis, and related data assessments. Over the past few years we have created social communities around sports, pets, and other personal interests. Although we have long been recognized in the sports community through our iconic Allianz Arena "spaceship" in Munich, our Facebook "Football for Life" page, Formula One, and other sponsorships, many people are surprised to learn about the pet community. In fact, it is a vocal, loyal community that is drawn to our pet insurance but shares information with other specific groups concerning our operational excellence across the insurance lifecycle — claims, customer responsiveness, and related services.

Infrastructure and Security

Allianz's value proposition is to be "the most trusted partner for all stakeholders." To achieve this objective, it is vital that we keep our customer and business-critical data secure and away from prying eyes. One of our major IT tasks is to capture, store, and manage data safely within the boundaries of the Allianz Group.

Consequently, one of our most important infrastructure projects is the expansion of the Allianz private cloud. The cloud enables us to perform two critical activities: (1) manage our critical customer and product data independently from public cloud providers and (2) maintain full control of our data and data processing. To finalize our private cloud infrastructure, we are investing €1billion over the coming five years. The cloud is comprised of three integral parts: consolidated data centers, a global network, and virtualized applications. All three components are protected by a security framework.

At the same time, our data center consolidation project is transforming our fragmented data center landscape — 140 centers scattered throughout the world — into 7 regional, highly secure hubs for our global private cloud. To implement this project we are collaborating with next-gen data center providers like IO, who are pioneering "modular data centers" comprised of modules about the size of a standard shipping container. These models offer additional physical security because only authorized people can enter them. Moreover, they enable us to easily move the entire module from one location to another so we can enjoy greater geographic flexibility.

In addition to the areas discussed above, advanced analytics offers the following benefits for Allianz:

- The Allianz Global Network (AGN) provides a secure, high-capacity connection between the data centers and the operating entities.

- Virtualized applications enable our operating entity to utilize data without the need to store it locally.

- Carefully selected security measures, such as a global identity and access management, protect the cloud from being compromised.

In summary, to be successful in the long run, Allianz needs to carefully balance the opportunities and the risks generated by massive volumes of customer and product data. To meet this challenge successfully we need to build solutions that accommodate customer expectations as well as Allianz's business needs while protecting our most valuable asset: trust.

Dr. Ralf Schneider is Group Chief Information Officer of Allianz Group

15

Think Over Constraints, Think About Sharing

We are living in a world with vast cloud computing capacity, broadband bandwidth, web services providers, and global talent pools populated by digital natives. In this "brave new world," traditional borders and constraints need to be revisited. The digital world is a world of sharing. People share ideas, assets, any resources that can be used by more people, and any problems where the crowd — that is, internet users — can be tapped to propose solutions.

The digital world decentralizes the classic major centralized investments into personal micro-investments. The business models employed by Google and Facebook are based on the fact that billions of input devices are bought and paid for by the input providers; that is, the users. These models would not work if the companies had to pay the bills for their input devices themselves, as happens in the analog world. The crowd providing the input is sharing through the internet, through Wikipedia, through YouTube videos, through social networks, through traffic information agents, and through a seemingly endless array of information and communication technologies.

Removing the constraints of the analog world in companies and in societies opens the door for crowd-based problem solving. The key is to incentivize collaboration. Companies can promote collaboration through reward systems and competition. Societies can foster large-scale cooperation by providing value such as time savings, cost reductions, 24/7 support, and insight into government open data pools.

The culture of participation, the decentralization of investments, and combinations of classic and new media-dissemination technologies are all tools to overcome classic or analog constraints in the digital world.

Although it is now a distant memory, it is worth remembering that companies across multiple business sectors spent hundreds of billions of dollars on Year 2000 remediation. The root cause was that a few decades earlier many organizations squeezed data into fixed-field 80 character records on punch cards. To accomplish this task they truncated four-digit year codes into only the final two digits while leaving "19" constant. This configuration generated a near-panic at the turn of the century when people realized that "1999" would not automatically convert to "2000."

A major theme in the history of IT has been to rethink expensive or insufficient storage, memory, bandwidth, and other resources. In the past few years, the digital revolution has succeeded in removing many of these constraints. To highlight this process, let's examine how computing infrastructure, bandwidth, and talent pools have increased and how digital strategy has evolved as a result of these developments.

Infrastructure

On a given weeknight, the millions of users who are watching Netflix movies online account for almost one-third of all downstream web traffic in North America. Significantly, instead of building its own data centers, Netflix uses the cloud resources provided by Amazon Web Services (AWS).[228] One of AWS's value propositions is "With traditional infrastructure, it can take weeks to get a server procured, delivered, and running. These long timelines stifle innovation. With cloud computing, you can provision resources as you need them. You can deploy hundreds or even thousands of servers in minutes, without talking to anyone."[229] Going further, you can finance all of these operations with a credit card if you wish, thereby significantly streamlining the financial process.

The impact of cloud computing is even more dramatic for companies with global coverage. "With traditional infrastructure, it's hard to deliver great performance to a broadly distributed user base, and most companies focus on one geographic region at a time to save costs and time. With cloud computing, the game changes — you can easily deploy your application in any or all of the nine AWS regions around the world."[230] As an example, Netflix uses its Dublin region to service its European users, but it services its South American users from Northern Virginia, although it could just as easily do so from Miami if usage patterns were to change. We could not have dreamed of this type of infrastructure flexibility just a few short years ago.

Of course, many enterprises cannot use public clouds like those from Amazon due to security or privacy concerns. Even these enterprises, however, use public clouds for testing or "sandbox" environments. In addition, provisioning speed and economic benchmarks from the public cloud are reshaping private clouds and hosting services. The net result is that infrastructure planning and provisioning have become much less cumbersome, especially for large-scale deployments, over the past few years.

Another dramatic change in technology infrastructure is the maturing of in-memory computing. Traditional analytics were constrained by the size of the database and the latency between the storage device and the server. Significantly, in-memory databases have been around since the 1980s. The problem has always been the cost and the limited amount of RAM that database servers could handle. Then there was the advantage of back-up and recovery and monitoring techniques that were programmed into traditional databases using spinning disks. So, in-memory applications were limited to modeling by Wall Street "quants" and defense agencies.

In 1985 a megabyte of RAM cost around $300. More recently, a gigabyte of NAND flash memory has fallen below $1. Tools like Terracotta's BigMemory that utilize the greatly enhanced memory, the capabilities of multicore processors, and compression techniques like columnar databases are showing that trend. These kinds of tools enable users to execute mainstream analytics at blazing speeds to leverage instant visualization of large datasets.

Bandwidth

Innovations of mobile devices and applications in recent years have been breathtaking. Even more remarkable is the fact that these devices utilize only a thin sliver of the radio spectrum. Portable phones, garage door openers, microwaves, TVs, home Wi-Fi, Bluetooth headsets, airline Wi-Fi, microwave transmissions, toll transponders, ham radios, and AM, FM, and XM radio all coexist without interfering with one another.

At the same time, communication opportunities for enterprises and consumers continue to expand. Below are some examples of new business opportunities that have emerged in the past few years.

JetBlue Airlines is planning to roll out in-flight Wi-Fi using ViaSat's Exede satellite internet service, which the airline claims is capable of delivering 12 Mbps to each connected passenger.[231] Competing in-flight services are based simply on an aggregate amount of bandwidth to the plane that often leaves passengers contending with one another for service. Making that level of bandwidth available to all passengers could lead to a dramatic increase in airline usage, as fliers come to enjoy a new generation of shopping, entertainment, travel, productivity, and other apps.

Meanwhile, Google has become a telecom carrier by offering 1-gigabit internet connections in Kansas City — nearly 100 times faster than the U.S. average.[232] Although the service is aimed primarily at the consumer market, it is spawning a surge of startups in the region as businesses seek to leverage the very affordable bandwidth. Indeed, some observers have begun to refer to the area around Kansas City as "Silicon Prairie." Google has also announced plans to offer a similar high-speed fiber service in Austin, Texas, and Provo, Utah. In addition, the company is putting pressure on incumbent telcos and cable companies to offer higher speeds at reasonable rates.

In the communications industry, a combination of consumer ingenuity and provider flexibility involving prepaid calling cards versus monthly charges has increased the number of mobile subscribers in India to nearly 900 million. This number represents a remarkable turnaround led by new-age mobile carriers such as Reliance and Airtel in a country where customers previously waited for decades to receive landline phones from state-run telecom companies. The impact on all sectors of the population has been significant. An example from the Indian state of Gujarat involves the Rudibens, a co-operative that sells organic agro-products through its network of more than 3,000 saleswomen.[233] A mobile app for inventory management funded by the Cherie Blair Foundation (wife of former UK Prime Minister Tony Blair) and Vodaphone India Foundation has significantly reduced the previous phone usage and physical travel times. In some cases, the resulting time savings and increased profits now provide the saleswomen with two meals a day.[234]

Technology Talent

Thomas Friedman's 2005 bestseller *The World Is Flat* catalogued the emergence of India as a major technology talent hub. The city of Bangalore played a major role in the book. Since Friedman's book was published, Indian outsourcers and their customers are increasingly exploiting the resources available in a wide range of smaller Indian cities including Hyderabad, Pune, and Noida. Going further, sophisticated customers of the outsourcers have pushed for "follow the sun" models where teams can work on their projects 24/7. For example, Tata Consultancy Services (TCS), an IT and business solutions company and India's largest outsourcer, pitches its "global delivery model" in which it can leverage staff in more than 40 countries.[235] Most multinationals take advantage of technology talent pools located in regions such as China, Eastern Europe, and South America. Nevertheless, Nasscom, the Indian outsourcing trade association, attracts a number of international delegations to its events as countries around the world try to emulate the Indian model of developing their own technology talent pools.[236]

Summary

The history of IT has always been about living with constraints — computing capacity and speed, bandwidth (speed), and economics. Today's Digital Enterprise still has to be savvy about how to procure IT tools. However, their economics have become much more attractive, and their provisioning speed has become much quicker. These innovations allow IT executives to "dream bigger" than was possible just a few years ago.

Now let's look at a practitioner perspective. Prof. Dieter Kempf, CEO of DATEV, explains how his company is providing countless small and mid-sized market clients with the digital leverage that much larger enterprises have.

DATEV

Prof. Dieter Kempf, Chief Executive Officer, DATEV eG

DATEV is a registered cooperative society (a German "eingetragene Genossenschaft" or "eG") that provides information services to tax professionals, accountants, and attorneys. We also provide backup, storage, IT, and other services to a number of other small businesses. In 2012 our 6,400 employees generated revenues of €760 million.

Although there is plenty of excitement in IT markets about cloud computing, DATEV has been providing versions of cloud-like, shared services since our founding in 1966. We service more than 40,000 customers who then use our technology to service hundreds of their accounting and legal clients. Every month, 11 million wage and salary slips are created using DATEV software. In addition, 2.5 million enterprises — primarily medium-sized German companies — utilize our software for their accounting and reporting functions.

Our different constituencies benefit from several emerging technologies. Larger enterprises have digitized many of their financial processes. In contrast, in the small-to-middle-sized market that our members service, much of the workflow is still paper based, and it ends up in their executives' physical offices. As Extensible Markup Language (XML) and eXtensible Business Reporting Language (XBRL) standards become more widely implemented, however, we are witnessing a growth in electronic documents and financial statements. DATEV provides multiple services to assist its members with this transition.

In another development, our members are increasingly leveraging scanning and optical character recognition (OCR) technologies to digitize the entire business process from document entry to storage. We regularly review scanning technologies — for example, intelligent character recognition (ICR) and optimal mark recognition (OMR) — to advise our members on how best to scan documents for maximum legibility while minimizing file sizes. The resulting ability to view structured entry data alongside document images is a significant productivity improvement for our members. To automate the subsequent document processing as much as possible, we apply classification methods to interpret the text recognized by OCR. The booking assistant in our programs recognizes items such as the date and number of scanned invoices, and it supports the user in posting invoices by initializing the detected values in the accounting record. We are eagerly awaiting legislative changes to allow a process flow that is based entirely on electronic processing and the immediate archiving of business documents.

On the legal side, lawyers are increasingly relying on semantic searches and voice recognition to deal with the ever-expanding volumes of documents. Additionally, our mobile app for lawyers allows them to access court fees and fine information and to calculate blood alcohol content and other useful information on the move.

DATEV provides mobile apps for our other markets as well. For example, the DATEV-App offers useful information and helpful tools for our members when they are out of the office. This information is accessible anytime and anywhere via smartphone or tablet. The information includes, for example, a selection of current documents from LEXinform tax, law, and economics. In addition, our members can access all of the free service information as well as any professional information they have subscribed to. Moreover, an upcoming feature, called the DATEV Controllingreport mobil, will be our first application that allows users to access sensitive corporate data securely on their smartphones and tablets.

To address the data protection and privacy needs of our professional members, DATEV has always invested heavily in security technology. For example, we have long required two-factor authentication with security tokens via smartcards that enable various security and verification features for client access to data stored in the DATEV data center, for email encryption, and account access. Of course, the same security measures must be applied to tablets and mobile devices. Going further, in the future mobile access to sensitive data in the cloud — starting with applications for the iPhone and iPad — will be possible via a smartcard. This technology will enable devices to communicate by Bluetooth with the new DATEV mIDentity air, a card reader that incorporates a smartcard in a micro-SIM format.

Going further, DATEV employs security specialists to constantly monitor our antivirus and firewall systems. Our client network, DATEVnet, offers features like reverse scan. This network checks all emails several times in a central storage buffer. Moreover, the virus scan does not end when you retrieve your mail. We also examine a copy of messages for 12 hours, always using the most current virus signatures. With this system we trap 20–30 malicious documents every month. We also use DATEV Web-Radar to populate and constantly update a list of malicious websites in the security zone. We block access to these sites centrally to protect DATEVnet users from the risk of infection.

DATEV's services help our members to digitize their processes and to keep their systems more secure. We also provide them with many other benefits. As our "cloud" eliminates the need for dedicated physical offices, our members are expanding their geographies and consolidating their offices. A growing number can now work "anytime, anywhere, with any device."

In sum, DATEV is bringing to thousands of small and mid-sized businesses the capabilities, convenience, and security that dedicated IT staff provide in much larger companies.

Prof. Dieter Kempf is Chief Executive Officer of DATEV eG and President of the industry association BITKOM.

16

Go Over Risk Scenarios

As societies become digitized they also become vulnerable to new scenarios of cyberwarfare, surveillance, electronic fraud, and hacking and other intrusion by criminals and even states. As a result, traditional security practices such as sample testing, blacklists, and entirely physical security systems have become outdated. In the digital world, both personal and business data need to be protected against misuse.

Let's take a closer look at the privacy aspect of modern technologies. Every Facebook user cedes ownership of his or her private data to that service. Moreover, because the internet has an infinite memory, those data will *never* be deleted. Therefore, young people who are publishing any type of personal data must be protected so they do not suffer negative consequences from these data in later life.

On the organizational level, businesses must guarantee the secrecy of all of the information they transmit via phone, internet, and any other media. Consider the following scenario. Two companies are competing for a big bid. In general, the key to obtaining the contract is for a company to differentiate itself from its competitors. A company that could and would hack into its competitors' information (a serious criminal act) would obtain a distinct advantage in that bid, to the disadvantage of all other stakeholders. As a general observation, the digital economy would come to a standstill if secrecy could not be guaranteed.

The published information regarding the Prism program conducted by the U.S. National Security Agency (NSA) has reduced the trust that digital users place in the level of secrecy in the internet. Common, international rules to protect secrecy and make information more secure are overdue in the globalized world of the digital societies.

A new acronym — SIRF — has emerged in the past few years. SIRF stands for "stolen identity refund fraud," and it works as follows: An individual (1) files U.S. income tax returns electronically via software like TurboTax, (2) claims fraudulent returns based on stolen identities, and then (3) uses the debit cards issued by the Internal Revenue Service for the refunds to minimize the audit trail. In fiscal 2012, the IRS claimed that it prevented the issuance of more than $20 billion in fraudulent refunds, up from $14 billion the year before.[237]

The McAfee annual survey of digital threats provides this caution in its 2013 edition:

"Cybercriminals and hacktivists will strengthen and evolve the techniques and tools they use to assault our privacy, bank accounts, mobile devices, businesses, organizations, and homes."[238]

Of course, much of that cybercrime originates with petty criminals. At the other extreme are state-sponsored cyberattacks. Recent examples are:

- The Russia-Georgia War of 2008, which involved a series of distributed denial-of-service (DDoS) attacks against government websites and banks[239]

- The 2010 discovery of the Stuxnet virus, which attacked Iran's nuclear plant in Natanz[240]

- The disclosures of the U.S. NSA Prism program and other surveillance and hacking episodes in 2013[241]

In addition, an increasing number of other global incidents point to the growing role of cyberattacks in modern warfare.

After NATO disclosed the evaluation of various war scenarios, there has been growing debate as to whether cyberspace now represents the "fifth dimension" of warfare after land, sea, air, and space. Indeed, a publicly available Atlantic Council study has identified a ten-stage spectrum of state responsibility for cyberattacks that ranges from "State-Prohibited" to "State-Ordered" to "State-Integrated."[242]

In previous chapters, we have highlighted many positive developments for Digital Enterprises. Here we explore some of the threats against which these organizations need to "protect the franchise" as innovative social, mobile, cloud, smart product, and sensor technologies are themselves introducing new risks and related liability issues. In addition, Digital Enterprises need to plan for the effects of cyberwarfare scenarios on their businesses.

Social Networking

As we share more personal information via Facebook and more organizational and professional information via LinkedIn, and as we increasingly follow links on YouTube and other social networks, sophisticated "spear phishing" and identity theft are becoming much easier to execute. Spear phishing fools a significant portion of recipients because it incorporates a vast amount of personal data about the user, much of which can be easily obtained from social graphs. Similarly, identity thieves obtain password clues from personal data shared on social sites. Facebook apps and shortened URLs on Twitter often lead users to malicious websites that download Trojan horses or keyloggers to the user's device.

Bring Your Own Device (BYOD) Policies

After resisting pressures to allow employees and contractors to use their personal mobile devices at work, many CIOs have relented and adopted BYOD policies. However, it is estimated that only a third of organizations have policies in place to ensure that employee-owned devices don't pose a security threat.[243] Even worse, organizations that prohibit BYOD often have a "shadow" BYOD infrastructure in which the mobile devices have even less visibility and are therefore much more difficult to monitor.

The BYOD risks arise from the millions of mobile apps that we are tempted to try out and then connect to corporate networks. Other risks involve lost or stolen mobile devices that continue to rely on passwords and other network-access features. Incorporating corporate data into personal emails and cloud sites poses still other risks. Geo-fencing — which, for example, disables cameras in high-security areas — is difficult to implement on BYOD devices.

Protection against Malware

The information security, or InfoSec community, is highly aware of what the MITRE Corporation calls "common weaknesses." MITRE maintains the Common Weakness Enumeration (CWE) website, with the support of the U.S. Department of Homeland Security's National Cyber Security Division (NCSD). The CWE site provides detailed descriptions of hundreds of programming, design, and architectural errors that can lead to exploitable vulnerabilities, along with guidance for mitigating and avoiding them.[244] Unfortunately, hackers continue to add to that list.

There is a growing acceptance that most commercially available antivirus software cannot keep up with the speed and intensity of the attacker community. Also, if attackers are going to target an enterprise directly, they are likely to use a new technique that most antivirus products will miss. Consequently, at least some CIOs are reducing their firewall and antivirus software spend and are shifting their resources to other security tactics. However, some executives continue to rely on traditional software products because industry regulations or customer contracts mandate their use.

Industrial Systems

Infrastructure industries from utilities to transportation networks rely on software and firmware for process control, distributed control systems (DCS), and supervisory control and data acquisition (SCADA) functionality. These industries represent attractive targets for sophisticated attacks.

Consider, for example, the Stuxnet virus, which attacked a nuclear plant in Iran. Sources claim that Stuxnet caused the engines' centrifuges in the plant to increase and decrease their speed, eventually rendering them unworkable. A reverse-engineering project on the Stuxnet virus conducted by Symantec, the security software company, concluded: "Stuxnet represents the first of many milestones in malicious code history — it is the first to exploit four 0-day vulnerabilities, compromise two digital certificates, and inject code into industrial control systems and hide the code from the operator."[245]

Intelligent Machines

As companies develop smart products, they are learning about "generally accepted traditions in the tech industry." One such tradition involves tearing down products as soon as they become available to obtain knowledge of their components and functionality. Photos of components, guesses as to their likely suppliers, likely costs, and product margins show up on blogs and websites like iFixit. "Jailbreaking," initially performed on iPhones, quickly translated to other platforms as well. A similar process called "rooting" is common on Android devices, as Barnes & Noble discovered with their Nook eBook reader.

As intelligent machines and M2M networks grow by leaps and bounds, they pose other challenges. To an even greater extent than mobile devices, these technologies involve a physical risk, especially with devices "in the wild" and the potential need to wipe their data and continued access. Many mobile devices transfer unencrypted data to save on processor cycles and battery life.

Old Risks Continue

In addition to the newer risks we have just discussed, many older risks continue to plague businesses, especially smaller enterprises that do not have dedicated security staff. These risks include the following:

- Delayed patching of commercial software

- Risks from unscanned USB drives, external hard drives, CDs, or DVDs that may be infected

- Exposure to hosted/outsourced storage, which replaced the traditional onsite file server, which historically managed access rights and audit logs

An even more sobering assessment from *InfomationWeek* involves the business continuity role that IT has long been tasked with. Respondents to its 2013 Backup Technologies Survey "are scrambling to keep up with fast-evolving IT architectures and security and business demands. While the percentage who perform test restores for most of their applications at least once per year increased from 38% in January 2011 to 44% in our March 2013 survey, that still leaves more than half who test sporadically, at best. Admins too often exclude some systems from not only their nightly but also their weekly backups and neglect to back up data at the remote or branch offices they support. Yet 84% are somewhat or very satisfied with their current backup systems. Go figure."[246]

Protection

Enterprises are learning to adapt to the growing risks associated with digital technologies. Rather than using a blacklist to block known threats — the conventional method employed by antivirus software — many IT shops assume that everything is suspect, and they test programs in a safe "sandbox" before allowing them to run on a machine. In addition, policies such as acceptable use for employee behavior on social networks can offset some of the threats. Perhaps the ultimate protection is to educate all employees to become more security savvy.

Summary
As Digital Enterprises innovate every aspect of their business, the "bad guys" are not sitting still. Therefore, information and physical security also need to innovate around newer social, mobile, and cloud technologies as well as around most traditional IT areas.

Now let's look at an academic perspective on cloud security from Prof. Dr. Peter Buxmann at Technische Universität Darmstadt in Germany.

Technische Universität Darmstadt

Prof. Dr. Peter Buxmann, Chairman, Information Systems Faculty, Technische Universität Darmstadt

As digital innovation expands throughout the world, so does the list of potential vulnerabilities. Moreover, as information technology becomes a key part of the fabric of every economy, the associated risks are not limited to technology users and vendors. Rather, they extend to entire societies and, ultimately, to the global economy. In our view, innovation in information security has to keep pace with digital innovation in clouds, mobile, social networks, cyber-physical systems, and other technologies.

My team in the Information Systems department at Technische Universität (TU) Darmstadt is involved with a number of emerging technology topics. These topics fall into three general categories: the future internet economy, the software business, and information management. Below I identify the key issues in each of these categories.

The Future Internet Economy

- Business models for social media and online social network providers
- Risk and privacy issues in online social networks
- The economic value of information and customer data
- Social HR

The Software Business

- Business models and strategies for the software industry
- SaaS and cloud computing
- R&D and innovation management

Information Management

- IT security and risk management

- Standardizing IT landscapes and enterprise architecture management

- IT organization and outsourcing

IT security is a significant focus for our department. Along with the Darmstadt University of Applied Sciences and the Fraunhofer Institute for Secure Information Technology (Fraunhofer SIT), we are part of the Center for Advanced Security Research Darmstadt (CASED) cluster, a key node in the global security network. Figure 16-1 identifies our partners in the CASED framework.

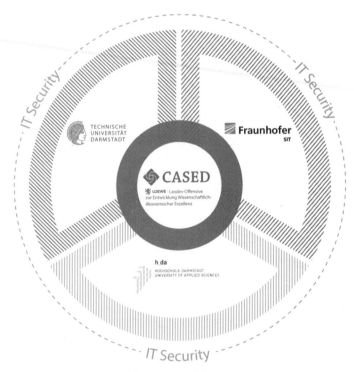

Figure 16-1: The CASED partnership

Below I describe some of the security projects CASED is currently working on. I then discuss some of our efforts to enhance security for cloud computing.

Current Projects

In this section I summarize some of the current security topics being researched at TU and CASED.

- Secure Software Engineering
  These projects focus on translating the security by design principle into action by incorporating security issues at the beginning of the software engineering process.

- Cryptography
  Among our research areas at TU are algebraic cryptanalysis, cryptographic protocols, public key infrastructures, and post-quantum cryptography. The relevance of these topics increases in light of the public debates concerning the eavesdropping on (encrypted) emails and telephone calls over Skype by government agencies such as the U.S. NSA.

- Privacy and Trust
  Users are increasingly concerned that their privacy is being violated, and they want to assess the trustworthiness of their counterparts, both human and digital. To address these concerns, we are working to innovate trust and reputation models. Obviously there is a trade-off between privacy and trust. To resolve this trade-off, our researchers are pursuing solutions in the field of identity management, inventing new technologies and enhancing existing ones like pseudonyms and anonymity management.

- Cyber-physical Systems
  Cyber-physical systems (CPS) involve a variety of mobile and embedded devices that combine IT and physical devices. CPS offer an enormous potential for a variety of applications; for

example, in the automotive sector and in the field of supply chain management. The growing popularity of CPS makes them attractive targets for all kinds of software and hardware attacks, including viruses, Trojan horses, and side channels. Traditional security measures and concepts are proving inadequate to protect computers from these malware attacks. Therefore, we are researching next-gen security solutions.

Cloud Computing Security

Over the past few years we have conducted studies of various cloud computing models — SaaS, IaaS, and so on. In general, we are focused on the subjective perceptions of IT security and the behavioral and organizational aspects of IT security in the context of cloud computing. The IT security risks in the cloud computing environment are based on six distinct risk dimensions, represented in Table 16-1, that we have developed using extensive literature review, Q-sorting, and expert interviews.

ID	Brief risk description: Risk of ...	ID	Brief risk description: Risk of ...
	Confidentiality risks		**Performance risks**
1	eavesdropping communications	16	network performance problems
2	supplier looking at sensitive data	17	limited scalability
3	disclosure of data by the provider	18	deliberate underperformance
4	disclosure of internal system data	19	performance issues of internal systems
	Integrity risks		**Accountability risks**
5	manipulation of transferred data	20	identity theft
6	data manipulation on the provider side	21	insufficient user separation
7	accidental modification of transferred data	22	insufficient logging of actions
8	accidental data modification on the provider side	23	access without authorization
9	data modification in internal systems	24	missing logging of actions in internal systems
	Availability risks		**Maintainability risks**
10	service discontinuity	25	limited customization possibilities
11	unintentional downtime	26	incompatible business processes
12	attacks against availability	27	incompatible with new technologies
13	loss of data access	28	limited data import
14	data loss on provider side	29	proprietary technologies
15	insufficient availability of internal systems	30	insufficient maintenance
		31	unfavorably timed updates

Table 16-1: The six dimensions of security risks in cloud computing

In our first study we used the framework highlighted in Table 16-1 to investigate the perceptions of IT security risks of cloud computing providers utilizing an empirical study that involved roughly 70 executives of provider firms. The results, which are summarized in Figure 16-2, revealed that individual vendors viewed their competitors' solutions as presenting substantially greater risks than their own solutions did.

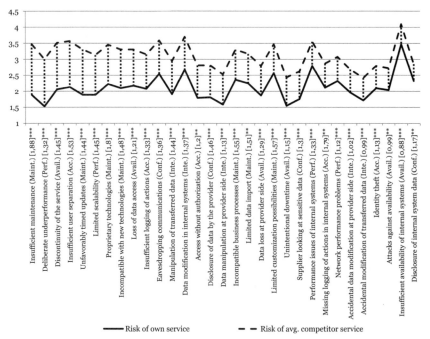

Figure 16-2: Perceptions of security risks: Vendors versus competitors

In a second study, we surveyed 73 IT vendor executives and 304 potential customer firms to compare their perceptions of the risks associated with the vendors' IT products. The responses, summarized in Figure 16-3, indicated that on average the providers scored the IT security risks significantly lower than their potential users did.

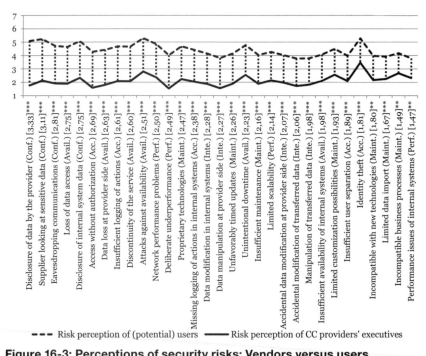

--- Risk perception of (potential) users —— Risk perception of CC providers' executives

Figure 16-3: Perceptions of security risks: Vendors versus users

Both surveys suggest that cloud computing vendors may be too optimistic about the robustness of their security infrastructures. Our goal is not to slow down the adoption of cloud models, but, hopefully to (1) help users to exercise better due diligence with their vendors and (2) help vendors to better benchmark how their competitors are delivering similar services.

Our next project will be a conceptual model of the information security behaviors of cloud computing providers. This project represents an infusion of technology adoption and established psychological theories.

With such a wide range of researchers covering emerging technologies, we are excited about all of the innovation opportunities available to Digital Enterprises. We will continue, however, to push the security agenda as well. Innovation in information security is just as important as innovation in mobile, social, and cyber-physical technologies. By merging technology developments with improved security, we plan to enable innovative business models.

Prof. Dr. Peter Buxmann is Chairman of Information Systems Faculty at Technische Universität Darmstadt

17

Reexamine Your Stakeholders

As societies become increasingly digitized, businesses' relationships with investors, unions, government agencies, customers, and citizens have to evolve to reflect this transformation. Digital natives, the young generation who grew up in a high-tech universe, demand digital participation not only in private life, but also in the enterprises they are working for. Digital citizens demand digital access to government services rather than waiting in line in government agencies. Enterprises need multichannel digital access to their customers, including a back channel for feedback. And, for all of these activities, the new digital hours of operation for all stakeholders are 24 hours/7 days a week.

The expression "time is getting faster" is synonymous with "accessible at all times." The digital revolution has created an environment in which almost any event happening anywhere can have an immediate, worldwide impact.

Another major consequence of the digital revolution is that virtual relationships are becoming more and more real. In the world of commerce, for example, digital natives don't differentiate between talking to a human agent and talking to an automated voice, as long as their request is resolved to their satisfaction. The loss of the real-world shopping experience is compensated for in the digital world by speed, comprehensive overview and instant action, and shopping opportunities available at your fingertips.

Digitization has also redefined the relationships between businesses and government agencies. Consider, for example, a scenario in which a business plans to transport hazardous materials by truck from one country to another across the Alps. In the analog world the approval process can take longer than the transportation itself. In contrast, in the digital world, this process takes only a fraction of that time. A pilot project between Austria and Bavaria that is currently testing the digital approval process has achieved great first results.[247]

A popular precept asserts that the flapping of butterfly wings in Australia can explain a hurricane in the Atlantic a few weeks later. This scenario is an effective metaphor for our interconnected universe. It also highlights an essential feature of the Digital Enterprise. Modern businesses maintain relationships and connections with a broad array of stakeholders who are dispersed globally to an unprecedented degree. Consequently, decisions made in one location can have a ripple effect worldwide. Therefore, as Digital Enterprises modify their practices and policies in response to rapidly evolving technologies, they need to redefine their relationships with their stakeholders, who can range from business partners to entire societies.

Consider the case of tantalum. Tantalum is a lightweight metal used to make the electronic components of mobile phones compact and powerful. It is mined from an ore called coltan. The Democratic Republic of the Congo (DRC; formerly Zaire) is rich in coltan reserves. Various armed militias mine and then sell coltan to finance a civil war in that country that has led to widespread death and suffering.[248] As a result of this practice, coltan and three other mineral ores found in the DRC have been labeled "conflict minerals." The United States responded to this situation by enacting legislation that requires companies to audit their supply chains to make certain that their mineral purchases are not fueling the conflict in the DRC.[249]

Other metals, known as rare earth elements (REEs), possess strong magnetic fields, which make them a critical component in technologies such as computer hard drives, self-powered flashlights, and motors for electric and hybrid vehicles. The Chinese region of Inner Mongolia has large reserves of REEs. In 2010, a diplomatic dispute led China to temporarily suspend shipments of REEs to Japan, a move that has alerted the world to the strategic importance of these minerals.[250]

Tantalum and REEs formerly were of interest primarily to geologists. Now they are a hot button for many technology companies. The technology world is increasingly affected by "flapping butterfly wings" from many sources, and technology itself causes ripples across a number of constituencies.

Prof. Dr. Henning Kagermann, president of acatech, the German National Academy of Science and Engineering, writes in his guest column in this chapter about the wide range of stakeholders he has to deal with compared to his previous role as CEO of SAP.

Let's review a few areas where Digital Enterprises have to revisit their relationships with stakeholders.

Investors

More companies are learning to communicate with their investors in technical terms. For example, Jeff Bezos began his 2010 annual letter to Amazon shareholders as follows:

> "Random forests, naïve Bayesian estimators, RESTful services, gossip protocols, eventual consistency, data sharding, antientropy, Byzantine quorum, erasure coding, vector clocks ..."[251]

In his 2011 letter he explained more of Amazon's technologies:

> "The most radical and transformative of inventions are often those that empower others to unleash their creativity — to pursue their dreams. That's a big part of what's going on with Amazon Web Services, Fulfillment by Amazon, and Kindle Direct Publishing."[252]

This is Amazon's way of informing investors that the company is not simply a retailer. Rather, it also makes significant capital investments in its Amazon Web Services (AWS) data centers, Kiva robots, Kindle readers, and other technologies.

Another company whose products encompass a broad array of technologies is 3M. Figure 17-1 displays the 3M website with its "Periodic Table" that lists its 45 "technology platforms." Click on "Bi," for example, and the site takes you to a page that details 3M's Biotechnology products. Similarly, "Mr" takes you to Microreplication, and so on. This is an effective way for 3M to convey information with investors and other interested parties about the wide range of both its products and its investments.

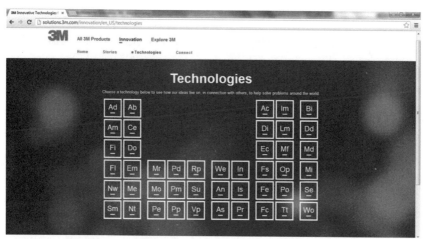

Figure 17-1: 3M's "Periodic Table" of technologies[253]

Society

Prof. Herman Tavani teaches philosophy at Rivier University in Nashua, New Hampshire.[254] His book *Ethics and Technology* was first published in 2004. Tavani has since updated every subsequent edition to highlight the ever-expanding societal impact of the latest technologies. In the 2012 edition, he included new issues that had emerged since the previous edition just three years earlier:[255]

- Ethical and social aspects of cloud computing, including concerns about the privacy and security of users' data that are increasingly being stored in the cloud

- Concerns about the increasing "personalization" of search results based on queries entered by users on search engines such as Google

- Controversies surrounding WikiLeaks and the tension this organization creates between free speech and responsible journalism

- Concerns affecting "net neutrality" and whether internet regulation may be required to ensure that service providers do not unduly control the content delivered via their services

- Recent controversies affecting "machine ethics" and the development of "moral machines" or autonomous systems that will be embedded with software designed to make moral decisions

- Questions about our conventional notions of autonomy and trust — Can machines be autonomous? Can we trust machines to act in ways that will always be in the best interest of humans?

Consider the fact that many hospitals can quickly convene an ethics committee that frequently includes doctors, attorneys, chaplains, nurses, and community members. The committee is available to a doctor or to someone close to a patient to consult on an ever-expanding set of issues. Digital Enterprises will increasingly be expected to establish similar ethics committees to address the impact of their technologies on different segments of society.

Regulators

In sector after sector regulators struggle to keep up with the technologies they are commissioned to oversee. Consider the following examples:

- The UN's nuclear watchdog, the International Atomic Energy Agency (IAEA), came under fire for what its critics claimed was its failure to properly analyze the threats posed by Japan's nuclear crisis as well as its record in monitoring global nuclear safety.[256]

- Financial regulators around the world have struggled to keep up with new derivatives and other complex products and practices made possible by the previously unimaginable capacity of computers to run highly complex models and algorithms.

- The U.S. Patent Office has accumulated such an overwhelming backlog that applications don't get looked at for years. It is not uncommon for patents to take three to five years to get issued. In the meantime, patent litigation has dominated industry headlines for several years.[257]

On the best of days, there is an uneasy relationship between businesses and regulators. When regulators are lagging technologically, these tensions increase. Difficult as it may be, Digital Enterprises will have to do their part to help regulators recruit and train appropriate technical talent and generally cooperate with them to serve the public interest.

Summary
The digitization of products and services has a ripple effect on a wide range of interests. Digital Enterprises need to revisit their traditional approach to investors, employees, regulators, and a broader range of stakeholders than was the case even a generation ago.

Now let's look at a perspective from Prof. Dr. Henning Kagermann, president of acatech, the German National Academy of Science and Engineering, about the wide range of stakeholders his organization deals with.

Germany's Digital Journey

Prof. Dr. Henning Kagermann, President, acatech (German National Academy of Science and Engineering)

The National Academy of Science And Engineering — known as acatech — represents the interests of the German scientific and technological communities. The academy functions as the voice for science and engineering at the national and international levels.

Founded in 2002, acatech is relatively young compared to similar academies in other countries. The Royal Swedish Academy of Sciences, for example, is nearly 300 years old. Germany was a bit late in accepting the precept that engineering is different from science. To me, science is about discovering and acquiring knowledge and understanding the world. In contrast, engineering is about solving problems; it is about innovation; it is about shaping the world, and not just understanding it.

Starting in 2006, the recently elected Chancellor Angela Merkel encouraged Germany to embrace a significant high-tech focus. Two examples of this focus are the IT Summit and the so-called Industry-Science Research Alliance, which has a broad scope, as illustrated in Figure 17-2.

ꞮꞮꞮ acatech
NATIONAL ACADEMY OF
SCIENCE AND ENGINEERING

**Focus on society's major challenges
and strategic projects**

Health & Nutrition	Climate & Energy	Mobility	Communication	Security
Expectation of life: One century	*Climate friendly and affordable*	*Always travelling best*	*Things learn to talk*	*Protect economy and society*

Industry 4.0

Key technologies

Source: BMBF

14   Science for Society: how? Prof. Dr. Kagermann | October 26, 2012

Figure 17-2: The Industry-Science Research Alliance

Let me describe a few of the initiatives that grew out of Merkel's High-Tech Policies.

   a. Industrie 4.0

      In April 2013 the working group, which was comprised of a broad range of Germany's industry leaders and academics, issued its final report.[258] The report concluded:

> "The first three industrial revolutions came about as a result of mechanization, electricity, and IT. Now, the introduction of the Internet of Things and Services into the manufacturing environment is ushering in a fourth industrial revolution, also known as Industrie 4.0."

The report further asserted that this development has a particular strategic value for Germany:

"Germany needs to draw on its strengths as the world's leading manufacturing equipment supplier and in the field of embedded systems by harnessing the spread of the Internet of Things and Services into the manufacturing environment so that it can lead the way towards the fourth stage of industrialisation."

As Figure 17-3 illustrates, there are several concepts that underpin the Industrie 4.0 vision.

Forschungsunion
Wirtschaft und Wissenschaft
begleiten die Hightech-Strategie

ſ⁻ acatech
NATIONAL ACADEMY OF
SCIENCE AND ENGINEERING

Vision for Industrie 4.0

- **Individualisation** (batch sizes of 1) at mass production prices will become a reality
- Manufacturing will be **highly flexible**, extremely productive (up to +50%), will use fewer resources (up to -50%) and will be sustainable in an urban environment
- **Dynamic design** of business and engineering processes
- **Work-life balance** taking account of availability of individual workers
- Older employees supported by **smart assistance systems**
- Existing infrastructure can be **upgraded gradually**
- A high-wage economy that is still **competitive**

---

13   Strategic initiative Industrie 4.0, July 3, 2013

Figure 17-3: The basic concepts that underlie Industrie 4.0

b. EIT Partnership

We are in close collaboration with the European Institute of Innovation and Technology (EIT),[259] whose mission is to turn

Europe into a global leader by integrating the knowledge triangle of education, research, and business. For example, EIT's Knowledge and Innovation Communities (KICs) operate a network of co-location centers to foster new ideas and to educate the next generation ICT professionals. These centers are based in Berlin, Germany; Eindhoven, Holland; Stockholm, Sweden; Helsinki, Finland; Trento, Italy; and Paris, France. They focus on emerging topics such as smart spaces, smart energy systems, health and well-being, digital cities of the future, future media and content delivery, and intelligent mobility and transportation systems.

c. National Platform for Electric Mobility (NPE)
    Germany's Federal Government has established a National Platform for Electric Mobility (NPE) with the goal of helping Germany become the leading market for and the leading supplier of electric mobility. Four ministries, eight industries, trade unions, and consumer representatives — in total 150 partners — participate in this novel cross-sectoral endeavor. Seven working groups focus on priority themes as part of a holistic "systemic approach" to facilitate the development of a climate-friendly and sustainable transformation of our transportation system.

d. Internet Privacy
    Recently, acatech published a position paper on internet privacy. The research team responsible for the paper included a number of our leading academicians from multiple disciplines as well as representatives from Google, Nokia, IBM, and Deutsche Post. The team's recommendations highlight the intricate balancing act between technology-driven innovation on the one hand and societal caution about such innovation on the other hand. The recommendations focus on developing education, regulation, business, and technology in a manner that protects internet privacy while ensuring that the internet can fulfill its potential

for supporting self-determination, democratic participation, and economic well-being.

e. The Innovation Dialogue between the Federal Government, and Business, and Science
    In October 2008, Chancellor Merkel, in collaboration with the Federal Ministry of Education and Research (BMBF) and the Federal Ministry of Economics and Technology (BMWi), commissioned acatech to design to advise the Federal Government on questions concerning research and innovation policies. Essentially, acatech provides a platform for discussions between the government, BMBF, and BMWi in which representatives from business, science, and society also participate. The academy's role is to organize the dialogue and the advisory process.

These examples indicate the wide range of stakeholders — from government to industry to academia to citizens — we factor into our research and initiatives. For example, we communicate with trade unions about the Industrie 4.0 vision described above.

Trade unions have historically been uneasy about automation and technology. Charlie Chaplin expressed these fears brilliantly in his 1936 classic *Modern Times*. To mollify these fears, we had to explain to union members that the next-generation agile robot is more of a personal assistant that actually gives workers more flexibility in performing their jobs. Unlike the previous generation of large, noisy robots in cages, these agile robots actually help create more pleasant working environments. Further, given Germany's aging workforce, these "assistants" allow the country to remain globally competitive. Going further, greener factories, which can be located closer to the towns and cities where workers live, encourage a better work/life balance.

As a business executive — a former CEO of SAP and the current director of global companies — I am well accustomed to dealing with a wide range of stakeholders, investors, customers, partners, employees, etc. Nevertheless, in my current role at acatech, I have been impressed how many more stakeholders are influenced by technology now than in the past.

Science and technology are helping us solve many business and societal challenges. At the same time, however, they are also creating new challenges. As executives build their own digital enterprises, I expect they will find — as we have — that they need to factor in a much wider set of stakeholders.

Prof. Dr. Henning Kagermann is President of acatech (German National Academy of Science and Engineering)

PART III

EVOLVING THE DIGITAL ENTERPRISE

18

Systems of Advantage

We are all familiar with *systems of record*. These are ERP-type systems that businesses utilize to manage their operations — our financials, HR, etc. They have to be precise, due in no small part to the fact that auditors and regulators rely on them. They are focused on controls and numbers.

Recent years have witnessed a growing shift toward *systems of engagement*, which "will overlay and complement our deep investments in systems of record." Systems of engagement are oriented towards making enterprise technology as usable and engaging as consumer technology by focusing primarily on the most current digital communication and collaboration technologies. Technology author Geoffrey Moore coined the term to reflect our growing reliance on social applications. Overall, these apps might be more appealing than traditional enterprise technologies. Even if this is true, however, these systems do not create well-designed products, apps stores, and efficient logistics to get the products to the customers in the first place. Significantly, systems of engagement do not typically support these functions.[260]

Today, many enterprises are entering a third phase: information systems for competitive advantage. You have read one example of these systems after another throughout this book. The personalities and companies that contributed cases to this book are embedding technology in their products and services, moving to technology-enabled business models, and utilizing technology to redefine their distribution channels. They are implementing digital technologies in both product-facing and customer-facing areas. This is technology that helps generate revenue, that helps to improve business results for companies in their social and economic environments, and that helps public agencies provide better citizen services. In short, it helps to create a better world.

Even more interesting is the fact that these examples are not localized in any one industry, such as automobiles, or in a specific region, such as Silicon Valley. For example, Coca-Cola Enterprises described how social, mobile, and crowdsourcing technologies are allowing them to evolve the consumer packaged goods market across Western Europe. Städel Museum in Frankfurt, Germany, demonstrated how even nonprofits can become remarkably innovative by utilizing emerging technologies. GE discussed how their wind turbines, locomotives, aircraft engines, and other industrial products provide vivid examples of the growing Internet of Things.

Within specific industries, companies are adopting diverse approaches. For example, *MAPFRE* described how they are leveraging telematics into the auto insurance industry. Allianz, a global insurance company, explained their applications of advanced analytics. Standard Chartered discussed the global rollout of their Breeze mobile banking application across many developing countries. BBVA explained how next-gen clouds and digital architectures have enabled them to catch up with their much larger global competitors in the corporate investment banking sector.

When you examine industries that have been radically transformed by technology over the past few decades, you can see how the survivors continue to morph and thrive. For example, Hubert Burda Media described their two-pronged strategy of launching new digital properties while simultaneously digitizing their existing print versions. TUI InfoTec explained how Big Data and mobile technologies are helping to reinvent the travel industry even further. Prof. Dr. Wolfgang Wahlster discussed how semantic memories promise to reshape the manufacturing and logistics of many products.

Several technology vendors described how their products and services have evolved as their customers have become more digitized. For example, Qualcomm explained how it morphs every few years with new mobile chips and other products. Accenture and Deutsche Telekom T-Systems now derive revenues from a radically different set of services than they did just a few years ago. Siemens continues to evolve its suite of product lifecycle management products.

Two traditional IT roles that remain critical are security and business continuity. Prof. Dr. Peter Buxmann made a convincing case for innovation in protecting the Digital Enterprise with the most current technologies for cloud computing and other forms of computing. Similarly, Prof. Dieter Kempf described how DATEV is utilizing next-gen security and business continuity services to protect tens of thousands of small and mid-sized enterprises as they proceed on their digital journeys.

These are exciting times for IT specialists. To some degree, the current landscape is a throwback to the 1960s and 1970s, when we dreamed of achieving competitive advantage through technology. During those years Sabre, the computer-driven airline reservation system, and American Hospital Supply were praised for transforming their industries.

Unfortunately, however, IT in many enterprises essentially stagnated for the next three decades. It focused primarily on products, costs, controls, and compliance — the systems of record. It did not focus on competitive advantage. In fact, IT costs and project overruns made many companies less rather than more competitive.

IT did not seem to be motivated even by the glorious last decade of innovation in consumer technology. Many business organizations dismissed iPhones and social networks as "toys" when they could have learned from the operational underpinnings that produced those innovations. Only recently have these enterprises started to appreciate achievements like the highly profitable Apple retail system, the hyper-efficient Amazon data centers, the massive Big Data architecture at Facebook, and the globally optimized Google network. We are now poised for an era of what GE is calling the Industrial Internet.

Enterprises are launching multidimensional, multimedia initiatives. For example, Echo Entertainment is utilizing facial recognition, RFID, mobile, and several other technologies to better service their VIP customers. Prof. Dr. Henning Kagermann conveyed the excitement in the German manufacturing sector about Industrie 4.0 — the promise of next-gen robotics, augmented reality training, wearable computers, and mass-customization technologies. Most of the companies profiled in this book are engaged in anywhere from 10 to 100 technology initiatives.

Most enterprises also realize that their "systems of advantage" provide only fleeting advantage. For example, innovative features in a high-end Mercedes can show up in just a few years in a modestly priced Škoda or even in a far cheaper Tata Nano.

So, enterprises are learning that the pace of systems of advantage has to be relentless. For example, Magne Frantsen described the technologies that allow Statoil to safely explore for energy sources in some of the most forbidding parts of the globe. Technologies that proved effective in the Norwegian Continental Shelf have to be modified for more recent forays into Canadian oil sands and U.S. shale reserves. Similarly, Nissan described technologies it is developing for markets in which electric vehicles are becoming mainstream. Finally, Dr. Michael Gorriz and Dr. Kai Holzweißig described Daimler's enthusiastic embrace of Linked Data.

All of the enterprises highlighted in this book are focused on the current wave of promising technologies. In the next chapter we explore technologies for the next generation of the Digital Enterprise. These innovations represent "The Next Big Thing" as defined by Digital Enterprises throughout the world.

19

"The Next Big Thing"

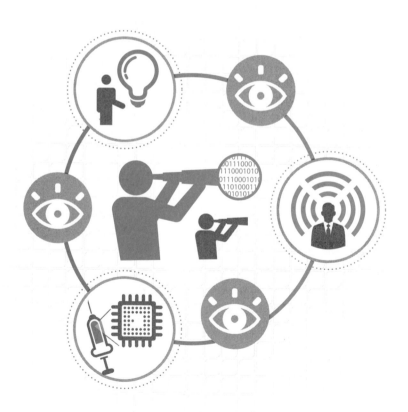

Corning Incorporated, the renowned maker of glass and ceramics, released a series of videos in 2011–2013 titled "A Day Made of Glass." These clips showcase a futuristic family as they interact with applications for photovoltaic, surface, and other specialty glass in the home, the classroom, and the hospital of the future. These highly acclaimed videos have attracted nearly 30 million YouTube views.[261]

People might be surprised to discover that a company like Corning can project such a striking vision of our technology-enabled future. In fact, Corning has been an integral part of technology markets for decades. Its Gorilla Glass protects more than 1.5 billion mobile devices.[262] In addition, the company has long been a major supplier of fiber optics, which serves as the backbone through which most global broadband traffic flows. Finally, Corning manufactures substrates for displays on LCD panel televisions, laptops, and other consumer electronics.

Similarly, in July 2013 GE's Appliance division created a Home 2025 exhibit for a gallery at the University of Louisville.[263] The exhibit showed off a futuristic washing/drying machine, a garbage disposal unit that creates compost, a beverage station with biometric readings to assess how hydrated people are, and even a 3D printer that can produce certain nonfood items.[264]

In many ways, Corning and GE are role models for most Digital Enterprises as they plan for their "Next Big Thing" — as in developing multiple technology waves and factoring conflicting technology trends into their strategies. "The future comes faster" these days — once you get onto the digital track you have to keep looking ahead. Of course, when businesses move out of consumer-focused markets, then the complexity of such planning increases exponentially.

More Complex Scenarios

This book opens with a reference to the keynote speech delivered by Dr. Thomas Enders, CEO of EADS, at CeBIT in March 2013. Dr. Enders challenged the IT industry to help Europe realize its vision of Flightpath 2050, an air transport system that will provide door-to-door service anywhere on the European continent in only 4 hours.[265] Despite his encouraging words, however, IT is currently facing long-term challenges in every industry.

Other industries need to implement this type of long-term technology planning as well. For example, Shell, the energy company, is well known for its long-term "scenario planning." The company claims its scenarios helped "anticipate, adapt, and respond to another oil shock in 1979, as well as the decline and eventual collapse of the Soviet Union in the 1980s."[266] Although these were geopolitical events, the energy business has increasingly become a technology business focusing on solar, wind, and other renewable energy sources. In one of its recent scenarios Shell stated: "Improvements in the technology known as hydraulic fracturing are unlocking huge volumes of oil and gas."[267] In 2012 the *MIT Technology Review* included Shell along with more mainstream technology companies among its "50 Disruptive Companies."[268]

Another example involves the small island nation of Singapore. Although the country possesses few natural resources, it is a major global player in sectors such as electronics, petroleum refining, shipping, financial services, and biomedicine. The country maintains its competitive position by constantly refreshing its labor force and its educational system through a sophisticated system of planning coordinated across the Ministry of Manpower, the Economic Development Board, the Ministry of Education, other government agencies, and local businesses. This integrated planning enables the nation's pool of talented workers to rapidly transition from one industry to another as the need dictates. In

2003 the government established the Workforce Development Agency (WDA) within the Ministry of Manpower "to help our workforce cope through training and skills upgrading."[269]

One of the WDA's recent initiatives is the "Individual Learning Portfolio." This initiative offers career-planning tools and information pertaining to labor markets and employment training to every citizen. At the same time, it benefits employers by providing visibility to talent sources and career choices that the market is showing preferences for as well as incentives for training and retraining workers for newer skills.[270]

In a different part of the world, the European Commission drafted its "Europe 2020" initiative aimed at securing global competitiveness. This initiative prioritized a wide range of technology areas. It also identified focus areas for R&D and other investments; for example, Nanotechnology, Space, and ICTs.[271]

A different set of technology trends factor into long-term planning at the U.S. Air Force. Its chief scientist, Dr. Mark Maybury, recently issued an unclassified report titled *Cyber Vision 2025*. This report highlighted the pressing need "to forecast future threats, mitigate vulnerabilities, enhance the industrial base, and develop the operational capabilities and cyber workforce necessary to assure cyber advantage across all Air Force mission areas."[272]

Of course, not every enterprise has the resources to invest in the significant amounts of technology tracking that Shell or the U.S. Air Force can. Instead, most enterprises rely on trend analysis provided by market watchers.

Market Forecasts
Enterprises have a wide range of research regarding technology trends that they can factor into their longer-term planning. For example, the

MIT Technology Review catalogs an annual list of breakthrough technologies. In presenting its 2013 list the journal explains:

> Our definition of a breakthrough is simple: an advance that gives people powerful new ways to use technology. It could be an intuitive design that provides a useful interface (see "Smart Watches") or experimental devices that could allow people who have suffered brain damage to once again form memories ("Memory Implants"). Some could be key to sustainable economic growth ("Additive Manufacturing" and "Supergrids"), while others could change how we communicate ("Temporary Social Media") .... Some are brilliant feats of engineering ....Others stem from attempts to rethink longstanding problems in their fields ("Deep Learning" and "Ultra-Efficient Solar Power").[273]

McKinsey & Company, the management consulting firm, has developed a similar list of disruptive technologies through its Global Institute. The institute's May 2013 report asserts:

> "The relentless parade of new technologies is unfolding on many fronts. Almost every advance is billed as a breakthrough, and the list of 'next big things' grows ever longer. Not every emerging technology will alter the business or social landscape — but some truly do have the potential to disrupt the status quo, alter the way people live and work, and rearrange value pools. It is therefore critical that business and policy leaders understand which technologies will matter to them and prepare accordingly."[274]

Technology research firms, of course, constantly keep track of market trends. Figure 19-1 illustrates what Forrester Research identifies as "the top 15 emerging technologies you need to start watching now, as they will have big impacts by 2018. Use it to maintain a technology watch list and identify hot opportunities for investment."[275]

Forrester Research's Top 15 Emerging Technologies By Category

End user computing technologies	Sensors and remote computing
• Next-generation devices and UIs	• Smart products
• Advanced collaboration and communication	• In-location positioning
• Systems of engagements	• Machine-to-machine network

Process data management	Infrastructure and application platforms
• Smart process applications and semantics	• Big data platforms
• Advanced analytics	• Breakthrough storage and compute
• Pervasive BI	• Software-defined infrastructure
• Process and data cloud services	• Cloud application and frameworks
	• New identity and trust models

Source: The Top Emerging Technologies To Watch: Now Through 2018, February 7, 2013

Figure 19-1: Forrester Research's "Top 15 Emerging Technologies"

Along similar lines, the "Enterprise Irregulars," a group of respected bloggers, were asked to project which technologies would become mainstream by 2018. Their forecasts include the following:[276]

- Home automation/control of everything (Z-wave, Zigbee hubs, and mobile apps)

- Google Glass-based devices will just be hitting mainstream (20M+ devices a year)

- TV/cable suddenly crumbles almost entirely to digital delivery over apps/IP-based devices

- The advent of One Device for everything (phone, apps, SLR quality video/photos, wallet, remote controls, secure enough for BYOD at work, everything)

- We are issued government digital identities and most Web sites require them for e-commerce, taxation, antiterrorism, censorship

- Recycling of old devices ageing out of the cloud becomes a big business and/or mandatory in many places

- Connected cars with built-in analytics. EVs will also have advanced to take a significant share of the market share

- Better password management through combination of biometric technologies (voice & facial recognition, for example)

- You won't need (much) manual labor to process payroll, issue benefits statements, insurance claims, invoices, receivables, manage systems

- Neural/computer interfaces….first for prosthetics and moving into even more advanced areas such as computation.

****

Whether they rely on outside advisers or have dedicated teams to track emerging technologies, whether they show off prototypes of their future technology-enabled products or keep their plans close to the vest, Digital Enterprises have to be continuously thinking about their "Next Big Thing." The pace of technological progress is relentless — customer expectations, competitor capabilities, industry standards, and government regulations continue to evolve rapidly. The digital world of the future promises to be very different from the one we inhabit today.

Let's use digital technology to bring about a better world. The possibilities are there, so we have no excuses not to.

Glossary

Augmented reality (AR) training: Training in which software algorithms and sensors present scenarios from the trainee's perspective; so-called because it occurs in a real-world environment that is supplemented, or augmented, by sensory data generated by modern computer technologies.

Automated Identification System (AIS): A maritime tracking system introduced in the 1990s that continuously analyzes real-time signals from a variety of sources, such as from a ship's onboard systems, that provide information such as location, speed, and direction.

Big Data: A widely used term for the massive and unprecedented volumes of unstructured data available to individuals and enterprises in the digital world.

Bring your own device (BYOD): Business policies that permit employees to bring personal mobile devices to work and connect those devices to the business networks.

Build-to-order (also *make-to-order*): A manufacturing system in which production begins only after a customer has submitted an order.

Business intelligence: A combination of technologies, processes, and theories that help enterprises acquire and utilize information to improve decision-making processes and enhance profitability and competitiveness.

Business process management (BPM): A management approach designed to optimize the performance and productivity of an enterprise's various business processes.

Complex event processing (CEP): A technology that enables organizations to extract information and create business value by correlating multiple events occurring across various levels inside or outside the enterprise.

Consumerization of IT: A current business trend in which employees often are technically better equipped at home than at work and consequently seek to use their personal devices in their jobs. See also **Bring your own device**.

Crowdsourcing: A strategy in which an enterprise shares a problem online with a large number of people (crowd) and invites them to provide input and offer solutions.

Cyber-physical systems (CPS): "Intelligent" technical systems whose sensor and actor technology, networked wirelessly via the internet and other services with standard protocols, increasingly allows autonomous actions and communication without operator control.

Digital babies: New startups that take advantage of the most current technologies; they typically challenge previous generations of enterprises.

Digital Enterprise: A business, government, or private organization that incorporates the most current information technologies into all of its processes and operations to achieve a competitive advantage and to better engage with customers, partners, and employees.

Digital natives: Individuals and organizations that were born into or established in a digital world.

Digital phoenixes: Enterprises that were in a state of decline but reestablished themselves by successfully utilizing digital technologies.

Distributed denial-of-service (DDoS): An attack in which a multitude of compromised systems assault a single target; the flood of incoming messages to the target system essentially forces it to shut down, thereby denying service to legitimate users.

Dynamic pricing: A business practice in which the price of goods fluctuates based on factors such as demand and customer characteristics.

Enterprise resource planning (ERP) systems: Management systems designed to integrate and automate the various processes performed within an organization.

Fourth Industrial Revolution: See **Industrie 4.0**.

Generation Y: Also known as *Millennials,* the age cohort born roughly 1980-2000; they are technologically savvy, and they seek greater flexibility and fewer constraints in their jobs.

Industrie 4.0: A term for the era of the connectedness of machines, based on a global network in which various digital systems, machines, sensors, and devices communicate directly with one another, enabling the integration of the mechanical and digital worlds, and in the process creating unprecedented opportunities for innovation and business value. It is also referred to as the *Fourth Industrial Revolution* and *Industry 4.0.*

Infrastructure as a service (IaaS): An IT model in which a vendor provides the basic operating system to the enterprise but the enterprise must create its own platform and manage the applications.

Just-in-time: A manufacturing system where the supplier provides the required material for an assembling or manufacturing process without strong buffers in stock but just in time. The objective is to minimize inventory.

Linked Data: A technology that explains the meaning of entities and their relationships in a machine-readable format by utilizing graphs known as *semantic networks*.

Machine-to-machine (M2M): Communication that takes place directly between two machines without any human intervention.

Mass customization: The capability of enterprises to mass-produce goods and services that are individualized for their customers and clients.

Mass production: The traditional large-scale manufacturing of goods that have essentially the same features; in the digital world it is being supplanted by mass customization.

Massive open online courses (MOOCs): Online courses that can attract thousands of participants, often on a global basis.

Master data management: A management strategy intended to provide all areas of an enterprise with a unified view of the organization's process-related data.

Micro-vertical: A subset of a vertical. For example, if an outsourcer for the financial services industry provides horizontal business process outsourcing (BPO) services for benefits administration, a micro-vertical outsourcer drills down further and performs BPO for benefits administration in wealth management.

Mobile device management: Software that enables an enterprise to monitor and integrate the myriad mobile devices — both corporate and employee owned — that are utilized in its various operations.

Near field communications (NFC): A set of standards for smartphones and similar devices to establish radio communication with each other by touching them together or bringing them into close proximity, usually no more than a few inches. Present and anticipated applications include contactless transactions, data exchange, and simplified setup of more complex communications such as Wi-Fi. Communication is also possible between an NFC device and an unpowered NFC chip, called a "tag". See also **Radio-frequency identification**.

On-premise IT systems: Systems in which the functionality resides within the enterprise itself; it is the alternative to cloud-based services.

Platform as a service (PaaS): A category of cloud computing services that provides an IT model in which a vendor maintains both the basic operating system and other software solutions to the enterprise but the enterprise must manage the applications.

Predictive maintenance: A digitally enabled approach to maintaining assets ranging from individual products to entire systems in which technologies can identify potential problems in advance so the problems can be addressed before the asset actually malfunctions. See **Industrie 4.0**.

Product lifecycle management (PLM): A management strategy that oversees all of the stages of creating and selling a product, from conception and design through sales and marketing.

QR code: Abbreviation for "Quick Response"; a type of 2-D barcode that can be scanned with the camera of mobile devices and deciphered by apps running on these devices (unlike a UPC barcode).

Radio-frequency identification (RFID): A wireless system in which tags with embedded microchips are attached to objects, which can then be tracked via radio signals.

Random access memory (RAM): A type of computer storage that is so-named because users can retrieve data in any order — that is, "randomly" — rather than in a predefined sequence.

Semantic product memory: A system in which a single memory stores product data for the entire lifecycle of the product.

Software as a service (SaaS): An IT model in which a vendor both provides and maintains the basic operating system, the IT platform, and the applications for the enterprise.

Systems of engagement: A concept developed by Geoffrey Moore that posits that enterprises will place a greater focus on collaborative technologies that "engage" and empower customers, partners, and employees as opposed to pure systems of record.

System of record: An information storage and retrieval system that serves as the key data source for a single piece of information that can exist on multiple systems within the enterprise.

Vertical disintegration: A business model in which an enterprise outsources segments of its supply chain; it is the opposite of vertical integration (below).

Vertical integration: A business model in which an enterprise owns all of the components of its supply chain.

Voice over Internet Protocol (VoIP): A technology in which telephone communications are conveyed over the internet.

Endnotes

1 http://cdn.idc.com/research/Predictions12/Main/downloads/
IDCTOP10Predictions2012.pdf

2 http://www.gartner.com/technology/research/nexus-of-forces/

3 http://prezi.com/_0lhq7of8i-d/copy-of-cebit-2013/

4 http://www.youtube.com/watch?v=-Cn_PFxmmMU

5 http://www.eads.com/eads/int/en/news/media.52bcc0e1-5a42-
4688-aef0-ab9288a7238d.-Tom+Enders%27+Speech+at+CeBIT+
%28English%29.html

6 http://ec.europa.eu/transport/modes/air/doc/flightpath2050.pdf

7 Remark about the Model T in 1909, published in his autobiography
My Life and Work (1922) Chapter IV, p. 71; this has often been para-
phrased, e.g.: "You can have any colour as long as it's black."

8 http://www.jcmit.com/memoryprice.htm

9 http://www.corning.com/news_center/corning_stories/gorilla_glass
.aspx

10 http://florence20.typepad.com/renaissance/2007/09/tiigrihppe--est
.html

11 http://www.webopedia.com/TERM/M/Moores_Law.html

12 http://www.gartner.com/technology/research/nexus-of-forces/

13 http://www.spiegel.de/wirtschaft/belastung-fuer-firmen-bundes-
buerokratie-verschluckt-30-milliarden-euro-a-513157.html

14 http://googleblog.blogspot.com/2010/10/what-were-driving-at.html

15 http://www.daimler.com/dccom/0-5-1210218-1-1462148-1-0-0-
1210228-0-0-135-0-0-0-0-0-0-0-0.html

16 http://www.bmw.com/com/en/insights/technology/connected-
drive/2013/index.html

17 http://florence20.typepad.com/renaissance/2013/04/the-tesla-mobile-app.html

18 http://hyundainews.com/us/en-us/Media/PressRelease.aspx?mediaid=37994

19 http://www.skoda-auto.com/SiteCollectionDocuments/Environment/Adaptivni_svetlomety_AFS_ENG_07_2008.pdf

20 http://www.tatamotors.com/media/pdf/Tata-Nano-Note.pdf

21 http://www.gerloff.com/qfive_02a_deu.htm

22 http://www.moen.com/iodigital

23 http://www.youtube.com/watch?v=aXV-yaFmQNk

24 http://www.businessweek.com/stories/2011-04-05/how-mattel-can-get-into-your-headbusinessweek-business-news-stock-market-and-financial-advice

25 http://www.digitalbuzzblog.com/lego-story-builder-augmented-reality-app/

26 http://www.forbes.com/sites/danielnyegriffiths/2013/03/05/mobile-makers-makielabs-3d-printed-dolls-get-ipad-app-safety-certification/

27 http://www.businessweek.com/stories/2009-09-21/intel-wants-you-to-age-gracefully-at-homebusinessweek-business-news-stock-market-and-financial-advice

28 http://www.hospira.com/products_and_services/infusion_pumps/

29 http://florence20.typepad.com/renaissance/2011/04/john-deeres-farmsight.html

30 http://florence20.typepad.com/renaissance/2013/06/lacaixa-mobile-banking-innovations.html

31 http://florence20.typepad.com/renaissance/2013/05/bank-branch-of-future.html

32 http://www.debeka.de/service/app/index.html

33 http://www.nationwide.com/newsroom/nw-iPhone-app.jsp

34 http://florence20.typepad.com/renaissance/2011/11/next-book-excerpt-case-study-4-estonias-tiigrihpe-tiger-leap.html

35 http://x-trans.eu/

36 http://www.prlog.org/11659709-leva-activates-forensic-video-analysis-response-team-to-support-vancouver-police-department.html

37 http://www.theverge.com/2013/4/16/4230820/in-boston-bombing-flood-of-digital-evidence-is-a-blessing-and-a-curse

38 http://www.mobilecommercedaily.com/mgm-mirage-launches-commerce-enabled-augmented-reality-iphone-app

39 http://www.tesh.com/story/pets-category/how-hotels-are-spying-on-us/cc/11/id/25023

40 http://www.theipadfan.com/york-plaza-hotel-features-ipad-room/

41 http://travel.usatoday.com/alliance/flights/boardingarea/post/2012/03/The-Cynical-Traveler---Radisson-8216Sleep-Number8217-bed/655068/1

42 http://ebw.evergreen.ca/move/feat/hong-kongs-octopus-card

43 http://www.computerworld.com.sg/resource/applications/why-you-dont-get-taxis-in-singapore-when-it-rains/

44 http://www.safelite.com/about-safelite/mobile-auto-glass-repair/

45 http://www.verizontelematics.com/press/releases/mbusa2.php

46 http://www.mbusa.com/mercedes/mbrace

47 http://www.sabre.com/home/about/sabre_history

48 http://aws.amazon.com/ec2/pricing/

49 http://www.cloudera.com/content/cloudera/en/about.html

50 http://evernote.com/premium/

51 http://www.inc.com/magazine/201112/evernote-2011-company-of-the-year.html

52 http://dynamicinsights.telefonica.com/479/about-us

53 http://news.cnet.com/8301-1023_3-57515522-93/gogo-quietly-hikes-up-its-in-flight-wi-fi-prices/

54 http://www.vonage.com/us-canada-calling-plans/unlimited-minutes?refer_id=WEBSR0706010001W1&lid=sub_nav_domestic_unlimited

55 http://support.apple.com/kb/ht2947

56 http://www.apple.com/de/itunes/itunes-match/

57 http://www.netflix.com/

58 http://www.redbox.com/facts

59 http://www.slashgear.com/amazon-prime-subscription-streaming-movie-bundle-tipped-incoming-02129925/

60 http://www.nytimes.com/subscriptions/Multiproduct/lp5558.html?campaignId=3HYHY

61 http://www.progressive.com/auto/snapshot-how-it-works/

62 http://climate.com/company/

63 http://www.amazon.co.uk/gp/help/customer/display.html?nodeId=200543730

64 http://florence20.typepad.com/renaissance/2011/06/groupons-global-rocket.html

65 https://foursquare.com/about/

66 http://www.pushpinsapp.com/about

67 http://www.amazon.com/Amazon-Services-LLC-Prime/dp/B00DBYBNEE

68 http://www.huffingtonpost.com/2013/06/28/tesla-direct-sales-auto-dealers-petition_n_3516836.html

69 http://carwoo.com/how_it_works

70 https://www.onstar.com

71 http://www.acura.com/CONCIERGESERVICE.ASPX

72 http://www.mbusa.com/mercedes/mbrace

[73] http://www.priceline.com/customerservice/faq/howitworks/howit-works.asp

[74] http://www.theguardian.com/politics/2009/aug/27/barnet-ryanair-pricing-model

[75] https://www.airbnb.com/about

[76] http://www.netjets.com/Life-as-an-owner/Owner-Journey/

[77] http://www.zipcar.com/about

[78] http://www.businessweek.com/magazine/natalie-massenet-on-starting-netaporter-12152011.html

[79] http://www.rutbergco.com/exitsanalysis.pdf

[80] http://finance.yahoo.com/news/strategy-analytics-global-smartphone-shipments-032900959.html

[81] http://www.kpcb.com/insights/2013-internet-trends

[82] http://florence20.typepad.com/renaissance/2013/06/will-mobile-apps-make-smarter-consumers.html

[83] http://www.businessinsider.com/15-facts-about-starbucks-that-will-blow-your-mind-2011-3?op=1

[84] http://florence20.typepad.com/renaissance/2012/02/freestyle-fountain-tour.html

[85] http://florence20.typepad.com/renaissance/2012/09/audis-digital-showroom.html

[86] http://politicalwire.com/archives/2013/04/18/romney_strategist_says_campaign_was_2_years_behind_obama.html

[87] http://newsfeed.time.com/2013/02/04/watch-oreos-snappy-super-bowl-blackout-ad/

[88] http://florence20.typepad.com/renaissance/2012/08/the-ikea-catalog-a-marvel-of-miniaturization.html

[89] http://bgr.com/2012/08/20/apple-store-stats-2012-300-million-50000-genius-bar/

[90] http://tech.fortune.cnn.com/2012/11/13/apple-stores-tops-tiffanys-in-sales-per-square-foot-again/

[91] http://florence20.typepad.com/renaissance/2011/07/grocery-shopping-at-your-subway-stop.html

[92] http://florence20.typepad.com/renaissance/2013/03/crowdsourcing-home-deliveries.html

[93] http://www.slideshare.net/Radian6/frontier-airlines-social-media-case-study-a-simple-idea-makes-a-huge-difference

[94] http://www.fvw.com/tui-germany-more-differentiated-products-for-next-summer/393/111598/11245

[95] https://fiber.google.com/about/

[96] http://googleblog.blogspot.com/2010/10/what-were-driving-at.html

[97] http://florence20.typepad.com/renaissance/2013/06/amazonfresh-webvan-20.html

[98] http://florence20.typepad.com/renaissance/2011/12/book-excerpts-case-study-6-virgin-america.html

[99] http://www.theguardian.com/business/2009/aug/31/disney-marvel-buy-out

[100] http://florence20.typepad.com/renaissance/2011/05/innovation-in-european-postal-services.html

[101] http://florence20.typepad.com/renaissance/2010/07/the-gogo-inflight-Wi-Fi.html

[102] http://www.csx.com/index.cfm/about-csx/projects-and-partnerships/fuel-efficiency/

[103] http://www.gettransportation.com/rail/rail-products/locomotives/fuel-savings-solutions/trip-optimizer.html

[104] http://aspnet.cob.ohio.edu/matta/mis2020/HotTopics/5.0%20Internet%20Of%20Things%20Updated.pdf

[105] http://www.nscorp.com/nscportal/nscorp/Investors/Financial_Reports/Investor%20Book/technology.html

[106] ZEW Industry Report — Results of the German Innovation Survey 2012, published in Jan. 2013

[107] Dr. Roman Friedrich, Partner, Booz & Company in his presentation "Future on Telecommunications." Event: Mobile Business Trends 2011, July 2, 2011 in Düsseldorf, Germany Organizer; eco, Association of the German Internet Industry

[108] http://florence20.typepad.com/renaissance/2013/07/chinas-amazing-infrastructure.html

[109] http://edition.cnn.com/2013/04/11/travel/china-high-speed-rail

[110] http://www.chinadaily.com.cn/china/2013-06/06/content_16580254.htm

[111] http://www.youtube.com/watch?v=twN6iUQXKqs

[112] http://www.digitaltrends.com/mobile/history-of-samsungs-galaxy-phones-and-tablets/

[113] http://www.samsung.com/us/guide-to-galaxy-smart-devices/galaxy-s-4-smartphone.html

[114] http://enswmu.blogspot.de/2013/04/workday-update-19-you-need-to-slow-down.html

[115] http://blogs.workday.com/Blog/the_power_of_one.html

[116] http://dealarchitect.typepad.com/deal_architect/2011/07/the-new-blitzkreig.html

[117] http://en.wikipedia.org/wiki/Black_Friday_%28shopping%29

[118] http://www.flextronics.com/about_us/default.aspx

[119] http://www.dirkzwager.com/?mod=content&section=AIS%20Services&id=257

[120] http://www.frogdesign.com/about

[121] http://www.euromoney.com/Article/3135672/Category/12/Channel Page/13/BBVA-builds-up-investment-banking.html?single=true

[122] http://www.utopy.com/index.php?mact=News,cntnt01,detail,0&cntnt01articleid=100&cntnt01returnid=125

[123] http://www.whitehouse.gov/state-of-the-union-2013

[124] www.nsf.gov/about/budget/fy2012/pdf/38_fy2012.pdf

[125] www.acatech.de/.../user.../Final_report__Industrie_4.0_accessible.pdf

[126] http://online.wsj.com/article/SB10001424052702303807404577434231377787826.html

[127] http://florence20.typepad.com/renaissance/2009/04/kiva-warehouse-robots.html

[128] http://www.daimler.com/dccom/0-5-7153-1-1556285-1-0-0-0-0-0-8-7145-0-0-0-0-0-0-0.html

[129] http://www.ehow.com/about_5460438_history-ink-jet-printers.html

[130] http://www.whitehouse.gov/state-of-the-union-2013

[131] http://ieeexplore.ieee.org/xpl/login.jsp?tp=&arnumber=5760480&url=http%3A%2F%2Fieeexplore.ieee.org%2Fxpls%2Fabs_all.jsp%3Farnumber%3D5760480

[132] http://ieeexplore.ieee.org/xpl/login.jsp?tp=&arnumber=5760480&url=http%3A%2F%2Fieeexplore.ieee.org%2Fxpls%2Fabs_all.jsp%3Farnumber%3D5760480

[133] http://www.wittenstein.de/en/innvoation-factory.html

[134] http://www.glaesernemanufaktur.de/en/

[135] http://www.who.int/bulletin/volumes/88/4/10-020410/en/

[136] http://www.idtechex.com/research/articles/opportunities_in_pharma_rfid_and_smart_packaging_00000487.asp

[137] http://www.arcweb.com/strategy-reports/2011-09-22/siemens-plm-software-2011-analyst-conference-1.aspx

138 http://www.acatech.de/fileadmin/user_upload/Baumstruktur_nach_
Website/Acatech/root/de/Publikationen/Stellungnahmen/acatech_
POSITION_CPS_Englisch_WEB.pdf

139 http://www.cruxialcio.com/supply-chain-support-1138#takeaways

140 http://hollis.harvard.edu/?itemid=|library/m/aleph|000473683

141 http://blogs.wsj.com/digits/2012/12/06/a-short-history-of-apples-
manufacturing-in-the-u-s/

142 http://www.kaiserpermanentejobs.org/university-connection/life-at-
kp.aspx

143 http://xnet.kp.org/newscenter/aboutkp/healthconnect/

144 http://www.usatoday.com/story/money/personalfinance/2012/10/23/
kaiser-health-care-costs/1639913/

145 http://www.bnsf.com/media/news-releases/2012/september/2012-
09-04a.html

146 http://ycharts.com/indicators/brent_wti_spread

147 http://www.kickstarter.com/

148 https://squareup.com/

149 http://transferwise.com/

150 http://www.iwoca.co.uk/

151 http://money.cnn.com/2008/01/16/news/international/brazil_soy
.fortune/index.htm?postversion=2008011917

152 http://ducknetweb.blogspot.de/2013/02/theres-algorithms-in-my-
orange-juice.html

153 http://www.brasil.gov.br/para/press/press-releases/march/brazil-
announces-phase-two-of-the-growth-acceleration-program/
br_model1?set_language=en

154 http://www.businesswire.com/news/home/20130131006018/en/
GE-Introduces-2.5-120-World%E2%80%99s-Efficient-High-Output-
Wind

155 http://www.metering.com/node/16985

156 http://www3.gehealthcare.com/en/Services/Hospital_Operations_Management

157 http://www.businesswire.com/news/home/20130610006645/en/GE-Healthcare-Invest-2-Billion-Software-Development

158 http://splash.alaskasworld.com/Newsroom/ASNews/ASstories/AS_20090708_050500.asp

159 http://webcache.googleusercontent.com/search?q=cache:cSWKqWUTH3YJ:www.getransportation.com/resources/doc_download/143-norfolk-southern-and-ge-announce-success-of-breakthrough-technology.html+&cd=1&hl=en&ct=clnk&gl=us

160 http://www.pcworld.com/article/2036305/pivotal-launched-from-vmware-emc-technologies.html

161 http://fordtechlane.com/tag/sync/

162 http://www.extremetech.com/extreme/125621-mercedes-benz-over-the-air-car-updates

163 http://www.whitehouse.gov/state-of-the-union-2013

164 http://intucellsystems.com/category/press/

165 http://florence20.typepad.com/renaissance/2011/05/toyota-friend.html

166 http://florence20.typepad.com/renaissance/2013/01/kinectcoke2pm-japns-got-talent.html

167 http://florence20.typepad.com/renaissance/2012/11/a-dairy-farmers-best-new-friend.html

168 http://www.linkedin.com/today/post/article/20130619125316-230929989-is-your-jet-engine-linked-in-connecting-minds-and-machines-to-drive-efficiency

169 https://www.coursera.org/

[170] http://www.onr.navy.mil/Media-Center/Press-Releases/2012/Augmented-Reality-Initiative-Progresses.aspx

[171] http://www.smartplanet.com/blog/pure-genius/q-a-moving-the-office-outside/9106?tag=nl.e660&s_cid=e660

[172] http://online.wsj.com/article/SB10001424127887324539404578342503214110478.html

[173] http://blog.ups.com/2009/12/07/birth-of-the-diad/

[174] http://florence20.typepad.com/renaissance/2013/01/mid-level-recruiting-goes-more-social.html

[175] http://hirevue.com/what-is-hirevue/

[176] http://hirevue.com/blog/impacting-sales-results-with-better-hiring-decisions/

[177] http://www.google.de/glass/start/what-it-does/

[178] http://florence20.typepad.com/renaissance/2013/01/the-golden-i-headset.html

[179] http://www.wearitatwork.com/

[180] http://inhabitat.com/elon-musk-unveils-his-iron-man-inspired-hand-manipulated-3d-holographic-technology/

[181] http://media.gmc.com/content/media/us/en/gmc/news.detail.html/content/Pages/news/us/en/2013/Apr/0430-sierra.html

[182] http://www.digitaltrends.com/car-videos/2013-ford-escape-hands-free-liftgate-demo-kick-the-bumper-to-open-the-trunk/

[183] http://www.bmw.com/com/en/insights/technology/technology_guide/articles/head_up_display.html

[184] http://www.mbusa.com/mercedes/mbrace/apps

[185] http://seekingalpha.com/article/1475701-nuances-acquisition-of-tweddle-connect-offers-big-growth-in-automotive-sector

186 http://www.bmw.com/com/en/insights/technology/connected drive/2013/services_apps/bmw_connecteddrive_services .html#mobileoffice

187 http://worldwide.hyundai.com/WW/Experience/ConceptCar/2013/ HCD-14/index.html

188 http://www.teslamotors.com/models/features#/interior

189 http://reviews.cnet.com/8301-13746_7-57552188-48/take-control-of-your-cars-tech-with-these-six-apps/

190 http://www.wired.com/autopia/2013/05/mercedes-qr-code/

191 http://venturebeat.com/2013/02/13/finally-a-fitness-tracker-that-actually-knows-what-youre-doing/

192 http://news.rice.edu/2012/08/20/brain-wave-reading-robot-might-help-stroke-patients-2/

193 http://www.iso.org/iso/catalogue_detail.htm?csnumber=41986

194 http://www.wired.com/thisdayintech/2008/06/june-26-1974-supermarket-scanner-rings-up-historic-pack-of-gum/

195 http://redpepperland.com/lab/details/check-in-with-your-face

196 http://florence20.typepad.com/renaissance/2012/11/50-ways-to-leave-your-lover-and-to-communicate-with-your-smartphone.html

197 http://www.shopperception.com/retailers.html

198 http://florence20.typepad.com/renaissance/2013/01/a-scanner-for-the-tsa-to-consider.html

199 http://www.myplace.sg/gaggenau-introduces-full-surface-induction-cooktop-cx-480/

200 http://florence20.typepad.com/renaissance/2011/07/the-de-dietrich-induction-hob.html

201 http://florence20.typepad.com/renaissance/2011/12/the-nest-learning-thermostat.html

202 http://www.adtpulse.com/home/how-pulse-works/mobile

[203] http://www.hulu.com/about

[204] http://www.car2go.com (05/31/2013)

[205] http://www.moovel.de (05/31/2013)

[206] King & Lytinnen (2004): Automotive Informatics: Information Technology and Enterprise Transformation in the Automobile Industry. Dutton, W.H., Kahin, B., O'Callaghan, R., and Wycoff, A. (Eds.): Transforming Enterprise, MIT Press, p. 1.

[207] Cf., e.g., Kagermann et al. (2013): Umsetzungsempfehlungen für das Zukunftsprojekt Industrie 4.0. Berlin: Büro der Forschungsunion im Stifterverband für die Deutsche Wissenschaft e.V.

[208] Cf. http://www.w3.org/standards/semanticweb/data and the corresponding subpages (05/31/2013)

[209] http://linkeddata.org and http://lod-cloud.net (05/31/2013)

[210] Several frameworks and standards can be used to complete this process. See http://www.w3.org/2001/sw/ and especially http://www.w3.org/2001/sw/wiki/Tools (09/12/2013)

[211] http://www.cemspot.com/2013/07/number-of-users-in-social-media.html

[212] http://florence20.typepad.com/renaissance/2013/01/the-big-data-of-water-leaks.html

[213] http://florence20.typepad.com/renaissance/2013/03/big-data-revolutionizing-farming.html

[214] http://www.imdb.com/title/tt1210166/

[215] http://dealarchitect.typepad.com/deal_architect/2013/05/bill-mcdermott-and-boston.html

[216] http://seatgeek.com/blog/ticket-industry/secondary-ticket-market-and-resellers

[217] http://florence20.typepad.com/renaissance/2012/08/british-cycling-the-technology-and-the-performance-improvements.html

[218] http://www.bartlett.ucl.ac.uk/casa

[219] http://dealarchitect.typepad.com/deal_architect/2013/06/complex-event-processing.html

[220] http://www.networksasia.net/content/dbs-bank-prevents-fraudulent-transactions-progress-software

[221] http://www.rfidjournal.com/articles/view?4225

[222] http://www.rfidjournal.com/articles/view?4225

[223] http://www.clarabridge.com/

[224] http://klout.com/corp/how-it-works

[225] http://www.lithium.com/

[226] http://www.openamplify.com/

[227] http://investors.progress.com/releasedetail.cfm?releaseid=690442

[228] http://florence20.typepad.com/renaissance/2013/06/netflix-the-broadband-monster.html

[229] http://aws.amazon.com/what-is-cloud-computing/

[230] http://aws.amazon.com/what-is-cloud-computing/

[231] http://www.jetblue.com/flying-on-jetblue/wifi/

[232] https://fiber.google.com/about/

[233] http://florence20.typepad.com/renaissance/2013/06/the-rudiben-mobile-app.html

[234] http://www.dnaindia.com/ahmedabad/1813468/report-rudiben-s-use-of-mobile-app-gets-cherie-blair-s-cheers

[235] http://www.tcs.com/Pages/default.aspx

[236] http://www.nasscom.in/vision-and-mission

[237] http://savillecpadallas.com/identity-theft/

[238] http://www.mcafee.com/us/about/news/2012/q4/20121227-01.aspx

[239] http://www.telegraph.co.uk/news/worldnews/europe/georgia/2539157/Georgia-Russia-conducting-cyber-war.html

[240] http://www.wired.com/images_blogs/threatlevel/2010/10/w32_stuxnet_dossier.pdf

[241] http://resources.infosecinstitute.com/prism-facts-doubts-laws-and-loopholes/

[242] *http://www.ccdcoe.org/publications/2012proceedings/1_2_Jason_Healey_WhenNotMyProblemIsntEnough.pdf*

[243] http://www.appstechnews.com/news/2013/oct/14/less-third-large-companies-have-byod-policies-samsung-finds/

[244] http://cwe.mitre.org/

[245] http://www.wired.com/images_blogs/threatlevel/2010/10/w32_stuxnet_dossier.pdf

[246] http://www.informationweek.com/storage/disaster-recovery/backup-bedlam-data-still-at-risk/240158878

[247] http://x-trans.eu/

[248] http://florence20.typepad.com/renaissance/2012/05/cleaning-up-the-tantalum-supply-chain.html

[249] http://www.ipc.org/ContentPage.aspx?pageid=Conflict-Minerals

[250] http://www.forbes.com/sites/china/2010/10/17/china-japan-rare-earth-fracas-continues/

[251] http://www.sec.gov/Archives/edgar/data/1018724/000119312511110797/dex991.htm

[252] http://www.sec.gov/Archives/edgar/data/1018724/000119312512161812/d329990dex991.htm

[253] http://solutions.3m.com/innovation/en_US/technologies

[254] http://www.rivier.edu/faculty/htavani/

[255] http://www.amazon.com/Ethics-Technology-Controversies-Questions-Strategies/dp/1118281721/ref=sr_1_1?ie=UTF8&qid=1376501506&sr=8-1&keywords=herman+tavani

[256] http://online.wsj.com/article/SB100014240527023049060045763717781243470772.html

[257] http://www.ipwatchdog.com/2013/02/14/the-rce-backlog-a-critical-patent-office-problem/id=35431/

[258] http://www.google.com/url?sa=t&rct=j&q=&esrc=s&source=web&cd=1&cad=rja&ved=0CC8QFjAA&url=http%3A%2F%2Fwww.acatech.de%2Ffileadmin%2Fuser_upload%2FBaumstruktur_nach_Website%2FAcatech%2Froot%2Fde%2FMaterial_fuer_Sonderseiten%2FIndustrie_4.0%2FFinal_report__Industrie_4.0_accessible.pdf&ei=gd0KUsjVEY7g8AS_wYCwDg&usg=AFQjCNFgZAn49pcgNucbzTDFXGjZ0reEiA&sig2=xXWpB0T5vNXv68NI3X_bcw

[259] http://eit.europa.eu/

[260] Moore, Geoffrey. (2011). "Systems of Engagement and The Future of Enterprise IT: A Sea Change in Enterprise IT." AIIM White Paper. Retrieved from http://www.aiim.org/~/media/Files/AIIM%20White%20Papers/Systems-of-Engagement-Future-of-Enterprise-IT.ashx.

[261] http://www.youtube.com/watch?v=PfgmlVxLC9w

[262] http://www.corning.com/news_center/features/gorillaglasssuccess.aspx

[263] http://insiderlouisville.com/news/2013/07/18/crazy-cool-ge-design-team-imagines-home-2025-appliances-of-the-future/

[264] http://www.wave3.com/story/22876813/ge-unveils-home-of-2025

[265] http://ec.europa.eu/transport/modes/air/doc/flightpath2050.pdf

[266] http://www.shell.com/global/future-energy/scenarios/40-years.html

[267] http://www.shell.com/global/aboutshell/media/speeches-and-webcasts/2013/getting-the-future-energy-mix-right.html

[268] http://www2.technologyreview.com/tr50/2012/

[269] http://www.wda.gov.sg/content/wdawebsite/L209-001About-Us/L209A-History.html

[270] http://www.wda.gov.sg/content/dam/wda/COS/ILP_Infographics.pdf

[271] http://ec.europa.eu/research/horizon2020/pdf/workshops/leadership_in_enabling_and_industrial_technologies/introduction_-_enabling_and_industrial_technologies_in_horizon_2020.pdf

[272] http://www.ndia.org/Divisions/Divisions/ScienceAndEngineering Technology/Documents/SET%20Breakfast%20Presentation.pdf

[273] http://www.technologyreview.com/featuredstory/513981/introduction-to-the-10-breakthrough-technologies-of-2013/

[274] http://www.mckinsey.com/insights/business_technology/disruptive_technologies?cid=disruptive_tech-eml-alt-mip-mck-oth-1305

[275] http://www.forrester.com/The+Top+Emerging+Technologies+To+Watch+Now+Through+2018/fulltext/-/E-RES82721?docid=82721 — Forrester Research, Inc.

[276] This list is reproduced from http://www.enterpriseirregulars.com/64541/eis-look-ahead-to-2018/

Bibliography

"10 Breakthrough Technologies 2013." MIT Technology Review, April 23, 2013. Retrieved from http://www.technologyreview.com/featuredstory/513981/introduction-to-the-10-breakthrough-technologies-of-2013.

"2014 Sierra Safety Alert Seat Aids Driver Awareness." GMC.com, April 30, 2013. Retrieved from http://media.gmc.com/content/media/us/en/gmc/news.detail.html/content/Pages/news/us/en/2013/Apr/0430-sierra.html.

3M website. Retrieved from http://solutions.3m.com/innovation/en_US/technologies.

"40 Years of Shell Scenarios." Shell website. Retrieved from http://www.shell.com/global/future-energy/scenarios/40-years.html.

"50 Disruptive Technologies 2012." MIT Technology Review. Retrieved from http://www2.technologyreview.com/tr50/2012.

"About Foursquare." Retrieved from https://foursquare.com/about.

"About Lightening Deals." Amazon.co.uk website. Retrieved from http://www.amazon.co.uk/gp/help/customer/display.html?nodeId=200543730.

acatech website. Retrieved from http://www.acatech.de.

Airnb website. Retrieved from https://www.airbnb.com/about/about-us.

"AIS Services." Royal Dirkzwager website. Retrieved from http://www.dirkzwager.com/?mod=content&section=AIS%20Services&id=257.

"Alaska Airlines, Horizon Air Pursue 'Greener Skies' Over Seattle." Alaska Airlines website, July 8, 2009. Retrieved from http://splash.alaskasworld.com/Newsroom/ASNews/ASstories/AS_20090708_050500.asp.

Alfred, Randy. "June 26, 1974: Supermarket Scanner Rings up Historic Pack of Gum." *Wired*, June 26, 2008. Retrieved from http://www.wired.com/thisdayintech/2008/06/june-26-1974-supermarket-scanner-rings-up-historic-pack-of-gum.

"Amazon EC2 Pricing." Amazon Web Services. Retrieved from http://aws.amazon.com/ec2/pricing.

Amazon Prime website. Retrieved from http://www.amazon.com/Amazon-Services-LLC-Prime/dp/B00DBYBNEE.

Anjum, Safar. "Why You Don't Get Taxis in Singapore When It Rains." *Computerworld*, October 3, 2012. Retrieved from http://www.computerworld.com.sg/resource/applications/why-you-dont-get-taxis-in-singapore-when-it-rains.

"Archived — AAC and MP3 Codecs (music file formats) compared." Retrieved from http://support.apple.com/kb/ht2947.

"Avoiding Danger, Providing Timely Warning, and Assisting." Daimler website. Retrieved from http://www.daimler.com/dccom/0-5-1210218-1-1462148-1-0-0-1210228-0-0-135-0-0-0-0-0-0-0-0.html.

"Award-winning Journalism. Award-winning Apps." *The New York Times*. Retrieved from http://www.nytimes.com/subscriptions/Multiproduct/lp5558.html?campaignId=3HYHY.

The Bartlett Centre for Advanced Spatial Analysis website. Retrieved from http://www.bartlett.ucl.ac.uk/casa.

"BBVA Receives an 'Innovation in Banking Technology' Award from *The Banker* Magazine for Speech Analytics Solution." Utopy.com. Retrieved from http://www.utopy.com/index.php?mact=News,cntnt01,detail,0&cntnt01articleid=100&cntnt01returnid=125.

"Belastung für Firmen: Bundesbürokratie verschluckt 30 Milliarden Euro." Spiegel Online Wirtschaft. Retrieved from http://www.spiegel.de/wirtschaft/belastung-fuer-firmen-bundesbuerokratie-verschluckt-30-milliarden-euro-a-513157.html.

Bezos, Jeffrey P. 2010 Letter to Shareholders. Retrieved from http://www.sec.gov/Archives/edgar/data/1018724/000119312511110797/dex991.htm.

Bezos, Jeffrey P. 2011 Letter to Shareholders. Retrieved from http://www.sec.gov/Archives/edgar/data/1018724/000119312512161812/d329990dex991.htm.

"BMW Connected Drive." BMW.com. Retrieved from http://www.bmw.com/com/en/insights/technology/connecteddrive/2013/index.html.

"BMW Head-up Display." BMW.com. Retrieved from http://www.bmw.com/com/en/insights/technology/technology_guide/articles/head_up_display.html.

"BNSF Expands Bakken Oil Transport Capacity to One Million Barrels per Day." BNSF News Release, September 4, 2012. Retrieved from http://www.bnsf.com/media/news-releases/2012/september/2012-09-04a.html.

Booth, Robert. "The Ryanair Pricing Model That Could Be a Route to Budget Care in Barnet." *The Guardian,* August 27, 2009. Retrieved from http://www.theguardian.com/politics/2009/aug/27/barnet-ryanair-pricing-model.

Bourne, James. "Less Than a Third of Large Companies Have BYOD Policies, Samsung Finds." Enterprise Appsworld. Retrieved from http://www.appstechnews.com/news/2013/oct/14/less-third-large-companies-have-byod-policies-samsung-finds.

"Brent WTI Spread." Retrieved from http://ycharts.com/indicators/brent_wti_spread.

Burgess, Chad. "The Expert Series: Guide to the Secondary Ticketing Market." SeatGeek.com, August 1, 2012. Retrieved from http://seatgeek.com/blog/ticket-industry/secondary-ticket-market-and-resellers.

Butcher, Dan. "MGM Mirage Launches Commerce-enabled Augmented Reality iPhone App." *Mobile Commerce Daily,* May 28, 2010. Retrieved from http://www.mobilecommercedaily.com/mgm-mirage-launches-commerce-enabled-augmented-reality-iphone-app.

car2go website. Retrieved from https://www.car2go.com/en/austin.

CarWoo! website. Retrieved from http://carwoo.com/how_it_works.

Chand, Rajeev. *Exits Analysis for Mobil.* Rutberg & Co., June 11, 2012. Retrieved from http://www.rutbergco.com/exitsanalysis.pdf.

"Check-ins Get a Facelift." Redpepper website. Retrieved from http://redpepperland.com/lab/details/check-in-with-your-face.

Chipman, Melissa. "Crazy Cool: GE Design Team Imagines HOME 2025, Appliances of the Future." Insider Louisville, July 18, 2013. Retrieved from http://insiderlouisville.com/news/2013/07/18/crazy-cool-ge-design-team-imagines-home-2025-appliances-of-the-future.

Chovanec, Patrick. "China-Japan Rare Earth Fracas Continues." *Forbes,* October 17, 2010. Retrieved from http://www.forbes.com/sites/china/2010/10/17/china-japan-rare-earth-fracas-continues.

Clarabridge website. Retrieved from http://www.clarabridge.com.

Clark, Andrew. "Disney Buys Marvel Entertainment." *The Guardian,* August 31, 2009. Retrieved from http://www.theguardian.com/business/2009/aug/31/disney-marvel-buy-out.

Climate Corporation website. Retrieved from http://climate.com/company.

Cloudera website. Retrieved from http://www.cloudera.com/content/cloudera/en/about.html.

Common Weakness Enumeration website. Retrieved from http://cwe.mitre.org.

"Concept Car: 2013 HCD-14 Genesis." Hyundai website. Retrieved from http://worldwide.hyundai.com/WW/Experience/ConceptCar/2013/HCD-14/index.html.

"Concierge Services." Retrieved from http://www.acura.com/ CONCIERGESERVICE.ASPX.

"Conflict Minerals." IPC website. Retrieved from http://www.ipc.org/ ContentPage.aspx?pageid=Conflict-Minerals.

"ConnectedDrive Services." BMW.com. Retrieved from http://www .bmw.com/com/en/insights/technology/connecteddrive/2013/ services_apps/bmw_connecteddrive_services.html#mobileoffice.

Cormier, Jeff. "New York Plaza Hotel Now Features an iPad in Every Room." The iPad Fan, February 14, 2013. Retrieved from http:// www.theipadfan.com/york-plaza-hotel-features-ipad-room.

"Corning Gorilla Glass Now Found on More Than 1.5 Billion Devices." Corning News Release, May 2013. Retrieved from http://www .corning.com/news_center/features/gorillaglasssuccess.aspx.

Coursera website. Retrieved from https://www.coursera.org.

Crawford, David, and Max Colchester. "IAEA Draws Fire over Japan Crisis." The Wall Street Journal, June 8, 2011. Retrieved from http:// online.wsj.com/news/articles/SB10001424052702304906004576 371781243470772.

Crawford, Katherine H. "Is This Real or Just Fantasy? ONR Augmented-Reality Initiative Progresses." Office of Naval Research, August 23, 2012. Retrieved from http://www.onr.navy.mil/Media-Center/ Press-Releases/2012/Augmented-Reality-Initiative-Progresses.aspx.

CSX website. Retrieved from http://www.csx.com/index.cfm/about-csx/ projects-and-partnerships/fuel-efficiency.

Cyber-Physical Systems: Driving Force for Innovation in Mobility, Health, Energy, and Production. acatech Position Paper, December 2011. Retrieved from http://www.acatech.de/fileadmin/user_upload/ Baumstruktur_nach_Website/Acatech/root/de/Publikationen/ Stellungnahmen/acatech_POSITION_CPS_Englisch_WEB.pdf.

"The Cynical Traveler — Radisson 'Sleep Number' bed." Retrieved from http://travel.usatoday.com/alliance/flights/boardingarea/post/2012/03/The-Cynical-Traveler---Radisson-8216Sleep-Number8217-bed/655068/1.

Davies, Chris. "Amazon Prime Subscription Streaming Movie Bundle Tipped Incoming." SlashGear.com, February 2, 2011. Retrieved from http://www.slashgear.com/amazon-prime-subscription-streaming-movie-bundle-tipped-incoming-02129925.

"A Day Made of Glass Extended Montage." YouTube video published May 1, 2013. Retrieved from http://www.youtube.com/watch?v=PfgmIVxLC9w.

"DBS Bank Prevents Fraudulent Transactions with Progress Software." Networks Asia, October 11, 2013. Retrieved from http://networksasia.net/article/dbs-bank-prevents-fraudulent-transactions-progress-software-1367284544.

Die Gläserne Manufaktur website. Retrieved from http://www.glaesernemanufaktur.de/en/.

Duffield, David. "The Power of One." Workday.com, November 10, 2010. Retrieved from http://blogs.workday.com/Blog/the_power_of_one.html.

Elmer-DeWitt, Philip. "Apple Stores Top Tiffany in Sales-per-Square Foot Again." *CNN Money,* November 13, 2012. Retrieved from http://tech.fortune.cnn.com/2012/11/13/apple-stores-tops-tiffanys-in-sales-per-square-foot, again.

Enders, Tom "Speech of EADS CEO Tom Enders at CeBIT." EADS website. Published March 6, 2013. Retrieved from http://www.eads.com/eads/int/en/news/media.52bcc0e1-5a42-4688-aef0-ab9288a7238d.-Tom+Enders%27+Speech+at+CeBIT+%28English%29.html.

European Commission. *Flightpath 2050: Europe's Vision for Aviation.* Report of the High-Level Group on Aviation Research, 2011. Retrieved from http://ec.europa.eu/transport/modes/air/doc/flightpath2050.pdf.

European Institute of Innovation and Technology (EIT) website. Retrieved from http://eit.europa.eu.

Falliere, Nicolas, Liam O. Murchu, and Eric Chen. "W32.Stuxnet Dossier." Symantec website, September 2010. Retrieved from http://www.wired.com/images_blogs/threatlevel/2010/10/w32_stuxnet_dossier.pdf.

Flextronics website. Retrieved from http://www.flextronics.com/about_us/default.aspx.

Ford, Henry, and Samuel Crowther. *My Life and Work.* Garden City, NY: Doubleday, Page, & Co., 1922.

Fowle, Scott. "Impacting Sales Results with Better Hiring Decisions." Hirevue.com. Retrieved from http://hirevue.com/blog/impacting-sales-results-with-better-hiring-decisions.

Freedman, David H. "Evernote: 2011 Company of the Year." Inc. website. Retrieved from http://www.inc.com/magazine/201112/evernote-2011-company-of-the-year.html.

Friedrich, Roman. "Future of Telecommunications." Presented at Mobile Business Trends 2011, July 2, 2011 in Düsseldorf, Germany.

frog website. Retrieved from http://www.frogdesign.com/about.

"Frontier Airlines Is Using Social Media to Reach Customers and Make It Right — A Simple Idea That Makes a Huge Difference." Retrieved from http://www.slideshare.net/Radian6/frontier-airlines-social-media-case-study-a-simple-idea-makes-a-huge-difference.

"Gaggenau Introduces Full-Surface Induction Cooktop CX 480." MyPlace.sg website, October 19, 2011. Retrieved from http://www.myplace.sg/gaggenau-introduces-full-surface-induction-cooktop-cx-480.

"Galaxy S2 vs. Galaxy S3 vs. Galaxy S4." YouTube video published May 20, 2013. Retrieved from http://www.youtube.com/watch?v=twN6iUQXKqs.

"GE Healthcare to Invest $2 Billion in Software Development over Next Five Years." *BusinessWire,* June 11, 2013. Retrieved from http://www.businesswire.com/news/home/20130610006645/en/GE-Healthcare-Invest-2-Billion-Software-Development.

"GE Introduces 2.5-120, the World's Most Efficient High-Output Wind Turbine—the First Brilliant Wind Turbine." *BusinessWire,* January 31, 2013. Retrieved from http://www.businesswire.com/news/home/20130131006018/en/GE-Introduces-2.5-120-World%E2%80%99s-Efficient-High-Output-Wind.

GE Transportation website. Retrieved from http://www.getransportation.com/rail/rail-products/locomotives/fuel-savings-solutions/trip-optimizer.html.

Gens, Frank. "Top 10 Predictions: IDC Predictions 2012: Competing for 2020." IDC.com, December 2011. Retrieved from http://cdn.idc.com/research/Predictions12/Main/downloads/IDCTOP10Predictions2012.pdf.

"Gerloff Magic Shower." Retrieved from http://www.gerloff.com/qfive_02a_deu.htm.

"Glass Once Used in Windshields and Spacecrafts Reborn into Cell Phones and Electronics." Corning website. Retrieved from http://www.corning.com/news_center/corning_stories/gorilla_glass.aspx.

Goodwin, Antuan. "Take Control of Your Car's Tech with These Six Apps." CNET.com, November 19, 2012. Retrieved from http://reviews.cnet.com/8301-13746_7-57552188-48/take-control-of-your-cars-tech-with-these-six-apps.

Google Fiber Website. Retrieved from https://fiber.google.com/about.

Google Glass website. Retrieved from http://www.google.de/glass/start/what-it-does.

Graziano, Dan. "Apple's Retail Dominance: 300M Visitors since October, 50,000 Daily Genius Bar Appointments." BGR.com, August 20, 2012. Retrieved from http://bgr.com/2012/08/20/apple-store-stats-2012-300-million-50000-genius-bar.

Grenoble, Ryan. "Tesla's Direct-Sales Model Exhausts Auto Dealers, Prompts White House Petition." Huffington Post, June 28, 2013.

Griffiths, Daniel Nye. "Mobile Makers: MakieLab's 3D-Printed Dolls Get iPad App, Safety Certification." Forbes, March 5, 2013. Retrieved from http://www.forbes.com/sites/danielnyegriffiths/2013/03/05/mobile-makers-makielabs-3d-printed-dolls-get-ipad-app-safety-certification.

"Growing Threat from Counterfeit Medicines." Bulletin of the World Health Organization, Vol. 88, No. 4 (April 2010). Retrieved from http://www.who.int/bulletin/volumes/88/4/10-020410/en.

Grozdanic, Lidija. "Elon Musk Uses Iron Man-Inspired Holograph 3D User Interface to Print a Rocket Part." Inhabitat.com, September 9, 2013. Retrieved from http://inhabitat.com/elon-musk-unveils-his-iron-man-inspired-hand-manipulated-3d-holographic-technology.

Hagerty, James R., and Miho Inada. "Robots Get a Makeover in Factories." The Wall Street Journal, May 31, 2012. Retrieved from http://online.wsj.com/news/articles/SB10001424052702303807404577434231377787826.

Hecht, Susanna B. and Charles C. Mann. "How Brazil Outfarmed the American Farmer." CNN Money, January 19, 2008. Retrieved from http://money.cnn.com/2008/01/16/news/international/brazil_soy.fortune/index.htm?postversion=2008011917.

Hennigan, Vincent. "The New MyFord Touch v3.6 Software Upgrade Is Here!" Ford Tech Lane, September 19, 2013. Retrieved from http://fordtechlane.com/tag/sync.

Hill, Simon. "A History of Samsung's Galaxy Phones and Tablets, from the S1 to the S4." Digital Trends, March 14, 2013. Retrieved from http://www.digitaltrends.com/mobile/history-of-samsungs-galaxy-phones-and-tablets.

"Hong Kong's Octopus Card." Retrieved from http://ebw.evergreen.ca/move/feat/hong-kongs-octopus-card.

Hopkins, Brian, and Frank E. Gillett with Leslie Owens, Sharyn Leaver, Christopher Mines, and Julian Keenan. *The Top Emerging Technologies to Watch: Now through 2018.* Forrester Report. Retrieved from http://www.forrester.com/The+Top+Em erging+Technologies+To+Watch+Now+Through+2018/fulltext/-/E-RES82721?docid=82721%20%E2%80%93%20Forrester%20 Research,%20Inc.

"Hospital Operations Management." Retrieved from http://www3 .gehealthcare.com/en/Services/Hospital_Operations_Management.

Howard, Bill. "Mercedes-Benz to Offer Over-the-Air Car Updates." ExtremeTech.com, April 10, 2012. Retrieved from http://www.extreme-tech.com/extreme/125621-mercedes-benz-over-the-air-car-updates.

"How Hotels Are Spying on Us." Intelligence for Your Life website. Retrieved from http://www.tesh.com/story/pets-category/how-hotels-are-spying-on-us/cc/11/id/25023.

"How Snapshot Works." Progressive.com. Retrieved from http://www .progressive.com/auto/snapshot-how-it-works/.

Hulu website. Retrieved from http://www.hulu.com/about.

"Hyundai's Premium Segment Success Sets the Stage for Next-Generation HCD-14 Genesis Reveal at the North American International Auto Show." Hyundai News and Press Releases, January 14, 2013. Retrieved from http://hyundainews.com/us/en-us/Media/PressRelease.aspx?mediaid=37994.

"IEC 60601-1-8:2006: Medical electrical equipment — Part 1-8: General requirements for basic safety and essential performance — Collateral standard: General requirements, tests and guidance for alarm systems in medical electrical equipment and medical electrical systems." ISO website. Retrieved from http://www.iso.org/iso/catalogue_detail.htm?csnumber=41986.

Immelt, Jeff. "Is Your Jet Engine Linked in? Connecting Minds and Machines to Drive Efficiency." LinkedIn. com, June 19, 2013. Retrieved from http://www.linkedin.com/today/post/article/20130619125316-230929989-is-your-jet-engine-linked-in-connecting-minds-and-machines-to-drive-efficiency.

"In-flight Wi-Fi Coming in 2013." JetBlue website. Retrieved from http://www.jetblue.com/flying-on-jetblue/wifi.

"Infusion Pumps." Hospira website. Retrieved from http://www.hospira.com/products_and_services/infusion_pumps.

Ingraham, Nathan. "Apple Announces 600 Million iOS Devices Sold, 93 Percent of Devices Running iOS 6." The Verge.com, June 10, 2013. Retrieved from http://www.theverge.com/2013/6/10/4415258/apple-announces-600-million-ios-devices-sold.

"Innovative Cooperation between Workers and Robots at Mercedes-Benz." Daimler website, December 4, 2012. Retrieved from http://www.daimler.com/dccom/0-5-7153-1-1556285-1-0-0-0-0-0-8-7145-0-0-0-0-0-0-0.html.

Intucell website. Retrieved from http://intucellsystems.com/category/press.

"IRS Conducts Nationwide Sweep to Crack Down on Identity Theft and Tax Refund Fraud." Saville, February 11, 2013. Retrieved from http://savillecpadallas.com/identity-theft.

"It Takes a Lot of Things to Be the Next Big Thing." Samsung website. Retrieved from http://www.samsung.com/us/guide-to-galaxy-smart-devices/galaxy-s-4-smartphone.html.

"iTunes Match." Retrieved from http://www.apple.com/de/itunes/itunes-match.

iwoca website. Retrieved from http://www.iwoca.co.uk.

Jackson, Joab. "Pivotal Launched from VMware, EMC Technologies." PCWorld, com, April 24, 2013. Retrieved from http://www.pcworld. com/article/2036305/pivotal-launched-from-vmware-emc-technologies.html.

Jiang, Steven. "China's High-Speed Trains Attract Frustrated Fliers." CNN.com, April 12, 2013. Retrieved from http://edition.cnn. com/2013/04/11/travel/china-high-speed-rail.

Kagermann, Henning, et al. *Umsetzungsempfehlungen für das Zukunftsprojekt Industrie 4.0. Berlin: Büro der Forschungsunion im Stifterverband für die Deutsche Wissenschaft e.V.* 2013. "Kaiser Permanente CIO on Saving Lives, Jobs." Interview with George Halvorson. USA Today.com, October 23, 2012. Retrieved from http://www.usatoday.com/story/money/personalfinance/2012/10/23/ kaiser-health-care-costs/1639913.

Kaiser Permanente website. Retrieved from http://www.kaiserpermanente jobs.org/university-connection/life-at-kp.aspx.

Katje, Chris. "Nuance's Acquisition of Tweddle Connect Offers Big Growth in Automotive Sector." Seeking Alpha, June 3, 2013. Retrieved from http://seekingalpha.com/article/1475701-nuances-acquisition-of-tweddle-connect-offers-big-growth-in-automotive-sector.

Kerr, Dara. "Gogo quietly hikes up its in-flight Wi-Fi prices." CNET.com, September 18, 2012. Retrieved from http://news.cnet.com/ 8301-1023_3-57515522-93/gogo-quietly-hikes-up-its-in-flight-wi-fi-prices.

Kickstarter website. Retrieved from http://www.kickstarter.com.

King, John Leslie, and Kalle Lytinnen. "Automotive Informatics: Information Technology and Enterprise Transformation in the Automobile Industry." In William H. Dutton, Brian Kahin, Ramon O'Callaghan, and Andrew W. Wyckoff (eds.), *Transforming Enterprise: The Economic and Social Implications of Information Technology.* Cambridge, MA: MIT Press, 2005.

King, Rachel. "How Mattel Can Get into Your Head." *Bloomberg Businessweek,* April 5, 2011. Retrieved from http://www.business week.com/stories/2011-04-05/how-mattel-can-get-into-your-head businessweek-business-news-stock-market-and-financial-advice.

Klout website. Retrieved from http://klout.com/corp/how-it-works.

Koetsier, John. "Finally! A Fitness Tracker That Actually Knows What You're Doing." VB website, February 13, 2013. Retrieved from http://venturebeat.com/2013/02/13/finally-a-fitness-tracker-that-actually-knows-what-youre-doing.

Lavrinc, Damon. "How a QR Code Could Save Your Life." *Wired,* May 28, 2013. Retrieved from http://www.wired.com/autopia/2013/05/mercedes-qr-code.

Lee, Peter. ""BBVA Builds Up Investment Banking." Euromoney .com, January 2013. Retrieved from http://www.euromoney.com/Article/3135672/Category/12/ChannelPage/13/BBVA-builds-up-investment-banking.html?single=true.

"Lego Story Builder." Digital Buzz, April 7, 2013. Retrieved from http://www.digitalbuzzblog.com/lego-story-builder-augmented-reality-app.

Lepore, Meredith. "15 Facts about Starbucks That Will Blow Your Mind." Business Insider, March 25, 2011. Retrieved from http://www.businessinsider.com/15-facts-about-starbucks-that-will-blow-your-mind-2011-3?op=1.

"LEVA Activates Forensic Video Analysis Response Team to Support Vancouver Police Department." PRLog Press Release, September 14, 2011. Retrieved from http://www.prlog.org/11659709-leva-activates-forensic-video-analysis-response-team-to-support-vancouver-police-department.html.

"Linking Open Data Cloud Diagram." Maintained by Richard Cyganiak and Anja Jentzsch. Retrieved from http://lod-cloud.net.

Lithium website. Retrieved from http://www.lithium.com.

Locker, Melissa. "Oreo's Snappy Super Bowl Blackout Ad." *Times NewsFeed,* February 4, 2013. Retrieved from http://newsfeed.time.com/2013/02/04/watch-oreos-snappy-super-bowl-blackout-ad.

Loudiyi, Ihssane. "Brazil Announces Phase Two of the Growth Acceleration Program." Growth and Crisis, March 30, 2010. Retrieved from http://blogs.worldbank.org/growth/brazil-announces-phase-two-growth-acceleration-program

"The Magazine Is an iPad That Does Not Work.m4v." THE YouTube video published October 6, 2011. Retrieved from http://www.youtube.com/watch?v=aXV-yaFmQNk.

Mallis, Laurie. "Birth of the Diad." UPS.com, December 7, 2009. Retrieved from http://blog.ups.com/2009/12/07/birth-of-the-diad.

Manyika, James; Michael Chui; Jacques Bughin; Richard Dobbs; Peter Bisson; and Alex Marrs. *Disruptive Technologies: Advances That Will Transform Life, Business, and the Global Economy.* McKinsey Global Institute Report, May 2013. Retrieved from http://www.mckinsey.com/insights/business_technology/disruptive_technologies?cid=disruptive_tech-eml-alt-mip-mck-oth-1305.

"Many Reasons to Go Premium." Evernote website. Retrieved from http://evernote.com/premium.

Marks, Howard. "Backup Bedlam: The Latest Survey Shows Data at Risk." *InformationWeek,* July 29, 2013. Retrieved from http://www.informationweek.com/storage/disaster-recovery/backup-bedlam-data-still-at-risk/240158878.

Massenet, Natalie. "Natalie Massenet on Starting Net-A-Porter." As told to Diane Brady. *Bloomberg Businessweek Magazine,* December 15, 2011. Retrieved from http://www.businessweek.com/magazine/natalie-massenet-on-starting-netaporter-12152011.html.

Maurtua, Inaki; Pierre T. Kirisci; Thomas Stiefmeier; Marco Luca Sbodio; and Hendrik Witt. "A Wearable Computing Prototype for Supporting Training Activities in Automotive Production." IEEE Xplore website.

Retrieved from http://ieeexplore.ieee.org/xpl/abstractAuthors.jsp? reload=true&tp=&arnumber=5760480&url=http%3A%2F%2F ieeexplore.ieee.org%2Fxpls%2Fabs_all.jsp%3Farnumber% 3D5760480.

Maybury, Mark T. *Air Force Cyber Vision 2025.* U.S. Air Force. Retrieved from http://www.ndia.org/Divisions/Divisions/ ScienceAndEngineeringTechnology/Documents/SET% 20Breakfast%20Presentation.pdf.

Mayfield, Cedra. "GE Unveils 'Home of 2025.'" Wave3.com, July 18, 2013. Retrieved from http://www.wave3.com/story/22876813/ ge-unveils-home-of-2025.

"mbrace2." Mercedes-Benz website. Retrieved from http://www.mbusa .com/mercedes/mbrace.

"McAfee Predicts Rapid Evolution of Cyberthreats in New Year." McAfee website, December 27, 2012. http://www.mcafee.com/us/about/ news/2012/q4/20121227-01.aspx.

McCallum, John C. Memory Prices: 1957-2013. (Feb. 27, 2013). Retrieved from http://www.jcmit.com/memoryprice.htm.

McDougall, Paul. "In Supply Chain, the Customer Isn't Always Right." CRUXIALCIO, September 17, 2013. Retrieved from http://www .cruxialcio.com/supply-chain-support-1138#takeaways.

"Media Center." Redbox website. Retrieved from http://www.redbox .com/facts.

Meeker, Mary, and Liang Wu. "Internet Trends D11 Conference." Kleiner Perkins Caufield Byers (May 29, 2013). Retrieved from http://www .kpcb.com/insights/2013-internet-trends.

"Mercedes-Benz USA pushes automobile connectivity to the next level with the launch of mbrace2 at CES 2012." Hughes Telematics, Inc., Press Release, January 10, 2012. Retrieved from http://www .verizontelematics.com/press/releases/mbusa2.php.

Mirchandani, Vinnie. "'Tiigrihüppe' -Estonia's wired 'tiger leap.'" New Florence New Renaissance. Retrieved from http://florence20 .typepad.com/renaissance/2007/09/tiigrihppe--est.html.

Mirchandani, Vinnie. "50 Ways to Leave Your Lover — and to Communicate with Your Smartphone." New Florence New Renaissance. Retrieved from http://florence20.typepad.com/ renaissance/2012/11/50-ways-to-leave-your-lover-and-to-communicate-with-your-smartphone.html.

Mirchandani, Vinnie. "A Dairy Farmer's Best New Friend." New Florence New Renaissance. Retrieved from http://florence20.typepad.com/ renaissance/2012/11/a-dairy-farmers-best-new-friend.html.

Mirchandani, Vinnie. "A Scanner for the TSA to Consider?" New Florence New Renaissance. Retrieved from http://florence20.typepad.com/ renaissance/2013/01/a-scanner-for-the-tsa-to-consider.html.

Mirchandani, Vinnie. "Amazon Fresh: Webvan 2.0." New Florence New Renaissance. Retrieved from http://florence20.typepad.com/ renaissance/2013/06/amazonfresh-webvan-20.html.

Mirchandani, Vinnie. "Audi's Digital Showroom." New Florence New Renaissance. Retrieved from http://florence20.typepad.com/ renaissance/2012/09/audis-digital-showroom.html.

Mirchandani, Vinnie. "Bank Branch of Future." New Florence New Renaissance. Retrieved from http://florence20.typepad.com/ renaissance/2013/05/bank-branch-of-future.html.

Mirchandani, Vinnie. "Big Data Revolutionizing Farming." New Florence New Renaissance. Retrieved from http://florence20.typepad.com/ renaissance/2013/03/big-data-revolutionizing-farming.html.

Mirchandani, Vinnie. "Bill McDermott and Boston." Deal Architect, May 20, 2013. Retrieved from http://dealarchitect.typepad.com/ deal_architect/2013/05/bill-mcdermott-and-boston.html.

Mirchandani, Vinnie. "Book Excerpts: Case Study 6 — Virgin America." New Florence New Renaissance. Retrieved from http://florence20

.typepad.com/renaissance/2011/12/book-excerpts-case-study-6-virgin-america.html.

Mirchandani, Vinnie. "BP CTO and Innovative Technology around the Gulf Spill." New Florence New Renaissance. Retrieved from http://florence20.typepad.com/renaissance/2010/10/bp-cto-and-innovative-technology-around-the-gulf-spill.html.

Mirchandani, Vinnie. "British Cycling: The Technology and the Performance Improvements." New Florence New Renaissance. Retrieved from http://florence20.typepad.com/renaissance/2012/08/british-cycling-the-technology-and-the-performance-improvements.html.

Mirchandani, Vinnie. "China's Amazing Infrastructure." New Florence New Renaissance. Retrieved from http://florence20.typepad.com/renaissance/2013/07/chinas-amazing-infrastructure.html.

Mirchandani, Vinnie. "Cleaning Up the Tantalum Supply Chain." New Florence New Renaissance. Retrieved from http://florence20.typepad.com/renaissance/2012/05/cleaning-up-the-tantalum-supply-chain.html.

Mirchandani, Vinnie. "Complex Event Processing." Deal Architect, June 30, 2013. Retrieved from http://dealarchitect.typepad.com/deal_architect/2013/06/complex-event-processing.html.

Mirchandani, Vinnie. "Crowdsourcing Home Deliveries." New Florence New Renaissance. Retrieved from http://florence20.typepad.com/renaissance/2013/03/crowdsourcing-home-deliveries.html.

Mirchandani, Vinnie. "Freestyle Fountain Tour." New Florence New Renaissance. Retrieved from http://florence20.typepad.com/renaissance/2012/02/freestyle-fountain-tour.html.

Mirchandani, Vinnie. "Grocery Shopping at Your Subway Stop." New Florence New Renaissance. Retrieved from http://florence20.typepad.com/renaissance/2011/07/grocery-shopping-at-your-subway-stop.html.

Mirchandani, Vinnie. "Groupon's Global Rocket." New Florence New Renaissance. Retrieved from http://florence20.typepad.com/renaissance/2011/06/groupons-global-rocket.html.

Mirchandani, Vinnie. "Innovation in European Postal Services." New Florence New Renaissance. Retrieved from http://florence20.typepad.com/renaissance/2011/05/innovation-in-european-postal-services.html

Mirchandani, Vinnie. "John Deere's FarmSight." New Florence New Renaissance. Retrieved from http://florence20.typepad.com/renaissance/2011/04/john-deeres-farmsight.html.

Mirchandani, Vinnie. "Kinect+Coke machine+AI+2PM = Japan's Got Talent." New Florence New Renaissance. Retrieved from http://florence20.typepad.com/renaissance/2013/01/kinectcoke2pm-japns-got-talent.html.

Mirchandani, Vinnie. "Kiva Warehouse Robots." New Florence New Renaissance. Retrieved from http://florence20.typepad.com/renaissance/2009/04/kiva-warehouse-robots.html.

Mirchandani, Vinnie. "LaCaixa Mobile Banking Innovations." New Florence New Renaissance. Retrieved from http://florence20.typepad.com/renaissance/2013/06/lacaixa-mobile-banking-innovations.html.

Mirchandani, Vinnie. "Netflix: The Broadband Monster." New Florence New Renaissance. Retrieved from http://florence20.typepad.com/renaissance/2013/06/netflix-the-broadband-monster.html.

Mirchandani, Vinnie. "Next Book Excerpt — Case Study 4 — Estonia's 'Tiigrihüpe' — Tiger Leap." New Florence New Renaissance. Retrieved from http://florence20.typepad.com/renaissance/2011/11/next-book-excerpt-case-study-4-estonias-tiigrihpe-tiger-leap.html.

Mirchandani, Vinnie. "The Big Data of Water Leaks." New Florence New Renaissance. Retrieved from http://florence20.typepad.com/renaissance/2013/01/the-big-data-of-water-leaks.html.

Mirchandani, Vinnie. "The Gogo In-flight Wi-Fi." New Florence New Renaissance. Retrieved from http://florence20.typepad.com/renaissance/2010/07/the-gogo-inflight-Wi-Fi.html.

Mirchandani, Vinnie. "The IKEA Catalog: A Marvel of Miniaturization." New Florence New Renaissance. Retrieved from http://florence20.typepad.com/renaissance/2012/08/the-ikea-catalog-a-marvel-of-miniaturization.html.

Mirchandani, Vinnie. "The Nest Learning Thermostat." New Florence New Renaissance. Retrieved from http://florence20.typepad.com/renaissance/2011/12/the-nest-learning-thermostat.html.

Mirchandani, Vinnie. "The New Blitzkrieg." Deal Architect, July 13, 2011. Retrieved from http://dealarchitect.typepad.com/deal_architect/2011/07/the-new-blitzkreig.html.

Mirchandani, Vinnie. "The Rudiben Mobile App." New Florence New Renaissance. Retrieved from http://florence20.typepad.com/renaissance/2013/06/the-rudiben-mobile-app.html.

Mirchandani, Vinnie. "The Tesla Mobile App." New Florence New Renaissance. Retrieved from http://florence20.typepad.com/renaissance/2013/04/the-tesla-mobile-app.html.

Mirchandani, Vinnie. "Toyota 'Friend': Green Meets Social Meets Mobile." New Florence New Renaissance. Retrieved from http://florence20.typepad.com/renaissance/2011/05/toyota-friend.html.

Mirchandani, Vinnie. "Will Mobile Apps Make Smarter Consumers?" New Florence New Renaissance. Retrieved from http://florence20.typepad.com/renaissance/2013/06/will-mobile-apps-make-smarter-consumers.html.

Mirchandani, Vinnie. New Florence New Renaissance. "The De Dietrich Induction Hob." Retrieved from http://florence20.typepad.com/renaissance/2011/07/the-de-dietrich-induction-hob.html.

Mirchandani, Vinnie. "EIs Look Ahead to 2018." Enterprise Irregulars, July 25, 2013. Retrieved from http://www.enterpriseirregulars .com/64541/eis-look-ahead-to-2018.

Mirchandani, Vinnie. "Mid-level Recruiting Goes More Social." New Florence New Renaissance. Retrieved from http://florence20 .typepad.com/renaissance/2013/01/mid-level-recruiting-goes-more-social.html.

Mirchandani, Vinnie. "The Golden-i Headset." New Florence New Renaissance. Retrieved from http://florence20.typepad.com/ renaissance/2013/01/the-golden-i-headset.html.

"Mobile Auto Glass Repair." SafeLite AutoGlass website. Retrieved from http://www.safelite.com/about-safelite/mobile-auto-glass-repair.

Moen website. Retrieved from http://www.moen.com/whats-new/ innovation/iodigital.

Moore, Geoffrey. (2011). *Systems of Engagement and the Future of Enterprise IT: A Sea Change in Enterprise IT.* AIIM White Paper, 2011. Retrieved from http://www.aiim.org/~/media/Files/AIIM%20 White%20Papers/Systems-of-Engagement-Future-of-Enterprise-IT.ashx.

"Moore's Law." *Webopedia.* Retrieved from http://www.webopedia .com/TERM/M/Moores_Law.html.

moovel website. Retrieved from https://www.moovel.com/en.

"More Differentiated Products for Next Summer." FVW.com, November 9, 2012. Retrieved from http://www.fvw.com/tui-germany-more-differentiated-products-for-next-summer/393/111598/11245.

Morgan, Hazel. "The History of Ink Jet Printers." eHow.com. Retrieved from http://www.ehow.com/about_5460438_history-ink-jet-printers .html.

Murphy, Chris. "Union Pacific Delivers Internet of Things Reality Check." *InformationWeek,* August 8, 2012. Retrieved from http://aspnet.cob

.ohio.edu/matta/mis2020/HotTopics/5.0%20Internet%20Of%20 Things%20Updated.pdf.

Nasscom website. Retrieved from http://www.nasscom.in/vision-and-mission.

National Science Foundation. *FY 2012 Budget Request.* "Advanced Manufacturing." Retrieved from http://www.nsf.gov/about/budget/ fy2012/pdf/38_fy2012.pdf.

"Nationwide Mobile Application Now Available on Apple App Store." Nationwide Press Release, April 22, 2009. Retrieved from http:// www.nationwide.com/about-us/042209-nw-iphone-app.jsp.

Netflix website. Retrieved from https://signup.netflix.com.

NetJets website. Retrieved from http://www.netjets.com/Life-as-an-owner/Owner-Journey.

The Nexus of Forces: Social, Mobile, Cloud, and Information. Gartner Special Report, 2013. Retrieved from http://www.gartner.com/ technology/research/nexus-of-forces.

"Norfolk Southern and GE Announce Success of Breakthrough Technology to Help Railroads Move Freight Faster and Smarter." Press Release, June 7, 2010. Retrieved from http://webcache .googleusercontent.com/search?q=cache:cSWKqWUTH3YJ:www .getransportation.com/resources/doc_download/143-norfolk-southern-and-ge-announce-success-of-breakthrough-technology .html+&cd=1&hl=en&ct=clnk&gl=us.

O'Connor, Mary Catherine. "Tracking Temperatures from the Inside out." RFID Journal, August 1, 2008. Retrieved from http://www .rfidjournal.com/articles/view?4225.

Obama, Barack. 2013 State of the Union Address. Delivered February 12, 2013. Retrieved from http://www.whitehouse.gov/ state-of-the-union-2013.

OnStar website. Retrieved from https://www.onstar.com/web/portal/ home?g=1.

Open Amplify website. Retrieved from http://www.openamplify.com.

"Opportunities in Pharma RFID and Smart Packaging." IDTechEx website. Retrieved from http://www.idtechex.com/research/articles/opportunities_in_pharma_rfid_and_smart_packaging_00000487.asp.

Petrilla, Molly. "Q&A: Moving the Office Outside." Smartplanet.com, November 26, 2012. Retrieved from http://www.smartplanet.com/blog/pure-genius/q-a-moving-the-office-outside/9106?tag=nl.e660&s_cid=e660.

Priceline.com website. Retrieved from http://www.priceline.com/customerservice/faq/howitworks/howitworks.asp.

Prince, Marcelo, and Willa Plank. "A Short History of Apple's Manufacturing in the U.S." *The Wall Street Journal,* December 6, 2012. Retrieved from http://blogs.wsj.com/digits/2012/12/06/a-short-history-of-apples-manufacturing-in-the-u-s.

"Prism — Facts, Doubts, Laws, and Loopholes." Infosec website. Retrieved from http://resources.infosecinstitute.com/prism-facts-doubts-laws-and-loopholes.

"Progress Software Customer, Turkcell, Wins Gartner & 1to1 Media CRM Excellence Award." Progress.com, July 10, 2012. Retrieved from http://investors.progress.com/releasedetail.cfm?releaseid=690442.

Protalinski, Emil. "Mark Zuckerberg: Facebook Minimum Age Limit Should Be Removed." ZDNet.com, May 20, 2011. Retrieved from http://www.zdnet.com/blog/facebook/mark-zuckerberg-facebook-minimum-age-limit-should-be-removed/1506.

Pushpins website. Retrieved from http://www.pushpinsapp.com/about.

Quinn, Gene. "The RCE Backlog: A Critical Patent Office Problem." IPWatchdog.com, February 14, 2013. Retrieved from http://www.ipwatchdog.com/2013/02/14/the-rce-backlog-a-critical-patent-office-problem/id=35431.

"Results of the German Innovation Survey 2012." ZEW Industry Report, January 2013.

"Romney Strategist Says Campaign Was 2 Years Behind Obama." Taegan Goddard's Political Wire, April 18, 2013. Retrieved from http://politicalwire.com/archives/2013/04/18/romney_strategist_says_campaign_was_2_years_behind_obama.html.

"Sabre History." Sabre.com. Retrieved from http://www.sabre.com/home/about/sabre_history.

"San Diego Gas & Electric — a Smart Meter Leader." February 15, 2010. Retrieved from http://www.metering.com/node/16985.

Securing the Future of German Manufacturing Industry: Recommendations for Implementing the Strategic Initiative INDUSTRIE 4.0. Final report of the Industrie 4.0 Working Group, April 2013. Retrieved from http://www.acatech.de/fileadmin/user_upload/Baumstruktur_nach_Website/Acatech/root/de/Material_fuer_Sonderseiten/Industrie_4.0/Final_report__Industrie_4.0_accessible.pdf.

"Semantic Web Development Tools." W3C website. Retrieved from http://www.w3.org/2001/sw/wiki/Tools.

"Semantic Web." W3C website. Retrieved from http://www.w3.org/standards/semanticweb.

Shah, Jumana. "Rudiben's Use of Mobile App Gets Cherie Blair's Cheers." DNA, March 20, 2013. Retrieved from http://www.dnaindia.com/ahmedabad/report-rudiben-s-use-of-mobile-app-gets-cherie-blair-s-cheers-1813468.

Shah, Neil. "More Americans Working Remotely." *The Wall Street Journal,* March 5, 2013. Retrieved from http://online.wsj.com/news/articles/SB10001424127887324539404578342503214110478.

Singapore Workforce Development Agency (WDA) website. Retrieved from http://www.wda.gov.sg/content/wdawebsite/L209-001About-Us/L209A-History.html.

Singapore Workforce Development Agency (WDA). Individual Learning Portfolio (ILP). Retrieved from http://www.wda.gov.sg/content/dam/wda/COS/ILP_Infographics.pdf.

Škoda Auto website. Retrieved from http://new.skoda-auto.com/en.

Slansky, Dick. "Siemens PLM Software 2011 Analyst Conference." ARC Advisory Group, September 22, 2011. Retrieved from http://www.arcweb.com/strategy-reports/2011-09-22/siemens-plm-software-2011-analyst-conference-1.aspx.

"SOS: Hilfe im Ausland" — die Debeka-App für Ihr Smartphone." Debeka website. Retrieved from http://www.debeka.de/service/app/index.html.

Square website. Retrieved from https://squareup.com.

"Strategy Analytics: Global Smartphone Shipments Reach a Record 700 Million Units in 2012." Press release, January 24, 2013. Yahoo! Finance. Retrieved from http://finance.yahoo.com/news/strategy-analytics-global-smartphone-shipments-032900959.html.

Strohmeier, Rudolf, and Zoran Stančič. *Enabling and Industrial Technologies in Horizon 2020 — The Framework Programme for Research and Innovation.* European Commission. Retrieved from http://ec.europa.eu/research/horizon2020/pdf/workshops/leadership_in_enabling_and_industrial_technologies/introduction_-_enabling_and_industrial_technologies_in_horizon_2020.pdf.

Stroud, Matt. "In Boston Bombing, Flood of Digital Evidence Is a Blessing and a Curse." *The Verge,* April 16, 2013. Retrieved from http://www.theverge.com/2013/4/16/4230820/in-boston-bombing-flood-of-digital-evidence-is-a-blessing-and-a-curse.

Swaine, John. "Georgia: Russia 'Conducting Cyber War.'" *The Telegraph,* August 11, 2008. Retrieved from http://www.telegraph.co.uk/news/worldnews/europe/georgia/2539157/Georgia-Russia-conducting-cyber-war.html.

"Take the Sales Back to Your Store." Shopperception website. Retrieved from http://www.shopperception.com/retailers.html.

"Talent Interaction Platform." Hirevue.com. Retrieved from http://hirevue.com/what-is-hirevue.

Tata Consultancy Services website. Retrieved from http://www.tcs.com/Pages/default.aspx.

"Technology Enhances Customer Service, Operating Efficiency." Norfolk Southern website. Retrieved from http://www.nscorp.com/nscportal/nscorp/Investors/Financial_Reports/Investor%20Book/technology.html.

Telefónica website. Retrieved from http://dynamicinsights.telefonica.com/479/about-us.

Tesla website. Retrieved from http://www.teslamotors.com/models/features#/performance.

"There's Algorithms in My Orange Juice — Good Example on How Corporate USA Models Work, They Have Many Available to Slip in to Place When New Laws are Created, Planned Out Ahead of Time to Use, Coca-Cola Uses This Planning to Create Nice 'Tangible' Products." Medical Quack website. Retrieved from http://ducknetweb.blogspot.de/2013/02/theres-algorithms-in-my-orange-juice.html.

Thrun, Sebastian. "What We're Driving At." October 29, 2010. Retrieved from http://googleblog.blogspot.com/2010/10/what-were-driving-at.html.

"Tom Enders Inaugurates CeBIT 2013." YouTube video published March 7, 2013. Retrieved from http://www.youtube.com/watch?v=-Cn_PFxmmMU.

TransferWise website. Retrieved from http://transferwise.com.

Ulger, Cem. "Number of Users in Social Media Increase the Necessary Storage Capacity." Cemspot.com, July 4 2013. Retrieved from http://www.cemspot.com/2013/07/number-of-users-in-social-media.html.

"U.S. & Canada Unlimited." Vonage website. Retrieved from http://www .vonage.com/us-canada-calling-plans/unlimited-minutes?refer_ id=WEBSR0706010001W1&lid=sub_nav_domestic_unlimited.

Van Camp, Jeffrey. "2013 Ford Escape Hands-free Liftgate Demo — Kick the Bumper to Open the Trunk." Digital Trends, November 17, 2011. Retrieved from http://www.digitaltrends.com/car-videos/2013- ford-escape-hands-free-liftgate-demo-kick-the-bumper-to-open- the-trunk.

Voser, Peter. "Getting the Future Energy Mix Right: How the American Shale Revolution Is Changing the World." Speech delivered to the Chief Executives Club of Boston, March 21, 2013. Retrieved from http://www.shell.com/global/aboutshell/media/speeches-and- webcasts/2013/getting-the-future-energy-mix-right.html.

"W3C Semantic Web Activity." W3C website. Retrieved from http:// www.w3.org/2001/sw.

wearIT@work website. Retrieved from http://www.wearitatwork.com.

Weintraud, Arlene. "Intel Wants You to Age Gracefully, at Home." *Bloomberg Businessweek,* September 21, 2009. Retrieved from http://www.businessweek.com/stories/2009-09-21/intel-wants- you-to-age-gracefully-at-homebusinessweek-business-news-stock- market-and-financial-advice.

Wen, Wang. "Number of Chinese Civil Airports Will Exceed 200 by 2014." Chinadaily.com.cn, June 6, 2013. Retrieved from http:// www.chinadaily.com.cn/china/2013-06/06/content_16580254.htm.

"What Is Cloud Computing?" Amazon Web Services. Retrieved from http://aws.amazon.com/what-is-cloud-computing.

Williams, Mike. "Brain Wave-reading Robot Might Help Stroke Patients." Rice University News & Media, August 20, 2012. Retrieved from http://news.rice.edu/2012/08/20/brain-wave-reading- robot-might-help-stroke-patients-2.

Wittenstein website. Retrieved from http://www.wittenstein.de/en/ innvoation-factory.html.

"Workday Update 19 — You Need to Slow Down to Hurry Up." Enterprise Software Musings, April 22, 2013. Retrieved from http://enswmu .blogspot.de/2013/04/workday-update-19-you-need-to-slow-down.html.

x-trans.edu website. Retrieved from http://x-trans.eu.

"Your Smartphone Just Got Smarter." ADT Pulse website. Retrieved from http://www.adtpulse.com/home/how-pulse-works/mobile.

Zipcar website. Retrieved from http://www.zipcar.com/about.

Index

W

Wahlster, Prof. Dr. Wolfgang, 6, 139,
143–9, 205, 275
Wearable computers, 142, 188, 192,
277
wearable computing, xi
WearIT@work, 192
Web
    connectivity, 144
    services, 63, 173, 230–1, 260–1
    technologies, 130
    traffic, 82
webMethods (Software AG), ix
Weltbild, 118
West Texas Intermediate (WTI), 162
Whirlpool, 110
Wi-Fi, 4, 53, 74, 111–12, 192, 233
WikiLeaks, 262
Wikipedia, 230
Williams, Robbie, 114–15, 119
Wind Turbines, 8, 167–8, 179, 275. *See
also* General Electric.
Wipak Walsrode, 148. *See also*
    TalkPack.
Wittenstein AG, 142
Workday, 125
Workforce Development Agency
    (WDA), 282
Workplaces of the future, 155
WorldInsight, 63–4
World is Flat, The, 234. *See also*
    Friedman, Thomas.

X

x-trans.eu, 53

Y

Yahoo!, v
YCAR, 52, 58–9
Year 2000 remediation, 230–1
Yelp!, 56
Yield management, 73, 77
YouTube, 33, 35, 75, 230, 244, 280

Z

Zappos, 140
ZipCar, 78. *See also* Avis.
Zipments, 96–7
Zynga, 111